Becoming a Computational Thinker

Becoming a Computational Thinker: Success in the Digital Age has a single purpose: to help everyone become computational thinkers. Computational thinking (CT) is thinking informed by the digital age, and a computational thinker is someone who can apply that thinking everywhere and anywhere. Through practical examples and easy-to-grasp terminology, this book is a guide to navigating the digital world and improving one's efficiency, productivity, and success immediately.

Given their pervasiveness, knowledge and experience of computation are a cornerstone of productivity, and improved thinking will only lead to advances in every aspect of one's life. In this way, CT can be thought of as the mutual reinforcement of thinking and knowledge of computation in the digital age. Comprising a rich collection of self-contained articles that can be read separately, and illustrated by pictures, images and article-end crossword puzzles, this book is an engaging and accessible route to 'Becoming a Computational Thinker' and achieving 'Success in the Digital Age'.

Aimed at the general reader, this book provides insights that can be applied across the full spectrum of industries and practices, helping readers to not only adapt and function in the digital world but also take advantage of new technologies and even innovate new ways of doing things.

Paul S. Wang is an author, computer scientist, researcher, consultant and academic. He is a PhD and faculty member of MIT with over 40 years of experience in teaching and book publishing. His current interest is in introducing computational thinking to all.

Becoming a Computational Thinker
Success in the Digital Age

Paul S. Wang

CRC Press
Taylor & Francis Group
Boca Raton London New York

CRC Press is an imprint of the
Taylor & Francis Group, an **informa** business

A CHAPMAN & HALL BOOK

First edition published 2024
by CRC Press
2385 NW Executive Center Drive, Suite 320, Boca Raton FL 33431

and by CRC Press
4 Park Square, Milton Park, Abingdon, Oxon, OX14 4RN

CRC Press is an imprint of Taylor & Francis Group, LLC

© 2024 Paul S. Wang

ISBN: 978-1-032-56899-7 (hbk)
ISBN: 978-1-032-56898-0 (pbk)
ISBN: 978-1-003-43768-0 (ebk)

DOI: 10.1201/b23382

Typeset in Latin Modern Font
by KnowledgeWorks Global Ltd.

Publisher's note: This book has been prepared from camera-ready copy provided by the authors.
Access additional online resources at https://computize.org/CTer/

Contents

Preface

Hello, welcome to the delightful pages of

Becoming a Computational Thinker: Success in the Digital Age

The book has a single purpose: to help everyone become a ***computational thinker***. A computational thinker is someone who has acquired computational thinking (CT) and can apply that thinking everywhere, every day. Reading the book, you can better navigate the digital world and improve your efficiency, productivity, and success immediately.

You'll find many interesting and practical articles on CT. We call them *CT Articles*. Each CT Article is short, sweet, and an independent self-contained unit. Each CT Article is written in plain language and amply illustrated by pictures and images. To enjoy the book, you don't need a background in computing, just a sense of curiosity.

Collectively, the CT Articles paint an increasingly complete picture of computing and digital technologies as well as mental skills inspired by them. You can pick a CT Article that strikes your fancy and read it. There is no need to stick to the sequential ordering. But it is good to start at the beginning.

You'll find the information revealing, interesting, and practical. The CT Articles' applications can be found everywhere, every day. Simply allow the CT Articles to guide your digital journey to better understanding, sharper mental skills, wiser decisions, and more success in everything you do.

To make the book more useful, there is a companion website at `computize.org/CTer` where you can find answers to article-end crossword puzzles, interactive demos, and more.

Companion Website QR Code

So go ahead, kick back, get a cup of tea or coffee, and start reading.

Welcome to the

Overview

Preface

Contents

Crossword
Puzzle

Demos

Updates

Author

Companion Website

It is great to welcome you here. On this site, you can access answers to the crossword puzzles and play with the interactive demos.

If you don't already have a copy of the book, take a look at the preface and the table of contents. If you like what you see, why not get a copy? You can order from amazon.com or directly from the publisher. You'll find that a good investment of your time and lots of fun too.

Your feedback will be most appreciated. Please send feedback by email to the author directly.

Thank you again very much for your interest in this book.

Companion Website: `computize.org/CTer`

Acknowledgments

I'd like to thank my dear wife Jennifer Wang (葛孝薇) who encouraged me to embark on this project, read all drafts, and provided great feedback, sometimes with specific ideas and wording changes. I am very grateful to her.

Some CT Articles are derived from my CT blog. Some blog articles have also appeared in the online *aroundKent* magazine published by Matt Keffer of Kent Ohio. I am grateful to him for his encouragement and support. The crossword puzzles have been made using `CrosswordLabs.com`, an excellent website for creating and customizing crossword puzzles.

I'd also like to thank Prof. Michael Mikusa and Mark Weiseman for reviewing the book proposal. I express my deep appreciation to the editors at CRC Press, Randi (Cohen) Slack, Solomon Pace-McCarrick and Michele Dimont, for their help and guidance, and thank the copyeditor Samar Haddad for a careful and thorough job.

Paul S. Wang, Kent, Ohio

王士弘

Computational Thinking: An Introduction

Computers brought us the digital revolution. People in the digital age have such wonderful things as laptops, smartphones, satellite navigation, drones, the Internet, the web, social media, streaming video, artificial intelligence (AI), and more. We are experiencing the *fourth industrial revolution* brought by significant applications of digital technologies and ever-increasing automation in all parts of our economy.

Such changes are tremendously beneficial as well as challenging. For example, we can *ask Google* or *chatGPT* any questions we may have on just about any subject and usually get answers instantly. The Internet spans the globe and brings all parts of the world within instant reach. But in the global village, rumors and fake news can spread quickly. Worse yet, hackers also could steal sensitive information or even hold our computers for ransom.

As modern citizens, we want to take advantage of digital technologies while wisely mitigate the complications and risks brought by them. That's where *computational thinking* (CT) can come into play. When we acquire CT and become *computational thinkers*, we can navigate the "digital sea" more effectively and apply CT every day to make ourselves more successful.

What Is Computational Thinking?

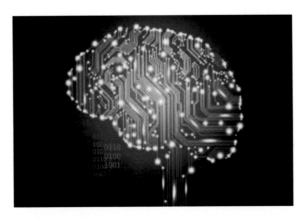

FIGURE 1: *Computational Thinking*

Thinking is and has always been a mental activity informed by experience, knowledge, and logic. Computational thinking (CT) is thinking informed by the computing age.

Knowledge and experience of computation will enhance thinking for all people in the digital age (Figure 1). And improved thinking will also lead to advances in every aspect of our lives, including computing as well as other areas of study.

> ***Thus, computational thinking is the result of mutual reinforcement between thinking and computational knowledge in the digital age** .*

Specifically, *CT is the mental skill and orientation to apply fundamental concepts and reasoning, derived from modern computing and digital technologies, in all areas, including day-to-day activities.*
CT involves our understanding of computing, its advantages, limitations, and potential problems. CT also encourages us to keep asking questions such as, "*What if we automate this?*", "*What instructions and precautions would we need if we were asking young children to do this?*", "*How efficient is this?*", and "*What can go wrong with this?*".

CT can expand our minds, help us solve problems, increase efficiency, avoid mistakes, and anticipate pitfalls, as well as interact and communicate better with others, people, or machines. A *computational thinker* (CTer) is anyone who has acquired the ability to use and apply CT. A CTer can not only adapt and function well in the digital world, but also take good advantage of new technologies and even innovate and create new ways to do things. A CTer strives to apply CT everywhere everyday.

A Powerful Way of Thinking

OK great, CT is important. But what exactly are the concepts and methodologies it provides? Here is a list of some main aspects of CT:

- Simplification through abstraction—Abstraction is a technique to reduce complexity by ignoring unimportant details and focusing on what matters (Figure 2). For example, a driver views a car in terms of how to drive it and ignores how it works or is built. A user cares only about which mouse button to click and keys to press and generally overlooks how computers work internally.

- Power of automation—Arranging matters so they become routine and easy to automate. Working out a systematic procedure, an algorithm,

FIGURE 2: *Abstraction Is Commonplace*

for carrying out recurring tasks can significantly increase efficiency and productivity.

- Iteration and recursion—Ingeniously reapplying the same successful techniques and repeatedly executing the same set of steps to solve problems.

- An eye and a mind for details— Small things such as characters in upper-case versus lowercase or with an extra space can make all the difference. Any piece of data may be subject to interpretation depending on the context. You need eyes of an eagle, mind of a detective, and a careful and meticulous approach. Overlooking anything can and will lead to failure.

- Precision in communication—Try telling the computer to do what you mean and not what you say ;-). You need to spell it out precisely and completely. Don't spare any details. Vagueness is not tolerated. And contexts must be made explicit.

- Logical deductions—"Cold logic" rules. Causes will result in conse-quences, whether you like it or not. There is no room for wishful or emotional thinking. Don't we all wish some of this seeps into such things as our politics?

- Breaking out of the box—A computer program executes code to achieve any task. Unlike humans, especially experts, it does not bring experience or expertise to bear. Coding a solution forces us to think at a dumb computer's level (as if talking to a one-year-old) and get down to basics (Figure 3). This way, we will naturally need to think outside any "boxes."

- Anticipating problems—Automation relies on preset conditions. All pos-sible exceptions must be met with prearranged contingencies. Ever said "I'll take care of that later"? Because there is a chance you might forget,

FIGURE 3: *Breaking out of the Box*

according to CT, you should have a contingency plan ready in case you do forget. Otherwise, you have set a trap for yourself.

These are just some of the main ideas. CT offers you many more concepts and ways to think that can be just as, if not more, important. You'll find these CT principles highlighted in articles throughout this book.

Computational Thinkers Computize

In the author's textbook *From Computing to Computational Thinking* (CRC Press, 2015), a new word was introduced.

Definition: **computize**, verb. To apply computational thinking. To view, consider, analyze, design, plan, work, and solve problems from a computational perspective.

When considering, analyzing, designing, formulating, or devising a solution/answer to some specific problem, computizing becomes an important additional dimension of deliberation.

Therefore, a computational thinker is anyone who understands and applies CT, who computizes as a rule, and who can take better advantages of new technologies in the digital age.

CT Protects against Disasters!

People say, "hindsight is 20/20." But, since automation must deal with all possible applications in the future, we must ask "what if" questions and take into account all conceivable scenarios and eventualities. Let's look at a specific example. Hurricane Sandy was one of the deadliest and most destructive hurricanes in US history (Figure 4).

FIGURE 4: *NYC Subway Flooding (Hurricane Sandy)*

With CT at multiple levels, dare we say that many of the disasters from Sandy might have been substantially reduced?

- The New York City subway entrances and air vents are at street level. What if streets are flooded? What if flood water enters the subway?

- What if we need to fight fires in a flooded area? Do we have fire boats in addition to fire trucks? Do we have firefighters trained for boats?

- Most portable emergency power generators run on gasoline. What happens if gas runs out and gas stations are flooded?

- What if the drinking water supply stops? Can we provide emergency water from fire hydrants? In that case, can we use a mobile contraption that connects to a hydrant, purifies the water, and provides multiple faucets?

- What if emergency power generators are flooded? Should we waterproof generators in designated at-risk buildings?

- What if cell towers lose power? How hard is it to deploy portable or airborne (drone?) cell towers in an emergency?

- What if we simulate storm damage with computer modeling and find out ahead of time what to prepare for?

So let's computize at multiple levels and do our best to get 20/20 hindsight beforehand.

CT and DNA: a Success Story

In computing, performing the same set of steps repeatedly to achieve a certain goal is a technique known as *iteration* which is an important concept in CT.

Iteration of a process has led to the invention of the *polymerase chain reaction* (PCR), a technique in molecular biology to generate thousands to millions of copies of a particular DNA sequence.

FIGURE 5: *Dr. Kary Mullis, TED Talk, 2009*

Developed by Dr. Kary Mullis (Figure 5) in 1983, PCR is now indispensable in medical and biological research and applications, including DNA testing and genetic fingerprinting. The impact of automated PCR is huge and far-reaching. Mullis was awarded the 1993 Nobel Prize in Chemistry for his part in the invention of PCR (Figure 6).

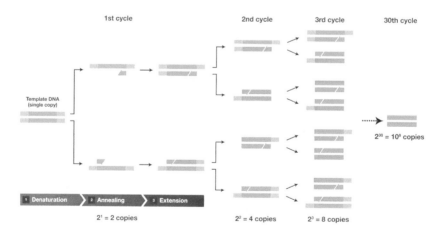

FIGURE 6: *Polymerase Chain Reaction (PCR)*

In recounting his invention, Dr. Mullis wrote in his book *Dancing Naked in the Mind Field*:

> *I knew computer programming, and from that I understood the power of a reiterative mathematical procedure. That's where you apply some process to a starting number to obtain a new number, and then you apply the same process to the new number, and so on. If the process is multiplication by two, then the result of many cycles*

is an exponential increase in the value of the original number: 2
becomes 4 becomes 8 becomes 16 becomes 32 and so on.

If I could arrange for a short synthetic piece of DNA to find a
particular sequence and then start a process whereby that sequence
would reproduce itself over and over, then I would be close to
solving my problem.

At the time of the invention, the "polymerase" and other related DNA dupli-
cation techniques were already known. It was the "chain reaction" part that
was missing. Well, we have Dr. Mullis and his computational thinking to thank
for the invention.

And what a significant invention! *The New York Times* described it as
"highly original and significant, virtually dividing biology into the two epochs
of before P.C.R. and after P.C.R.". Today, DNA technologies have been applied widely and changed our lives in countless ways, in medical science, law
enforcement, biology, and so on.

Furthermore, major breakthroughs attributable to CT also include weather
modeling and prediction, machine learning in Artificial Intelligence (AI) and
many other disciplines. Such advances help motivate CT in all areas.

Problem-Solving

A central idea in CT is problem-solving. Some CT experts would even say
"CT is nothing but problem-solving." Not everyone is willing to go that far,
But, it is certainly true that problem-solving is at the center of CT.

The usual or colloquial meaning of '*problem*' is often a certain difficulty
to overcome when trying to do something. But, from the CT point of view,
**almost anything one does becomes a problem of how to apply CT
to it**.

Thus, to a CTer, a problem can be any or a combination of these: a project,
task, mission, goal, challenge, difficulty, effect, outcome, or purpose. And the
meaning of *solving that problem* becomes "finding a systematic, ingenious,
step-by-step, effective, and efficient way to achieve, perform, or overcome it."
Such solutions can potentially be automated using well-designed algorithms
or procedures.

Here we define a new word *problemize*:

Definition: **problemize**, verb. To consider or treat something as a problem of
how to apply CT to it.

Realizing the power of CT, CTers have the attitude to problemize, no matter
how annoying and tedious it may seem.

CT Article 1, "*Everyday Computational Thinking Can Save Lives*" will discuss how to *problemize daily activities* such as leaving the house and going to bed. Hence, we can say that CTers tend to problemize all the time.

Time Well Spent

One does not become a computational thinker overnight. But reading CT Articles here is definitely a direct and enjoyable approach. As history has demonstrated time and again, a person who is better educated in the next dominating technology and who can absorb new thinking into common sense will have a significant competitive edge. You know we are talking about a computational thinker.

Happy Reading!

1

Everyday Computational Thinking Can Save Lives

Algorithms and their design and implementation are critical to modern computing.

Today we live in a global village. The Internet, the web, and the computer in its many different forms are providing instant communication across vast distances and changing almost every aspect of our lives. All the wonderful changes have been made possible by ingenious algorithms running on computing machines.

Here we'll see what an algorithm is and how flowcharts can help us envision procedures and formulate step-by-step solutions to problems. The knowledge is basic and key to computational thinking (CT).

Also in this CT Article, we will explain how algorithm-inspired CT can be applied by everyone in everyday situations and how it can make important differences and even save lives.

What Is an Algorithm?

Remember the hugely successful movie *The Social Network* (2010)? It told the story of Mark Zuckerberg and how he created Facebook. The motion picture also introduced the term *algorithm* to much of the world for the first time.

Simply put, *an algorithm is a step-by-step procedure designed to perform a particular task or to solve a specific problem*. Such a procedure forms the basis for writing a program that will perform the procedure on a computer. Thus, algorithms are fundamental to computing and therefore important for computational thinkers.

The origin of the word "algorithm" traces back to the surname Al-Khwārizmī of a Persian mathematician (780–850 CE), who was well known for his work on algebra and arithmetic with Indian numbers (now known as Arabic numbers). The modern-day meaning of algorithm in mathematics and computer science relates to an effective step-by-step procedure to solve a given class of problems or to perform certain tasks or computations (Figure 1). Specifically, a procedure becomes an algorithm if it satisfies all of the following criteria:

FIGURE 1: *Creating an Algorithm*

- **Finiteness**: The procedure consists of a finite number of steps and will always terminate in finite time.

- **Definiteness**: Each step is precisely, rigorously, and unambiguously specified.

- **Input**: The procedure receives certain data (or none) as input before it starts. Possible values for the data may vary within limitations.

- **Output**: The procedure produces results as its output.

- **Effectiveness**: Each operation in the procedure is basic and clearly doable.

For a given problem, there usually are multiple algorithms for its solution. The design and analysis of algorithms are central to computer science and programming.

What do algorithms have to do with everyday computational thinking? Good question. Well, it has to do with setting goals, devising concrete steps to achieve them, anticipating problems, and arranging solutions in advance. That's pretty important for everything every day, right?

Flowcharts

An algorithm is basically a procedure to achieve a certain goal.

A *flowchart* presents a procedure visually with words and diagrams. For any procedure, we can use a flowchart to plan the sequences of steps, to refine the solution logic, and to indicate how to handle different possibilities. Here is a simple flowchart (Figure 2) for the task of "getting up in the morning." We begin at the `Start` and follow the arrows to each next step. A diamond shape is used to indicate a fork in the path. Which way to turn depends on the conditions indicated. Obviously, we use diamond shapes to indicate

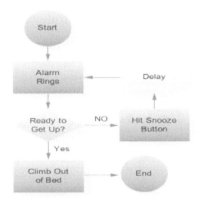

FIGURE 2: *A Wake-Up Flowchart*

possibilities. The snooze option leads to a branch that repeats some steps. In programming, such a group of repeating steps is called a *loop*. The procedure ends when the person finally climbs out of bed.

As another example, let's look at a flowchart for troubleshooting a lamp (Figure 3). The very first step after Start is significant. Although the purpose

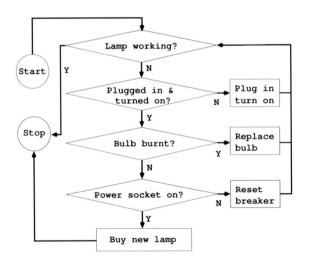

FIGURE 3: *Lamp Fixing*

of the procedure is to troubleshoot a lamp, we, nonetheless, make no implicit assumption that the lamp is not working. Without this step at the beginning, the procedure would potentially troubleshoot a perfectly good lamp, and, worse yet, would decide to replace it with a new lamp!

Each of the next three steps tests for a particular problem and makes a fix. Then the same procedure is reiterated by going back to step one to determine if the lamp is now working. This flowchart is a bit more complicated. Yet, it is worth careful examination (Figure 4) by following the steps. That is also a good way to get into the head of a programmer.

FIGURE 4: *Following a Flowchart*

All you need is pencil and paper to start drawing your own flowcharts. Try it and you may find it not so difficult. To make nice looking flowcharts, you can find many tools on your computer as well as online.

Correctly setting goals and guarding against potential problems are important aspects of devising a procedure. We want to avoid fussy, vague, confused, wishful, emotional, impulsive, optimistic, or pessimistic thinking. We want to practice CT any time and anywhere we can. We want to set clear goals, have a sequence of steps to achieve them, anticipate problems, and prepare solution plans in advance.

CT and Driving

Take driving a car for example. What is the goal? It is to get to a destination safely. It is not enjoying the sound system, watching the scenery, or engaging in conversation, although we have nothing against any of that as long as it does not get in the way of safe driving. Texting and driving is never safe.

Stopped at a traffic light, we wait for the light to turn green. But, we may need to run the red light if an 18-wheeler is about to crash into us from behind. That means we need to be checking our rearview mirror while waiting for the green light. When the light turns green, do we blindly rush into the intersection? What if a car is running the tail end of the yellow light or the red light?

Thus, the goal is not to obey traffic signals, but to ensure safety. In the United States, a car crash kills a person every 12 minutes on average. If you are thinking straight, is a car a fun machine or a dangerous one? CT can keep you focused on the goals, make you pay attention to details, plan for contingencies, and shield you from distractions. CT can save the day, and perhaps even your life!

FIGURE 5: *Preflight Checklist*

Now let's apply CT to the task of "getting ready to drive a car" and write down an algorithm-inspired predrive checklist like the one used by airline pilots (Figure 5).

1. Am I ready to leave? Forgot to bring anything?

2. Walk around the car, check windows, tires, lights, back seat, and any objects and activities near the car.

3. Get in the car, foot on brake, close and lock all doors.

4. Adjust seat and steering column positions as needed. Check positions of all rear-view mirrors, buckle up.

5. Check the instrumentation panel, pay attention to the fuel level.

6. If necessary, familiarize yourself with the controls for lights, turn signals, wipers, heat/AC, and emergency signal. Make sure they are working properly.

7. Release the hand brake, start the engine, shift gear.

8. Make sure the gear is in D or R as intended, then start driving.

Airlines have developed rigorous preflight checklists for safety. Incidents, sometimes fatal, happen when pilots and crew, failing computational thinking, do not follow the exact procedure. The same goes for doctors and nurses in hospitals, especially in operating rooms.

More Everyday Applications

Driving a car is not the only thing we do every day. Let's see how CT can be used to our advantage in other common activities.

We see an algorithm has a well-defined beginning and ending. This leads to the following CT principle:

> **CT concept–*Get ready before you start***: *If you are not prepared, forget something you need, or get underway in a hurry, you may often find yourself in trouble or even danger.*

Thus, when you leave home, work, school, or any other place, you need to get ready before you go! You don't want to leave anything behind or forget to bring anything you need later. Ever heard of people going to a show but forgot to bring tickets? In computing when you begin a procedure or algorithm, you need to make sure to set up the correct context. The same goes for daily living.

FIGURE 6: *Working in the Yard*

Leaving one place for another is the most frequent context change we do, and if we pay attention we can avoid trouble and be safer too. For example, when you go outdoors to work in the yard or garden (Figure 6), don't forget to wear sunglasses, hat, gloves, long pants, and working shoes. Apply sun screen lotion if necessary too. Oh, bring your cellphone with you in case someone might call. Surely you can think of many other daily situations where getting ready before you start becomes such good advice. How about forgetting to charge your phone or gas up your car before a trip? It can mean life or death indeed.

CT also encourages symmetric thinking. Getting ready at the beginning also reminds us to do the same at the end. When you leave a restaurant or some other such place, how often have you left your sunglasses, umbrella, hat, gloves, pen, or water bottle behind (Figure 7)? After finishing a call, you

FIGURE 7: *Sir, Your Water Bottle?*

might put the cellphone down casually? Put it back where it belongs. How many times have you misplaced your phone and can't find it? How about your scissors or another tool (Figure 8), car keys, sunglasses, even wallet? Hence, we have the symmetric CT principle:

FIGURE 8: *Where Is That Tool?*

CT concept–*Get set after the end*: *Returning things to their undisturbed state can help a lot in the future.*

All this CT leads to a good habit:

CT concept–*Checklisting*: *Write down a complete and detailed list for starting, performing, and finishing important tasks.*

Even a shopping list can be a good thing everyday.
We all go to bed at night and wake up in the morning every single day.

There are two chances per day to practice leaving one state and entering another. So get into a restful state for a good night's sleep and wake up to an energetic state ready to face a new day. Who said we couldn't practice computational thinking everyday?

A flowchart or an algorithm has another characteristic, namely sequencing of the steps. This leads to:

> **CT concept–*Activity sequencing***: *The order in which things got done matters.*

We all have loads of things to do every day, but we can become much more efficient if we plan ahead and decide what to do first and what next. Doing things in a logical order can make life go smoothly indeed.

Here we mentioned just several CT ideas inspired by a few computational techniques such as flowcharts and algorithms. As you know more about digital and computing technologies, by reading CT Articles here, for example, you'll discover many other CT ideas making you an even better computational thinker and helping you succeed in the digital age.

You Can Do It!

We have seen a sampling of computational thinking, inspired by algorithms and how computers follow step-by-step instructions. More importantly, we see how CT can be applied in everyday situations. We see the advantages CT can bring if applied well.

For most people, CT does not come naturally. Research has shown that snap judgment based on intuition and experience is the norm. But, by keeping CT in mind and consciously making it an added dimension to our deliberations, we can make it work for us.

By being creative, everyone can derive benefits from CT every single day. As a result, our community, even the entire society, will be better off by becoming more efficient and effective.

CT Crossword Puzzle

Basic Concepts

Across

2. Repeating a set of steps
4. Applying CT
5. Chart of a procedure
7. Data received

Down

1. Step-by-step procedure
3. In the beginning
5. At the end
6. Data produced

2

Digital Technology in the COVID-19 Fight

The World Health Organization (WHO) reported that, as of early May 2023, there have been 765,222,932 confirmed cases of COVID-19, including 6,921,614 deaths globally. And by the end of April 2023, a total of 13,344,302,744 vaccine doses have been administered worldwide.

According to WHO data, from January 3, 2020 to May 3, 2023 in the United States, there have been 103,266,404 confirmed cases of COVID-19 with 1,124,063 deaths.

The estimated cumulative financial costs of the COVID-19 pandemic related to lost output and health reduction were more than $16 trillion, or roughly 90% of the annual GDP of the United States. For a family of four, that would be nearly $200,000!

But the damage and cost due to the pandemic could have been much worse without active interventions worldwide. Therein, application of computing and digital technologies played a crucial role. People do their best in a crisis, and there are important lessons to learn for the world to better face the next one.

We will look at how digital technologies have been applied in the fight against COVID-19. The experience underscores the need for continued investment in public health, medical research, and technological innovations to prepare for future global health crises. Computational thinkers in all walks of life have been and will be contributing greatly.

COVID-19 Virus Identification

COVID-19 (coronavirus disease 2019) is a disease caused by a virus named SARS-CoV-2 (Figure 1). But no one knew anything about this deadly virus when it first broke out in Wuhan, China on January 10, 2020. It was very contagious and spread quickly in the 6th largest city in China, with a population of about 11 million, which is greater than either New York or London.

The Chinese central and local governments, with cooperation from city residents as well as the entire country, completely isolated Wuhan in a 76-day lockdown beginning on January 23, 2020. The global fight against the unknown disease suddenly began.

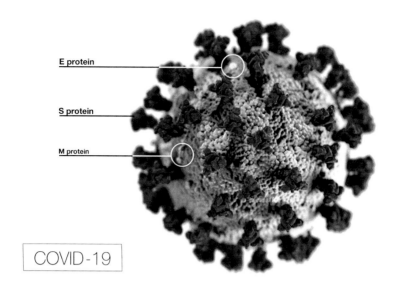

E protein

S protein

M protein

COVID-19

FIGURE 1: *Virus Illustration by the CDC*

The identification and DNA sequencing of the COVID-19 virus and its subsequent mutations relied heavily on digital technologies. The process involves multiple steps, including sample collection, DNA isolation, DNA sequencing, and data analysis.

- **Sample collection**: Samples of the virus were collected from patients using various methods such as swabs, saliva, or blood. Once collected, these samples were transported to the lab for further analysis. Digital tools were used to track and manage the samples during transportation and storage to ensure that they remained viable for analysis.

- **DNA isolation**: The next step involved isolating the DNA of the virus from the patient sample. This process required the use of digital tools such as pipettes, centrifuges, and automated DNA extraction machines, which help extract the DNA more efficiently and accurately.

- **DNA sequencing**: The isolated DNA was sequenced using advanced sequencing technologies such as Next-Generation Sequencing (NGS). NGS technology enabled researchers to sequence the entire genome of the virus in a matter of hours, compared to the weeks or months that would have been required using traditional sequencing methods.

- **Data analysis**: The DNA sequence data were analyzed using bioinformatics tools and software. The results helped researchers compare the genome of the virus to other known viruses and identify its genetic mutations. They also helped track the spread of the virus and predict its future mutations.

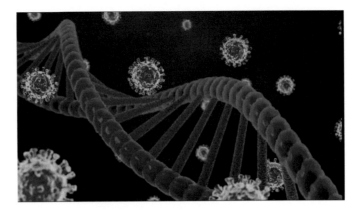

FIGURE 2: *COVID-19 Virus Can Affect Human DNA*

Researchers also demonstrated that SARS-CoV-2 damaged human DNA and triggered an altered DNA damage response (Figure 2).

These important digital technologies have been critical to identifying and sequencing the DNA of the virus, as well as its mutations, quickly and accurately. This gave people a significant advantage in the fight against this pandemic.

Evolution of DNA Technologies

DNA technologies have come a long way since the invention of Polymerase Chain Reaction (PCR) in the mid-1980s. PCR (Figure 3) revolutionized the field of DNA technologies, enabling scientists to amplify specific DNA sequences quickly and easily.

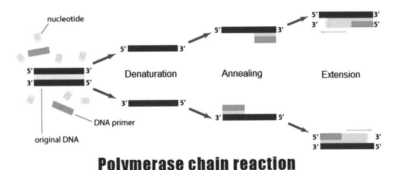

FIGURE 3: *PCR Steps*

Dr. Kary Mullis received the Nobel Prize in Chemistry 1993 for the invention of the PCR technique. Since then, there have been significant advances in

DNA technologies, which have further expanded our understanding of genetics and enabled new applications in medicine, agriculture, and forensic science.

Here are some of the key advances in DNA technologies since the invention of PCR:

- **Next-generation sequencing** (NGS): NGS technologies have transformed the way we sequence DNA, making it faster, cheaper, and more accurate. NGS can now sequence millions of DNA molecules simultaneously, allowing researchers to analyze complex genomes, identify genetic mutations, and study gene expression.

- **CRISPR-Cas gene editing**: The CRISPR-Cas system has revolutionized gene editing (Figure 4), allowing scientists to precisely and easily edit DNA sequences in living cells. This technology has the potential to cure genetic diseases, create new drugs, and increase productivity of crops.

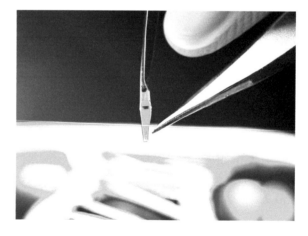

FIGURE 4: *CRISPR-Cas Gene Editing*

- **DNA microarrays**: The method is used to analyze gene expression, genotyping, and DNA methylation. This technology can simultaneously analyze thousands of DNA sequences, making it useful for medical diagnosis, cancer research, and pharmacogenomics.

- **Metagenomics**: It is a field of study that analyzes the genetic material of entire communities of microorganisms. This technology has enabled us to study the microbiome and understand its role in human health and disease.

- **Synthetic biology**: It involves creating new DNA sequences or modifying existing ones to create new biological systems. This technology has the potential to create new drugs, fuels, and materials and improve our understanding of fundamental biological processes.

These significant DNA technology advancements enabled us to understand genetics and apply it to various fields. It is our good fortune because these advances played a crucial role in the fight against COVID-19.

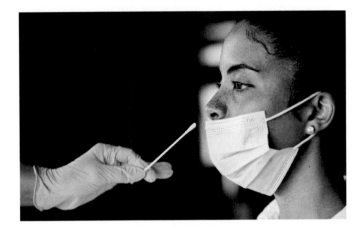

FIGURE 5: *COVID-19 Testing (image: COVID.gov)*

Here are the ways these advances have been used:

- **Patient testing**: PCR technology was widely used for COVID-19 testing (Figure 5) to identify individuals who had been infected with the SARS-CoV-2 virus. PCR testing can detect viral genetic material in patient samples and is highly sensitive and specific, making it a reliable tool for diagnosing COVID-19.

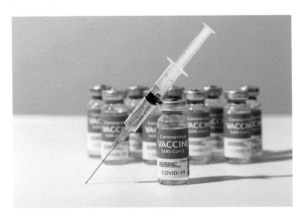

FIGURE 6: *COVID-19 Vaccines (image: Freepik)*

- **Mutation detection**: Genomic sequencing technology had been instrumental in identifying new variants of the SARS-CoV-2 virus, which was critical for tracking the spread of the virus and developing effective treatments and vaccines. Genomic sequencing had helped researchers to determine the genetic makeup of the virus, identify mutations that made it more/less transmissible or virulent, and monitor the spread of these variants.

- **Vaccine development**: Technologies such as genetic engineering and recombinant DNA technology played a significant role in the development of COVID-19 vaccines (Figure 6). The Pfizer and Moderna vaccines, for example, used a technology called *messenger RNA* (mRNA), which was a type of synthetic genetic material that instructed cells to produce viral proteins that would trigger an immune response.

- **Medication development**: Researchers used and are still using CRISPR gene-editing technology to create new treatments that can target and destroy the SARS-CoV-2 virus in the body.

In addition to DNA technologies, digital communications also played critical roles in the fight against the COVID-19 pandemic.

Contact Tracing

To reduce the transmission of COVID-19 and protect the public, the key is speed—that with which a society can find close contacts of confirmed and suspected cases and take immediate preventive measures to arrest the spread of the disease.

China, for example, implemented a digital contact tracing system using mobile apps and QR codes. The system collected data on a person's movements and activities and alerted them if they had been in close contact with someone who had tested positive for COVID-19. The people identified were then tested and observed for a while to make sure they were not infected, or they would be quarantined and treated and their close contacts traced.

Several states and cities in the US had implemented digital contact tracing apps, including Virginia's COVIDWISE, North Dakota's Care19, and California's CA Notify. These apps used Bluetooth technology to detect close contacts and notified users of potential exposure to the virus.

China also implemented a health QR code system that used color-coded QR codes (Figure 7) to indicate a person's health status. The codes were based on a person's travel history and health status and were used to control access to public spaces such as malls, restaurants, and public transportation.

South Korea has been widely praised for its effective use of digital technologies, including a mobile app that provided real-time information on the spread of the virus and contact tracing through GPS data and credit card transaction

FIGURE 7: *COVID-19 Health QR Code*

records. The country's aggressive testing and contact tracing strategies had helped to contain the spread of the virus.

Contactless Communications

Digital communications technologies enable people to avoid person-to-person contacts preventing virus transmission in great measure. During the pandemic, students and teachers went to online classes. People ordered takeout meals, shopped for groceries and necessities via e-commerce, watched videos at home instead of going to theaters, worked from home, held online meetings via services such as Zoom, and so on.

Telemedicine services became more widely used in the US during the pandemic, allowing people to consult with healthcare professionals remotely.

Many countries also implemented telemedicine services. Such services included video consultations and online prescription services.

This has helped to reduce the risk of transmission among healthcare workers and patients and increase access to healthcare services for people who are unable to visit hospitals or clinics in person.

Vaccine Distribution

Digital technologies enabled the efficient distribution of COVID-19 vaccines in the US as well as other countries. Effective distribution used online appointment scheduling, digital vaccine passports, and real-time tracking of vaccine supply and demand. Several states also implemented digital vaccine registries to keep track of who received what type of vaccines and when. The system also notified participants if and when they became eligible for booster shots.

Virus Monitoring and Information Sharing

The World Health Organization (WHO) of the United Nations established a website to provide up-to-date information on the global spread of the virus, confirmed cases, and deaths. The website also provides information on public health and social measures listing steps taken by countries, territories, and areas that enforce rules or guidelines to limit the spread of COVID-19.

The US Centers for Disease Control and Prevention (CDC) has utilized digital technologies to collect and analyze data on the spread of the virus, including the COVID-19 Data Tracker, providing real-time data on cases, hospitalizations, and deaths.

The Johns Hopkins Coronavirus Resource Center played an important role as well. After 3 years of around-the-clock tracking of COVID-19 data from around the world, the center's operations were discontinued as of March 10, 2023.

There are many other applications and areas where computational technologies have helped the fight against the pandemic. For example, drones and robots were used to deliver medical supplies, disinfect public spaces, and assist with temperature checks at airports and other public spaces.

Finally

The fact is that DNA techniques and computational technologies have been indispensable in the fight against COVID-19.

Without these technologies, it would have been much more challenging to diagnose the virus, track its spread, and develop effective treatments and vaccines.

We are fortunate to have access to these modern and effective ways to deal with such a pandemic. It would be unthinkable to do without them.

The COVID-19 pandemic has been a significant challenge for humanity, governments, and ordinary people worldwide. For computational thinkers, it has brought to light the importance of being prepared for unforeseen events that can have catastrophic consequences. Remember computational thinkers will always ask "what if" questions and plan ahead of time. Here are some important lessons:

- **Early warning systems**: Similar to fire fighting, early warning is of the utmost importance. Countries and international organizations should invest in early detection systems to identify and respond to potential health crises. These systems could involve the use of machine learning algorithms to monitor data from hospitals, nursing homes, social media, news outlets, and other sources to identify potential outbreaks.

- **Improved communication and collaboration**: Collaboration and communication between countries, healthcare professionals, and researchers are crucial. Governments should work together to share information, data, and best practices to prevent the spread of diseases.

- **Preparedness planning**: Governments and organizations should have contingency plans in place to respond to potential crises, including plans for ample medical and safety equipment, hospital beds, emergency shelters, quarantine spaces, testing, contact tracing, and vaccination campaigns.

- **Public education and awareness**: Every society must routinely and continuously educate the public on ways to prevent the spread of diseases and promote healthy behaviors.

As the COVID-19 pandemic wanes, people around the world must not be complacent and should continue to be vigilant in their defenses. We need to be prepared for the next big disaster, because we know it is not if but when it will strike again. Possibilities include: another germ/virus attack, nuclear or chemical accident, climate change or other natural disaster, power/Internet blackout, war, serious civil unrest, and so on. Of course, all of us, especially computational thinkers, must remember the lessons and unite in getting prepared for the next crisis. In case we succeed, all the deaths due to the pandemic would not have been in vain.

CT Crossword Puzzle

COVID-19 Fight

Across

3. PCR

7. Global public health organization

8. QR code can help contact

9. CDC

10. PCR

11. Work from home

Down

1. Meeting online

2. At a distance

4. PCR inventor

5. PCR use

6. Without contact

3

The Metamorphosis of TV

The digital revolution has brought many changes to our lives and altered our world in many basic ways. Among these is the transformation of television (TV) from analog to digital and then to a merging of TV and personal computer technologies.

As a result, we have profoundly changed the way we get news, watch shows, find and view all kinds of information, communicate and share ideas, learn, play, and even conduct meetings. Here we will explore and understand this extraordinary evolution.

In the Beginning: Analog TV

Television started with a simple idea, *capturing an image as a sequence of signals, then recreating the image from those signals.* The method is distinct from projecting images from a film, namely *motion pictures* or *movie*, developed in the late 19th century.

Early TV development from the *Grolier Encyclopedia*[1]:

> In the early part of the 1920s, a mechanical television system, scanning images using a rotating disk with holes arranged in a spiral pattern [the Nipkow disk 1884], had been demonstrated by John Logie Baird in England and Charles Francis Jenkins in the United States.
>
> Later on September 7, 1927, an electronic version of TV was first demonstrated by 21-year-old Philo Taylor Farnsworth in San Francisco. The system worked by capturing signals of an image, coding the signals onto radio waves and then transformed back into a picture on a screen. It would work fast enough to capture moving images.

In the 1930s, publicly available TV broadcasts began in a few countries, including Britain and the US. Analog broadcast signals were received with an

---

[1]Stephens, M. (1999) *The History of Television.* In Grolier Multimedia Encyclopedia (2000 ed.)

FIGURE 1: *Old CRT TV Set*

antenna connected to a Cathode-Ray Tube (CRT) TV set (Figure 1). That was the beginning of analog TV which offered very few channels and had limitations with picture quality and signal strength, often requiring antenna adjustments for better reception.

Yet, TV grew in popularity, achieved better image and sound quality, and remained for many decades the main source of news and entertainment for the masses. Then, we had the digital revolution.

Digital TV

The transition from analog to digital TV began in the late 1990s and continued into the early 2000s with different countries and areas following their own timeline. Digital TV transmits digitized audio and video signals, resulting in much better picture and sound quality than analog TV. It is because analog signals weaken, interfere with radio station and other signals as well as distort through transmission. Digital TV signals have no such problems and also allow for more efficient use of the broadcast spectrum, enabling broadcasters to transmit multiple channels simultaneously in a process known as *multiplexing*.

In the US, the Federal Communications Commission (FCC) mandated that starting June 12, 2009 all US-based television signals must be transmitted digitally. The great majority of US households (97.5%) were prepared for the digital transition in the weeks prior to the switch.

Consumers who relied on over-the-air analog TV signals had these options: upgrading to digital TV sets, installing digital-to-analog converter boxes, or subscribing to cable or satellite TV service.

Most homes chose the converter option for the change. The government offered a $40 coupon for such a converter. From that point onward, over-the-air analog TV broadcast ceased to exist in the US.

Digital Audio and Video

Digital Audio

Of course, digital TV uses digital representations for audio and video. Technically, audio refers to sound within the human hearing range. Sound is caused by vibration. A sound wave represents the amplitude (volume) and frequency (pitch) of sound. The continuous sound wave is **sampled** at regular time intervals, and the amplitude value at each sampling point is *quantized* to the nearest discrete level.

The resulting data are stored in binary format as a digital audio file. The higher the sample rate and the greater the bit depth (number of quantization levels), the higher the sound fidelity and the larger the file size (Figure 2). Let F be the highest frequency of an audio signal. The sampling rate must

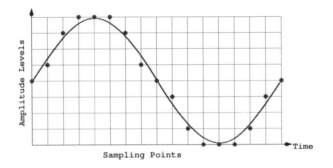

FIGURE 2: *Sampling and Quantization*

be at least $2F$ to represent the signal well. This is the so-called *sampling theorem*. Human hearing is limited to a range of 20 Hz to 20 KHz (cycles per second). Thus, the CD-quality sampling rate is often 44.1 KHz. Human speech is limited from 20 Hz to 3 KHz. An 8 KHz sampling frequency is high enough for telephony-quality audio.

Advances in digital audio brought increasingly sophisticated compression schemes to reduce the size of audio files while preserving sound quality. Compressed data can be transmitted much faster and decompressed at the receiving end. A compression-decompression scheme is called a *codec*. For example, the widely used MP3 is the audio compression standard ISO-MPEG Audio Layer-3 (IS 11172-3 and IS 13818-3). Other formats include *Advanced Audio Coding* (AAC), Ogg Vorbis (`xiph.org`), and *Free Lossless Audio Codec* (FLAC).

Let's turn our attention to digital video which has been a major factor in the evolution of TV.

Digital Video

A video is a sequence of images, called *frames*, displayed in rapid succession that is usually also played in synchrony with a sound stream. Similar to audio, an image can be digitized by sampling and quantization values of each pixel in the image. Each frame supplies a complete image, where each pixel is represented by a number of bits; the more pixels and bits per pixel, the better the picture quality. For smooth motion, a sufficient *frame rate*, about 30 frames per second (fps), is needed.

A video file usually supplies video tracks, audio tracks, and metadata. Tracks in a video file can also be organized into chapters that can be accessed and played directly. Such files are known as *video containers* and they follow well-designed *container formats*, which govern the internal organization of a video file.

The video and audio tracks in a container are delivered with well-established video compression methods. A video player must decompress the tracks before playing the data. Many compression-decompression algorithms exist. Generally speaking, video compression uses various ways to eliminate redundant data within one frame and between frames. There are many digital video codecs for different purposes, including DVD, Blu-ray™, HDTV, DVCPRO/HD, DVCAM/HDCAM, and so on.

Video Streaming

Video streaming is a technology that breaks down audio and video data into a sequence of packets that are transmitted, usually over the Internet, to a player that can piece together the flow of packets and play them back. Streaming TV, or applying streaming to TV data, has become a game changer, revolutionizing the way TV content is delivered and consumed.

Currently, for online video streaming, one of the most widely used video codec is H.265 or High Efficiency Video Coding (HEVC) due to its high-quality video with a smaller file size and broad compatibility. Even with sophisticated data compression algorithms, digital video files can be huge; the higher the image resolution and sound fidelity, the larger the file size.

For video streaming, the speeds of network transmission, encoding, decoding, and display rendering operations are critical. Enabling technologies include broadband Internet, high speed mobile network, video/graphics processing hardware/software, especially a powerful *graphics processing unit* (GPU) for display rendering.

Streaming TV allows the delivery of TV content over the Internet, giving viewers access to a wide variety of shows and movies on-demand, without the need for traditional broadcast or cable infrastructure and not limited by any program airing schedules.

Streaming services such as Netflix, Hulu, Amazon Prime Video, and others have gained immense popularity, providing viewers with flexibility and convenience in choosing what they want to watch, when they want to watch it, and on multiple devices. In addition, platforms such as YouTube, Vimeo,

FIGURE 3: *Live Video Streaming (image: Kampus Production)*

and TikTok enable easy creation, editing, uploading, and managing your own videos. The popularity of such services has ended the one-way nature of TV, allowing people to widely share video contents of their own creation. Such contents include DIY experiences, sports coaching, cooking demos, physical exercises, travel logs, product demos (Figure 3), and much more.

Convergence of TV and PC

The convergence or integration of TV, video streaming, and personal computer (PC) technologies has been an ongoing trend in consumer electronics. This convergence has been driven by advancements in technology, changing consumer behaviors, and evolving content consumption habits. For example, we wonder about the difference between a TV set and a PC monitor. And if we have a smartphone or tablet/laptop, who needs a TV set? These are good questions, especially for young computational thinkers.

Let's look at some key aspects of the convergence:

- **Smart TV**: A smart TV is a TV set that has built-in Internet connectivity (WiFi/Ethernet) and computing capabilities, allowing users to access online content and services, especially for audio and video, directly from their TV. Smart TVs often run on operating systems such as Android TV, webOS, Tizen, or Roku OS, which provide an interface for users to access streaming services, browse the web, and run apps. You can do all this with a well-designed remote control unit. A smart TV may also have additional features such as voice controls, content recommendations, and smart home integration, blurring the lines between traditional TV and computer experiences.

- **Smart TV Projector**: This is a portable projector with all the networking and streaming functions as a smart TV, but without the bulkiness. Projection lighting can be from a lamp, lasers, or LEDs. Some even come with HD or higher resolutions, brightness up to 2000 ANSI lumens, and perhaps also great built-in speakers.

- **Streaming Media Player**: A streaming media player, such as Apple TV, Roku, Amazon Fire TV, and Google Chromecast, is an external device that connects to a TV set to provide access to online streaming content and services. It is basically a smart TV without a display screen or tuner.

- **Gaming Console**: A gaming console, such as PlayStation, Xbox, and Nintendo Switch, is basically a specialized PC for playing video games. It often needs to be connected to a display with speakers, and offers multimedia functions, such as streaming video and music, browsing the web, and accessing social media. Some gaming consoles also support keyboard and mouse inputs, enabling users to interact with the console as they would with a PC.

- **Cross-Device Connectivity**: Another area of convergence between TV and PC is inter-connectivity. Users can connect their PCs, smartphones, tablets, and other devices to the TV to display content, mirror screens, or control the TV using apps or remote controls. Smart TVs can easily play contents on home Network Attached Storage. A PC can be connected to a TV via HDMI instead or in addition to a monitor. This allows for seamless integration and interaction between different devices, enabling users to access and share content across devices and platforms.

The merging of TV and PC has transformed the way people access, consume, create, and share content, offering a more integrated and personalized viewing experience. There is little difference nowadays between a TV display and a PC monitor. As technology continues to advance, we can expect further convergence between TV and PC technologies, creating new opportunities and challenges in the world of entertainment and media.

The Metamorphosis

Television has come a long way since its inception, and the digital age has brought about significant changes in TV sets and how TV programs are produced, distributed, and consumed (Figure 4). The original analog, black-and-

FIGURE 4: *A Smart TV*

white, over-the-air broadcast TV received with antennas and displayed on CRT screens was already magical. Yet, it is entirely possible for some people in some countries to have never seen CRT TV sets and instead only view TV on their phones. TV has indeed evolved into something even more wonderful and powerful that is impacting and bringing profound changes to consumers and society at large.

First of all, digital video offers a much better picture and sound quality. It also becomes more convenient and flexible to access and view TV programs and video contents on demand, not limited to TV's fixed airing schedules. Viewers can control and replay programs on different devices. Video and TV contents are often available free of charge. All you need is a good Internet connection. Besides, TV now is a two-way street, enabling user interactions, content creation, and sharing.

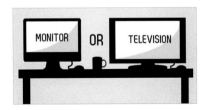

FIGURE 5: *Merging of TV and Monitor*

As TV and PC technologies merge, we have the best of two worlds. You can use a computer and its monitor as a TV, and a TV as a computer monitor as well (Figure 5). The old TV is gone. It has morphed into something more useful and beautiful—a story from which we all, computational thinkers in particular, can learn. We must be flexible, resilient, and diligent to keep up with the times so we can let changes in the digital age help, not hinder, our success. After all, we are the masters of our own fate.

.... CT Crossword Puzzle ....

Digital Video

Across

3. Continuous signal
5. PC
7. Continuous to discrete
8. Discrete signal
10. Internet video

Down

1. Over-the-air TV signal
2. Continuous to discrete
4. Computer display
6. Interactive video
9. TV

4

Smart about Smartphones

The modern smartphone suddenly, within the span of a few years, became a must-have device for most people (Figure 1). We use it for almost everything: phone calls, texting, web/Internet, taking pictures/videos, streaming shows, making payments, banking, control smart devices, managing fitness and health, getting directions, and much more. We can do all this right in the palm of our hands. The smartphone represents the convergence of many modern technologies in one lightweight handset. Without question the smart-

FIGURE 1: *Smartphones Are Popular*

phone has become a vital part of our daily lives. It is important for all of us to know it better and use it more effectively and appropriately.

Who Invented the Smartphone?

We know Alexander Graham Bell won the first US patent for the telephone in 1876. The smartphone, however, is another story.

As early as the 1940s, there were efforts to make phones *mobile* with radio transmissions so they could be used from automobiles, trains, and by the military in the field. In 1946-1948, AT&T introduced *Mobile Telephone Service* to a number of towns and highways in the US. The first mobile phones weighed 80 pounds each.

Mobile phones became *cellular phones* when coverage areas were divided into cells. Each cellular area has its own directional antennas on a transmission tower or tall structure. These *cell towers* (also called *cell base stations*) reuse radio frequencies and enable handing ongoing phone calls off from one cell to the next. The 1990s saw cell transmissions move from analog to digital and the development of the GSM (European) and CDMA (US) standards. The 2G era brought explosive growth of mobile phone use. In August 1994, IBM released

FIGURE 2: *IBM Simon 1994 (image: Irish Times)*

Simon (Figure 2) that rolled a cell phone, a pager, a fax machine, and a touch-screen PDA into one handheld device. Although not a commercial success (discontinued in February 1995), it is perhaps the first smartphone. Then came the successful BlackBerry from Research In Motion (Canada) which brought many advances to smartphones. Today, the company is no longer in business. In the meantime, the Apple iPod shaped how people used portable devices leading to the iPhone (2007) which was the best smartphone consumers had ever seen. With a price of about $500, people stood in line to buy the iPhone and subscribe to its exclusive carrier AT&T.

What Is Android? iOS?

Android and iOS are the two dominant mobile operating systems for smartphones and tablets. The iPhone runs *iOS* which is Apple proprietary and built upon the same kernel as macOS. *Android* is an open-source (free for all) system developed by Google based on the Linux kernel and other open-source software around 2007-2008. Name any smartphone other than the iPhone; chances are it runs a version of Android. According to `bankmycell.com`, for the quarter ending in June 2023, mobile operating system market share worldwide was for Android 71.63% and for iOS 27.71%.

Smartphones are wonderful. One convenient handset can combine a touch-screen tablet, mobile phone, still/video cameras, and additional devices such as microphone, speaker, flash light, global positioning system, and other sensors.

On top of all that hardware, you have a huge variety of software (apps); a few are built-in, but many others are easily installed by downloading them from the Apple App Store or Google Play (Figure 5). Remember the App

FIGURE 3: *Smartphone App Stores*

Store or Google Play is your central control for all apps where you may find, download/install, uninstall, update, and configure apps either individually or as a whole. For example, you may consider allowing automatic updates for all apps when the phone is connected to WiFi. The modern smartphone, providing so many useful functions, is no wonder a little complicated. Let's explore the many aspects of a smartphone.

Making Phone Calls

You can't call anyone except 911 if your phone does not have a Subscriber Identity Module (SIM) card from a wireless service provider such as Verizon, AT&T, T-Mobile, and so on. With a SIM inserted, all you need is a strong enough signal from a nearby cell tower to make/receive phone calls (Figure 4) and to send/receive text messages. Simply put, texting is nothing more than sending a textual message to a particular phone number. The phone will automatically log all calls and text messages made and received. Beware that your calls and text messages are carried over the public cellphone network and therefore subject to eavesdropping. There are apps to secure them by encryption. For example, the free *signal* app encrypts calls and messages end-to-end.

Some health issues can arise as a result of excessive use of smartphones. Be aware that prolonged phone use, especially texting or watching videos, can hurt your neck. The syndrome, known as *text neck*, is caused by the head bent downward and not moving, which puts additional pressure on the neck.

Radiation can be another concern. If you don't want the phone next to your ear, you can use the *speaker mode* which also allows several people around the phone to join the conservation. You can put the phone call *on hold* to pause

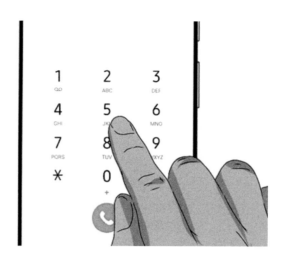

FIGURE 4: *Using a Smartphone*

the call and resume a bit later. While holding a call, you may use the phone to check email, look up a web page, or make another phone call.

While on the phone, you can answer another incoming call. You may also add a call to turn it into a conference call. An audio recording app, such as Easy Voice Recorder or Audio Recorder, allows you to record incoming phone calls or to make recordings in general. A video recording app, such as DU Recorder or AZ Screen Recorder, can record video calls.

You can customize the ring tone or put the phone in vibrate mode to avoid bothering others. It is polite to do so in movie theaters and such. If you don't want to be bothered at all, turn on the *airplane mode* which turns off all wireless transmissions including cellular, WiFi, bluetooth, and any Global Positioning System (GPS). Many also use this feature to save battery power. Airplane mode lets you use what you already have in the phone while preventing any wireless communication to/from it. Turn off airplane mode, and your phone comes back alive to the outside.

Other things you can do include block/unblock calls, call forwarding, log calls, and manage caller IDs.

Short Codes

The Unstructured Supplementary Service Data (USSD) is a protocol allowing cell customers to access/set account information and features by dialing *short codes* right from their phone. For example, dialing the short code `#BAL#` (`#225#`) displays your account balance, `#NUM#` (your phone number), `*#06#` (the International Mobile Equipment Identity or IMEI number).

Other codes control call forwarding, call waiting, voice mail, and so on. The complete list of short codes is available from your cell service provider. You can check them online and use them as you like.

Protecting Your Phone

Your SIM card stores data such as subscriber identity, billing information, mobile phone number, network authorization data, and personal security keys. It may also store contact lists and text messages.

Each SIM card comes with a default PIN code (usually "0000"). When you turn on your phone, it asks you to enter the PIN and connects to your cell network only after getting the correct PIN. This is important protection and you should always set your own PIN to replace the default one.

Make sure you remember your PIN. If incorrect PIN codes have been entered 3 to 5 times in a row, the SIM card becomes *locked*. But it can be unlocked with a PIN Unblocking Key (PUK) which is given to you when you first got your SIM card. Keep your PUK in a safe place away from your phone, as it is the key to unblocking your SIM, and establish a new PIN code. Note that if you enter the wrong PUK 10 times in a row, the SIM will be permanently blocked, and you'll need to purchase a new SIM card.

In addition to the SIM PIN, you should also set up a phone unlock pattern and/or fingerprint, or face recognition unlock feature. Some believe using the latter features can be less secure than strong PIN codes and unlock patterns.

In any case, to protect your smartphone, don't leave it lying around and always keep it with you. As a principle, don't let anyone else use your smartphone.

The Tablet Aspect of Smartphones

For your smartphone to function as a tablet computer, it needs an Internet connection. There are two ways: WiFi and cellular data connection. Of course, your home WiFi as well as public WiFi hot spots do not incur an additional cost. Data plans by cell carriers can be expensive.

Having connected to the Internet, you can make a *video call/chat* (Figure 5) which is, in many respects, better than phone calls because the calling parties can see one another and can share views of their surroundings. Why not make video calls, especially when they can often be made free of charge? Simply install a video call app from your App Store. Popular chat apps include: Skype, Google Duo/Chat/Meet, FaceTime, Viber, WhatsApp, WeChat, Facebook Messenger, Zoom meeting, etc. Better yet, these usually are free. But remember, the chat parties must first start and log into the corresponding video chat app on their end. A big advantage of video chat is the fact that

FIGURE 5: *Making a Video Call on a Smartphone*

you can share live images of people, objects, and scenery via the smartphone's front and back cameras. Most video call apps also support conferencing for holding meetings online (Figure 6). Playing video is of course popular and a

FIGURE 6: *Video Conferencing on a Smartphone*

smartphone allows you to stream video anywhere with an Internet connection. What displays on your small screen can usually also be *cast* to your big-screen smart TV. Basically, anything you can do on a laptop computer you can also do on your smartphone including listening to music, radio programs, and audio books. Of course, you can surf the web, send/receive email, shop online, and much more.

Working Out

Do you exercise for better fitness? You can use a smartphone to track the distance or count the number of steps while jogging or walking, not to mention playing your favorite music to keep you in rhythm. With various fitness apps and associated gear, you can time your workout, log your progress, monitor your heart rate, even estimate your blood pressure. You can also find many weight loss apps to manage your overall fitness.

Mobile Payments

You can use your smartphone to make payments at stores and vendors. It is convenient and contactless, avoiding physically touching the payment terminal.

Basically you first install a mobile payment app such as Apple Pay, Google Pay, WeChat Pay and Alipay (Figure 7). Then follow instructions to add one or more *payment methods*, usually credit cards, debit cards, PayPal and so on. Once set up, you can use your smartphone to make payments usually by

FIGURE 7: *Mobile Payment Systems*

simply placing it next to the vendor's payment terminal. Data is transferred via Near Field Communication (NFC) between two devices next to each other. Make sure your phone has NFC turned on. When you have no need for NFC, turning it off saves power.

For most people, mobile pay is simply pay by credit card without using the physical credit card. It is more convenient and also more secure. With mobile pay you can also directly send/request money from family and friends.

Vendors can receive payments with their smartphones. Popular apps include Square, PayPal/Venmo, Zelle, Cash, and Payanywhere. They all make sending and receiving cash/credit card payments via your phone quick and easy with little or no cost involved.

Get an app from your bank or other financial institution and you'll be able to deposit checks, transfer funds, make investments, and much more.

Voice Commands

Perhaps one of the most satisfying experiences with a smartphone is to say what you want and get it done (Figure 8). The underlying speech recognition and generation technology is amazing. But we won't go into details except to say that rapid speech recognition supported by Internet access is involved. Thus, the phone needs to be Internet-connected for voice commands to work. Personal assistant apps such as Google Assistant, Alexa, and Siri all rely on

FIGURE 8: *Command Your Smartphone To Do Things*

speech technologies to listen to user commands and to give verbal answers. When giving a voice command, we need to say a short *wake-up phrase* to activate the speech recognition program. Examples are *OK Google*, *Hey Google*, *Alexa*, and *Hey Siri*. You can also set your own wake-up phrase to something you like. It is also possible to touch a microphone icon or holding down the home button to give a voice command directly.

> **CT concept–*Use wake-up phrase with people***: *Avoid saying something to someone suddenly or unexpectedly. Get your conversation to a smooth start by politely and gently say hi, sir, mister, a name, pardon, excuse me, or guess what ... so the intended other party is ready to hear what you have to say.*

With your own voice, you can initiate a call or text (*'call Mom'*, *'text/tell Joe Smith'*), change settings (*'flashlight on/off'*, *'battery saver on/off'*, *'WiFi on/off'*, *'Bluetooth on/off'*), play music/radio/video (*'play Pandora'*, *'watch*

Star Wars'), set alarms, timers, calendar entries, reminders (*'set an alarm for 3:30 pm'*), get facts, ask for directions, and search the web (*'what is the weather?'*, *'what is the time/date in Beijing?'*, *'what is 15% of 58?'*), and much more.

Search for the complete list of voice commands for your phone online or say *'the complete list of voice commands'*. Remember voice recognition works not only in English, but also in other major languages such as Chinese, Spanish, French, etc.

Other apps that accept voice input include Google Translate, Google Maps, speech to text conversion apps, and many others. Increasingly, people use their phones to control smart devices, do remote home monitoring, and so on. Many of such apps would also support voice commands.

In-car Use

Whether you are driving or walking, modern GPS navigation devices make going to places as simple as following turn-by-turn directions. A smartphone can become a navigation tool because it usually has a built-in global positioning sensor. If you have that, plus a navigational map, then you are in business.

This usually means you need to have an Internet connection while moving or you had the needed maps already downloaded into your phone. For example, with the Google Maps app, you can download and save regional maps for offline use.

FIGURE 9: *No Texting and Driving (image: bmwblog.com)*

Dedicated GPS devices have built-in maps but that can become outdated. This means you need to update the maps. With the smartphone approach, you will be always working with the most current maps. You can pair your phone via Bluetooth to an in-car media system for an improved experience.

Apps such as Android Auto (from Google) and CarPlay (from Apple) are examples that pair with compatible car systems for hands-free phone calls, texting, audio streaming, and navigation.

Talking on the phone or texting while driving is dangerous (Figure 9). Set your phone's *drive mode* options to refuse incoming calls. The phone can even go into drive mode automatically when the car is moving.

Smartphone Cameras

The quality and capabilities of cameras on modern smartphones vary a lot, ranging from very good to just OK. Usually, you will find front and back cameras and a built-in camera app. You can take photos (with/without flash assist) in day/night mode, portrait/scenery mode, zoom in/out, take selfie (using the front camera), and so on (Figure 10). Timer delay is supported but is rarely useful. You can also take video in 720P, 1080P, and even 4K. Slow-motion videos are also possible. For better and more advanced camera

FIGURE 10: *Taking a Picture*

apps, search for recommendations online and download them from your app store. For more detailed control of the camera and how to take professional or studio quality photos/videos, you need to really study not just the manuals but learn digital photography, a subject beyond the scope here.

The best thing about taking photos/videos with your smartphone is that you can share them immediately with others by simply tapping the share icon in the camera app or the gallery app. For email, consider using the JPEG format with a 640×480 or 800×600 pixel size (4:3 aspect ratio). If your camera app does not have a setting for the pixel size, use a photo resizer app to scale down the full-resolution photos (usually too big to go through email) to the desired size before emailing.

Other apps use the camera to scan QR codes, barcodes (i-nigma), even documents (Adobe Scan). To capture your smartphone screen, you don't need a camera, just push the power button and choose screen capture to get an image of the screen.

Smartphone Security

Because you depend on your smartphone so much, because others use your phone to authenticate you (send security codes to you, for example), and because it stores so much private data, it is of the utmost importance that you keep your phone secure and always with you. Make sure you set up a lock screen for your phone, as it is easy and a necessary security measure (Figure 11). Always keep your SIM PIN and phone unlock key to yourself.

FIGURE 11: *A Lock Screen*

Keep them together with your other login information in an encrypted file on another computer. For convenience, you can keep that same file in your phone as long as it is encrypted with an app such as *TextSecure* and *Crypt4All*.

Don't download any file or open any email attachment from strangers. According to the British daily newspaper *The Guardian*, Amazon boss Jeff Bezos' iPhone was "hacked in 2018 after receiving a WhatsApp message that had apparently been sent from the personal account of the crown prince of Saudi Arabia ... included a malicious file."

Back up your contacts, list of apps, and their associated data as well as other useful information on cloud storage (Google Drive or Dropbox, for example). Phone backup/restore apps make this very easy.

What Is 5G?

In the US, most cell phones operate on 4G LTE networks which are up to 10 times faster than 3G networks. 5G is the next evolution sponsored by the 3rd Generation Partnership Project (3GPP) and the International Telecommunications Union (ITU). 5G got seriously underway in the US around 2020.

5G can support much faster speeds (up to 100 times faster than 4G) and many simultaneous mobile devices densely located in a given location such as a football stadium, concert hall, or factory. These 5G capabilities open the door for *Internet of Things*, *Smart Cities*, and more.

Because 5G uses new radio spectra and new tower stations, it takes time to roll out. The first stage involves adding new spectra to the existing 4G LTE for more speed (about 20% faster). Finally, 5G will be separated from 4G in stand-alone mode. Of course, you need a 5G compatible smartphone to enjoy the improvements. China has moved very quickly to deploy advanced 5G inside the whole country. The US is moving ahead quickly as well.

Too Much of a Good Thing?

Smartphones are convenient and powerful. But, as with any tool, misuse or overuse would be inappropriate or downright dangerous.

FIGURE 12: *Walking into an Accident?*

Have you ever seen a couple, sitting face-to-face across a table of fine food, looking down and playing with their phones and not talking or relating to each other? Is that not sad?

Smartphones can be a distraction in many other situations, including answering calls during a conversation or meeting. Doing so while walking or driving is known to cause accidents (Figure 12).

According to Reuters news agency[1]:

> *The train driver blamed for the worst U.S. train crash in 15 years was sending and receiving text messages seconds before his crowded commuter train skipped a red light and collided head-on with a freight train, federal investigators said on Wednesday.*
>
> *The Metrolink commuter train plowed into a Union Pacific freight locomotive on September 12 in Chatsworth, California, killing 25 people and injuring 135 in the worst train accident since 1993.*

This example is among many accidents worldwide related to operator cellphone use.

In the US, all states have passed their own distracted driving laws restricting or prohibiting cellphone use, especially texting, while driving.

Too much cellphone radiation might lead to health problems such as brain tumors and skin cancer. With nonstop use, light from the display screen can lead to eyestrain and sleep deprivation.

Overuse may also cause many psychological issues such as loneliness, being suspicious all the time, feeling self-centered, and so on. Texting too much not only isolates you from face-to-face human interactions but also can cause *text neck*.

Children, and some adults, can easily become addicted to the smartphone and that can cause many problems.

Another concern is privacy. Your smartphone gives away your location and your travels because cell towers track your phone. The phone also has several cameras, microphone, and many other sensors that can be accessed by apps (legitimately or not) to spy on you. Mobile phone carriers had been accused of making consumers' real-time location data available to third parties.

Remember, calling someone can often be a rude interruption. The receiver is almost forced to drop other things and answer a phone call. We need to be considerate and avoid making unexpected calls on a whim. Texting can be a good alternative. Some people elect to turn off their smartphones from time to time.

In short, too much of a good thing is always a bad thing. And we all need to be smart about smartphones.

---

[1]Reuters Staff. (2008, Oct. 2). reuters.com

Finally

Cellphones and online communication kept all of us going during the difficult days of the COVID-19 pandemic, making it easier to practice social distancing without becoming isolated or feeling alone.

Modern smartphones are great yet complicated. Basically, you have many devices rolled into one and even mastering one of the functions takes time and effort. Here is a place to practice CT and apply *abstraction*, focusing on the important features of a complicated system by ignoring unimportant details.

Smartphones are wonderful. But, remember, your smartphone can save or destroy your life; it is up to you to use it responsibly.

.... CT Crossword Puzzle ....

Smartphone

Across

5. Bring your phone for
7. APP
9. Smartphone OS
10. Early mobile phone brand

Down

1. SIM
2. From APP store
3. Sending short messages
4. Divided into cells
6. Can you hear me?
8. Screen lock

5

Cybersecurity–How Not To Be a Fish

Today the *cyberspace* where communication over computer networks takes place has become a must-have infrastructure for any modern society. However, in cyberspace, just like in physical space, bad things can happen. Such things include delivering unwanted or unwelcome materials, eavesdropping, breaking and entering, information theft, datanapping, and other cyber crimes. Surely, we want to take full advantage of the web/Internet while guarding against possible downsides.

Widely publicized security breaches range from information theft to influencing democratic elections to holding computers for ransom. No wonder why many individuals feel edgy about their own security and privacy online. You are not alone if you feel unsure or even helpless.

While cybersecurity is a vast area and involves many factors and players—Internet providers, computer software and hardware companies, search engines, social media, and government agencies—here we focus only on a basic understanding of safety measures for individual users.

We'll explain how to protect yourself and provide practical advice on ways to improve safety, spot dangers, and avoid falling victim to various baits and lures that come your way in cyberspace.

Cyberattacks

Let's first take a look at some high-profile cyberattacks in the recent past (Figure 1).

- **Minneapolis public school system data breach and leak (2023)**: The notorious Medusa (a group of hackers) took credit for the data breach and confirmed their involvement by leaking a sample of employee and student data to the dark web. The early March 2023 attack tied up computer systems and communications throughout Minnesota's largest school system for several days.

- **Colonial Pipeline ransomware attack (2021)**: In May 2021, the Colonial Pipeline, a major fuel pipeline operator in the United States, fell victim to a ransomware attack. The cybercriminal group known as

FIGURE 1: *Cyberattacks*

DarkSide was responsible for the attack, leading to the shutdown of the pipeline for several days and causing disruptions in fuel supply across the US East Coast.

- **SolarWinds cyberattack (2020)**: One of the most significant cyber attacks in recent history, the SolarWinds attack targeted the software company SolarWinds, allowing hackers to infiltrate its systems and gain access to numerous organizations worldwide. It is believed to have been carried out by a Russian hacking group, resulting in the compromise of sensitive data and networks.

- **WannaCry ransomware attack (2017)**: The WannaCry ransomware attack (Figure 2) affected hundreds of thousands of computers worldwide. It exploited a vulnerability in Microsoft Windows systems and spread rapidly, encrypting files and demanding ransom payments in Bitcoin. The attack targeted various organizations, including healthcare institutions and government agencies.

FIGURE 2: *WannaCry Ransomware Attack*

- **NotPetya cyberattack (2017)**: The NotPetya cyberattack was a destructive malware campaign that affected numerous organizations globally. It initially targeted Ukrainian businesses but quickly spread to other countries. NotPetya was disguised as ransomware but was later revealed to be a wiper, destroying data irrecoverably. The attack caused significant financial losses for several companies.

- **Equifax data breach (2017)**: In one of the most significant data breaches in history, the credit reporting agency Equifax suffered a cyber-attack that exposed personal information of approximately 147 million people. The breach occurred due to a vulnerability in the company's web application software, allowing hackers to access sensitive data, including social security numbers and credit card information.

- **Sony Pictures Entertainment hack (2014)**: A high-profile cyberat-tack targeted Sony Pictures Entertainment, leading to the leak of sen-sitive data, internal emails, and unreleased films (Figure 3). The attack was attributed to the hacker group known as Guardians of Peace and was believed to be motivated by geopolitical tensions. The incident re-sulted in significant financial losses and reputational damage to Sony.

FIGURE 3: *Sony Attack by Guardians of Peace*

- **Target point-of-sale systems attack (2013)**: Some of us still remem-ber that, one day after Thanksgiving 2013, the large retail chain Target suffered a security breach. Cybercriminals appeared to have focused on the point-of-sale systems in Target's retail stores, which collect informa-tion from customers' credit and debit cards, and potentially personal identification numbers, or PINs. The stolen information can be used to create counterfeit credit or debit cards.

Cybersecurity attacks can be launched by a single individual or a well-organized group, some, the so-called *advanced persistent threat* groups, could be connected to industry or even governments.

A *Bloomberg News* article[1] said, "Russian hackers hit systems in a total of 39 states."

Generally, a cybersecurity attack exploits one or more vulnerabilities in a system or network, including the Internet as well as phone networks. Here are some types of attacks that should concern end users.

- Phishing—Collecting private or confidential information such as user IDs, passwords, Social Security numbers, driver's license numbers, account numbers, phone numbers, PINs, addresses, and birth dates by tricking users to supply them through phone calls, emails, or fake websites (Figure 4). For example, an email may ask the user to increase email storage space, verify an online order, confirm a refund or payment, change login information, fix an old unpaid invoice, or manage a package delivery by clicking a link in the email. The link leads to an official-looking online form put up by the attacker. Or, a scam may inform you of a sudden wealth that you can receive by sending your bank account information and often a handling fee or tax!

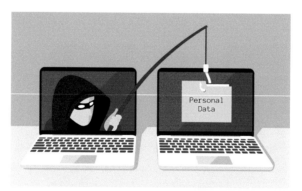

FIGURE 4: *A Phishing Attack*

- Spoofing—Pretending to be someone, at some IP address, from a certain website, sent from some email address, or located at certain GPS locations. Spoofing is usually done by falsifying data used in communication protocols. For example, the email sender (the `From` header) can be spoofed easily.

- Malware—Malicious software of all kinds including computer viruses, ransomware, worms (spreading themselves through the network), Trojan horses (hiding in seemingly legit applications), keyloggers, spyware, and rogue security programs.

---

[1]Riley, M. and Robertson, J. *Russian Hacks on U.S. Electoral System Wider Than Previously Known.* (2017, June 13). bloomberg.com

- Eavesdropping—Spying by secretly monitoring network communications or leaking electronic emissions from equipment. The man-in-the-middle attack carries this further by intercepting messages between two correspondents, and perhaps even altering the messages as they are passed along to the other end.

Cyber crimes are a serious and global concern. Governments, private sectors, and academic institutions have acted to produce countermeasures, including legislation, regulation, law enforcement, protection of communication infrastructures, and Computer Emergency Readiness Teams (CERTs) in the US and other countries.

Lock and Key

Security in cyberspace is not so different from that in physical space. In any case, there is no escaping the need to deal with our own security in cyberspace. It may be a bother, but there's no alternative.

How do we keep things safe in physical space? Is it not lock and key? The same goes for cyberspace. There, we want to keep our email account, bank account, online purchase accounts (Amazon or eBay account), memberships (LinkedIn, Netflix, NPR, ACM, or IEEE) and so on under lock and key as well. These are known as *protected resources* online.

To unlock and access a protected resource, the key is usually a *user ID-password* pair. Only the correct user ID and password can unlock the protected resource and give you access. This process is usually called *login* or *sign in*. The assumption is that only the owner has the key, and no one else does. Hence, we must do our best to keep it that way.

In cyberspace, the process of verifying the identity of a user in order to grant access to protected (locked) resources is known as *authentication*. The most common way of authentication for users is by user ID and password. For additional protection, some systems use the so-called *two-factor authentication* where an additional interactive step involving an email or text message is required. Furthermore, the login process may also involve *CAPTCHA* tests to guard against attacks by robots.

Taking Care of Passwords

In physical space we need to take care of our lock and key. In cyberspace, we must also safekeep our user ID and password.

- Avoid short passwords. Use 12 or more characters that include uppercase and lowercase letters, numbers, punctuation marks, and special symbols.

Keep your password easy to remember but hard to guess. Don't use family names, 1234, 0000, or whole words. For longer passwords, consider a secret phrase.

- Don't use the same password in different places. This way, if a password were compromised, the damage would be limited to one place. But, this means that you will have many passwords, one for each of your accounts online.

- Write down your user ID, password, and other authentication information (such as answers to security questions) somewhere safe. Consider saving them in a file kept offline (on a USB drive, for example). It is best to also encrypt the file.

- When setting up answers to security questions, avoid using real answers and invent your answers instead. For example, use a fake birthday, mother's maiden name, hobby, model of first car, and so on. Record these in your file, too.

- Change your passwords from time to time just to be extra safe.

- Make sure you are not being observed or video recorded when you log in. This is especially important when you are in a public place. Consider logging in to important places only from the privacy of your home. To be extra secure, set aside a computer for the sole purpose of doing important business online. Don't use that computer for any other purpose.

- Do not leave your computer or cellphone unattended after login. Lock the screen if you must leave for a short while. Always log out immediately after finishing your business. Close your browser or shut down your system afterwards.

- Use the browser auto-login feature, where your browser remembers your user IDs and passwords for different websites, only if you enable a *browser master password* to protect the saved login information from others who may gain access to your computer. Select your browser's advanced security option to set your master password.

Dear Me, My Password!

You are not alone in feeling frustrated when you cannot remember a certain password. It happens to all of us, including those who never thought it possible for them. It is tempting to cop out and use the same password at many different places, making it easier to remember. Of course, that is unsafe and ill advised. Saving your passwords in a secure file is a good solution.

It is always possible to reset your password. Usually, *forgot my password* is an option at login time. Clicking on that option starts a process where you need to answer questions to establish your identity and to demonstrate that you are the owner of an account. The answers you provide will be checked against data stored in your account (address, email, phone number, security question answers, and so on) for verification. When things check out, you will receive an email with instructions for setting up a new password.

Your email address, being a way to identify your account and to send information to you and you alone, is critical in this whole password reset process. Therefore, it is important for you to make sure that no one except you can receive your email. It is never a good idea to allow someone else to handle your email.

The point is, if someone could receive your email that person would potentially be able to reset the password to some other account of yours, such as, goodness forbid, your bank account.

The same goes for your cellphone. A text message to your cellphone can be an alternative to email for resetting your password. And no one needs to be reminded that losing your cellphone is bad.

Encrypting Your Sensitive Data

The most sensitive data are Personally Identifiable Information (PII) because those data can uniquely identify you as a person and often used to determine the identity of a person (Figure 5). To keep files with sensitive data, such as PII, safe on your computer, you should encrypt them. For example, you may store in files scanned copies of family driver's licenses, passports, birth certificates, stock certificates, and so on. It is a good idea to encrypt such files. The file with login info should be encrypted. Or use a password manager, such as LastPass, to store your passwords.

When a file is encrypted, it becomes a pile of scrambled garbage data to anyone but the person who knows the key to decrypt the file back to its original readable form. Many tools are available for file encryption including Microsoft Word, LibreOffice, and AES Crypt, just to name a few. Be careful, forgetting the key for decrypting a file means the file will be lost forever. It is OK to use the same master key for all your encrypted files. Just make sure that key is secure and not used for any other purpose.

Back up your encrypted files. You don't want to lose these files if something happens to your computer.

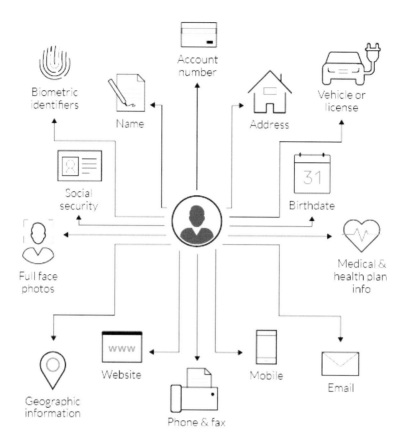

FIGURE 5: *Common Personally Identifiable Information (PII)*

Cybersecurity Habits

Organized countermeasures and the technologies on the web and Internet for identification, authentication, encryption, and so on are all well and good. But, the human factor is still the weakest link in cybersecurity. As users in cyberspace, we all need to do our best to tighten security, and hopefully we can collectively make cyberspace more secure for everyone.

Here are some suggested actions for individual users.

- Make sure system updates relating to security are installed as soon as possible.

- Enable firewalls and configure them correctly on your routers and computers. On your wireless router, use WPA2/WEP wireless security and turn off remote admin access.

- Download and install software only from known and trusted websites. Avoid free software that is too good to be true.

- Encrypt sensitive files on your computers and smartphones.

- Do not give your user ID or password in response to an email or a phone call.

- Back up your important files on external disks (detachable from your computer), on flash drives, or on the cloud in encrypted form.

- Do not access your online accounts from public places or use borrowed computers.

- Keep your laptops, tablets, and smartphones with you all the time. Close down your web browser after finishing with a login session. Lock the screen if you need to be absent for a short while. Do not leave them in your car or otherwise lying around!

- Be careful with flash drives and other similar free gift items. They may contain malware that can infect your computer.

- Be extra careful with Microsoft Windows; most security attacks target Windows applications due to their popularity. Consider using computers running Linux to be extra careful.

- For mobile devices, install apps only from official app stores, and enable the screen lock (and SIM card lock) features. Install an anti-virus app.

Do your best, and you'll be glad you did. If everyone does their part, cyberspace will be that much more secure.

Use Common Sense

When you receive an email with a fantastic deal that sounded too good to be true, it usually is. Do not open any attachments. Delete the email immediately.

To lure you in, phishing emails make up different stories such as online storage over quota, security policy changes, package delivery problems, and other clever tricks. Be suspicious, do not believe such stories without double checking on your own.

No legit business or organization will send email to a customer and give some excuse to ask for your user ID and password. Neither will they give you a clickable link to enter such information. If you receive an email like that, it may indeed lead you to a phishing site where any information you enter will be stolen. You can spot the phishing site by paying attention to the browser `Location` box where the site URL is displayed. Is the URL the official company site? Is there a lock icon next to the URL? If not, get out of there immediately.

Web browsers will display a secure icon in the form of a *closed padlock* when HTTPS (secure HTTP) is in use. This means data traffic between you and the site is encrypted to prevent eavesdropping. Clicking on the lock icon reveals the *digital certificate* of the site. Examine the certificate to ensure that the site is not counterfeit.

To be safe, avoid clicking any link in an email or strange site. Always go to your intended site directly on your own by typing in its URL such as: `bankofamerica.com`, `vanguard.com`, or `amazon.com`. Well-managed businesses and organizations usually send sensitive information to customers not by email but by messages placed in a secure inbox accessible only after login.

To avoid being swindled, you should never disclose personal information over email, by texting, by phone, or at a site not arrived to on your own initiative. Let's all refuse to become a phishing victim.

It is good practice to never send any sensitive information over email unless it is encrypted. Overlook this and suffer the consequences. Imagine, once upon a time, the US may have elected a different president if certain email documents were not leaked due to lax cybersecurity.

Reporting Cyberattacks

Immediately report email scams, phishing, web forgery, and other security attacks you encounter. In the US, forward suspected phishing email to:

`phishing-report@us-cert.gov`

or the Anti-Phishing Working Group at `reportphishing@apwg.org`.

Contact authorities or the legitimate businesses to alert them. Use your web browser's `Help->Report Web Forgery` option, or contact the Internet Crime Complaint Center (`ic3.gov`).

You Can and Need To Do It

We have discussed the basics to protect yourself in cyberspace. All this may seem complicated and not particularly urgent for you. Nothing bad has happened to you or your computer. But when it happens, it will be too late. Hopefully, by acting on some of the suggestions here, you'll start to make it safer. You don't have to do everything all at once. Make a step, and then I am sure you will become more confident to follow through.

CT Crossword Puzzle

Cybersecurity

Across

3. Make data unreadable

4. lock computer force payment

9. Verify identity

10. Pretending to be someone else

Down

1. Recover unreadable data

2. online attacks

5. the space online

6. Secure HTTP

7. Oh, I forgot my

8. Deceiving to obtain info

6

Computers: More Than Meets the Eye

Computers are pervasive in our daily lives, from smartphones and laptops to automated systems in various industries. It is obvious that a good understanding of computers is important for everyone.

People say you cannot judge a book by its cover. It is also true that you can't know a computer by looking at its display screen. That is similar to knowing a car by examining its steering wheel. An under-the-hood view will not only give you insights but also make you a better computational thinker.

Here we'll describe the modern computer in simple terms for everyone–its hardware, software, operating system, usage, files and folders, online use, and troubleshooting–just the basics, nothing fancy. We will also focus on computers for personal use and simply mention that other types of computers– supercomputers, mainframes, web servers, database servers, cloud servers, and so on–are more powerful and complicated.

Hardware

Modern personal computers (PCs) come in different forms: desktop, workstation, laptop, notebook, tablet, handheld, and smartphone. Computer hardware refers to the physical components of a computer. A component can be central or peripheral. Basic central components (Figure 1) include the Central Processing Unit (CPU), random access memory (RAM/DRAM), file and data storage devices (hard drives, solid-state drives), power supply and so on.

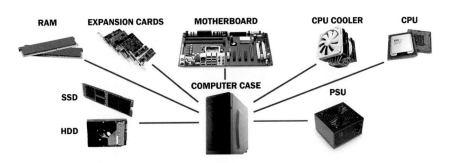

FIGURE 1: *Typical Hardware Components*

Peripherals can make a computer easier to use and simpler to add capabilities to it. Normally, a peripheral has its own power supply and is connected to the computer by special interface cables (for example, VGA, DVI, HDMI, or DisplayPort for monitors) or through wireless links such as WiFi or Bluetooth.

Commonplace peripherals include monitors, speakers, microphone, headphone, webcam, printers, scanners, mouse, keyboard, and so on (Figure 2).

FIGURE 2: *Computer Peripherals*

Operating System

A main function of the operating system (OS) is to control and utilize all the hardware and make the computer easily usable by people and by programs or apps.

It brings life to the innate electronic hardware components and orchestrates all activities on a computer. The same hardware under a different OS is literally a different computer. The operating system is a piece of software that is the master manager and controller of a computer, the whole computer. Figure 3 shows the most widely used operating systems: MS Windows, macOS, Android, and Linux.

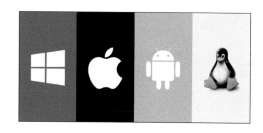

FIGURE 3: *Popular Operating Systems*

The OS provides service and control functions to users, administrators, programs, files, display monitors, printers, network connections, and everything else on a computer system. The *kernel*, the most central part of an OS, has CPU specific features to take better advantage of any particular model CPU. A computer OS is one of the most complicated and sophisticated objects humans ever built.

A modern OS consists of three main parts:

1. A *kernel*,

2. Interfaces for users, programs, devices, and networks, and

3. A set of commands and apps.

The kernel deals with central functions, including concurrent program execution, memory management, input/output (I/O), file services, networking and security. Commands and apps supply other operations such as file managers, text editors, email processors, web browsers, software package managers, audio/video and image processing tools, language compilers, and so on. Interfaces define and support communications among all the components.

For users, the OS provides easy-to-use Graphical User Interfaces (GUIs) in the form of *desktop environments* (Figure 4). An OS also provides efficient and effective Command-Line Interfaces (CLIs) in the form of *Shells*.

FIGURE 4: *Windows 10 Desktop*

Familiarize yourself with your system. Learn how to navigate the file system, manage files and folders, install and uninstall software, install updates, and customize system settings. For example, you can set language preferences, define keyboard shortcuts, and even choose a left-hand mouse setting.

Software Applications

The ultimate purpose of the hardware and OS combination is to run application programs (apps) in order to perform specific tasks. Today, we seldom use a disk, CD-ROM, or DVD to install a new app. We simply go to the *app store* (Figure 5) to choose, download, and install any available app we like with just a few mouse clicks. How convenient! Common apps include word processors (Mi-

FIGURE 5: *Windows App Store*

crosoft Word, Google Docs), spreadsheets (Microsoft Excel, Google Sheets), presentation software (Microsoft PowerPoint, Google Slides), and email clients (Gmail, Thunderbird, MS Outlook).

When an app runs it becomes a *process*, which is the name for a program in execution (being run by the CPU). The OS handles and manages all processes and is responsible for their creation, suspension, scheduling, resumption, finishing, and destruction. The OS also controls inter-process communications. Modern OSs allow *multitasking* on single-CPU computers, running processes concurrently by seamlessly and rapidly switching the CPU among the processes. The technique is known as *context switching*, saving the state of the running process and replacing it with the state of the switched-to process. If multiple CPUs exist on the computer, then the OS also supports *multiprocessing* using all available CPUs to run processes in parallel.

The desktop GUI allows you to run several apps simultaneously, each in its own window, and switch among them easily. Of course, these are in addition to other parallel activities that the OS coordinates and orchestrates, such as I/O, networking, printing, file transfer, display refreshing, and updating.

Files and Folders

A computer offers an electronic filing system, known as a *file system*. That is a great advantage indeed. Storing data as files that can be accessed immediately by the user and by programs is essential for modern operating systems.

Each item stored in the file system is called a *file* and is identified by a *filename*.

A file can contain other files; in which case, it becomes a *folder*. Thus, when we say files we usually mean files and folders.

FIGURE 6: *Tree Structure of Files*

Figure 6 shows the tree structure of files. In a file system there are separate *system-wide* and *per-user* storage spaces. System-wide files are common to all users while per-user files belong to a particular user. Unless achieving *administrator status*, users can only manage/access their own files. Each user has a separate *home folder* where per-user files are stored.

The data type of a file is known as its *file type*. For example, a file may contain an email, report, tax return, C++ program, compiled program, organized database, library of mathematical routines, picture/image, or audio/video clip. Often the file type is indicated by the filename suffix, such as `txt` (text file), `jpg` (image file), `mp3` (audio file), `mp4` (video file), `doc` (MS Word file), `xls` (MS Excel file).

The OS provides a consistent set of facilities allowing the user to create, store, retrieve, modify, delete, and otherwise manipulate files. The *physical* storage media (usually high-speed magnetic or solid-state disk drives) are divided into many *blocks* of *logical* storage areas. A file uses one or more of these blocks, depending on the amount of data in the file. Blocks are used and freed as files are created and deleted. The part of the OS kernel that creates, stores, retrieves, protects, and manages files is the *file storage system* (or simply file system).

Computer users, computational thinkers (CTers) especially, should become familiar with organizing and managing files and folders on the computer, including creating, copying, moving, and deleting files, as well as understanding file types and compatibility.

Internet and Web Browsing

Modern computers can hardly work without access to the Internet. Most functions of a computer have become Internet-dependent. Files, folders, even emails can be online. Other operations depend on the cloud. A computer/smartphone connects to the Internet through an Internet Service

Provider (ISP) by cable or 5G modem, DSL, ISDN, WiFi router (hotspot), or mobile data.

If the Internet connection goes down, it can bring serious disruptions to normal operations. The most obvious disruption is "no Internet no web access." That means no banking, shopping, video streaming, online chat, remote learning, video conferencing, shipping and delivery tracking, or many other operations.

Modern computers depend on networking and the Internet in almost all aspects. Some say it is hard to tell where the computer ends and where the network begins. Turn off the network and use your computer off-line to get a feel of what difficulties you would encounter. Without Internet access a computer cannot find the address of other computers and becomes an isolated island in the sea of all other computers and servers. The experience can be most frustrating indeed. For example, it cannot do email, software updates, or get the news. As you read more CT Articles in this book, you will realize the reasons and the scope of this network dependence. In fact, for a modern society, the Internet is as important an infrastructure as the power grid, an important concept for all CTers.

We need to understand web browsers (Google Chrome, Microsoft Edge, Firefox, Opera, Safari; see Figure 7), search engines, and the Internet in order to use them efficiently and effectively. In addition, we need to evaluate the credibility of online sources, and practice safe browsing habits.

FIGURE 7: *Major Web Browsers*

Network access brings convenience and productivity. Yet it is not without concerns. With Internet access also comes certain security risks. CTers need to familiarize themselves with concepts such as anti-virus software, firewalls, and safe online practices; understand the importance of strong passwords, software updates; and recognize and avoid phishing attempts. These are the prices to pay for the conveniences the computer and the Internet bring.

Troubleshooting

Computers provide such great capabilities, and we count on them. Yet, we all may have unpleasant experiences when somehow the computer or Internet stop working (Figure 8), and we need to fix it pronto. Here are some tips for troubleshooting:

FIGURE 8: *Oh No! The Computer or Internet Is Down*

1. *Check the power supply:* Ensure that the power cable is securely plugged into both the PC and the power outlet. Confirm that the power outlet is functioning by testing it with another device. If you're using a power strip, make sure it is turned on and functioning properly. Consider trying a different power cable or power supply, if available. Check power to the peripherals too. For a smartphone, laptop, or tablet, check the battery power.

2. *Check network connections:* If no Internet, check your network router and Internet modem. Also check the network settings on your computer. Try restarting the modem and router, wait 30 seconds or so before turning the device back on.

3. *Examine the PC for physical issues:* Check if any cables, such as the monitor cable or USB cables, are loose or disconnected. Inspect the PC for any signs of damage, such as bent pins, loose components, or burn marks.

4. *Restart the PC:* Press and hold the power button for about 5 seconds until the PC powers off. Wait for a few seconds, then press the power button again to turn it back on. Sometimes, a simple restart can resolve minor issues.

5. *Check monitor-related problems*: Ensure that the monitor is turned on and receiving power. Check that the monitor cable is securely connected to both the monitor and the PC. Try connecting the monitor to a different port (e.g., HDMI, VGA, DisplayPort) on the PC. If you have a spare monitor or a TV, connect it to the PC to determine if the problem lies with the monitor.

6. *Listen for error beeps*: If your PC emits beeping sounds during startup, it can indicate specific hardware issues. Consult the PC's manual or the motherboard manufacturer's website to identify the meaning of the beeps.

7. *Disconnect external devices*: Remove any external devices connected to the PC, such as printers, scanners, external hard drives, or USB devices. Sometimes, faulty peripherals can prevent the PC from starting up.

8. *Boot into Safe Mode*: If the PC powers on but fails to start properly, try booting into Safe Mode. Restart the PC and repeatedly press the F8 or Shift key (depending on the PC) during startup to access the advanced boot options. From there, select Safe Mode to boot with minimal drivers and services. This helps determine if a software or driver issue is causing the problem.

9. *Seek professional help*: If none of the above steps resolve the issue, consider contacting a help desk, a professional technician, or the manufacturer's support for further assistance.

Remember to exercise caution when working with hardware components and consult professional help if you're unsure.

Personal Computer Inspired CT

FIGURE 9: *CT Inspiration*

Here we can point out several computational thinking (CT) principles inspired by our understanding of the PC (Figure 9).

CT concept–*Central control*: *The OS is a model of total control over hardware, apps, files, users, peripherals, and networks.*

CT concept–*Connecting independent devices*: *Connect independent devices to make the combined mechanism more flexible, extendable, and scalable.*

CT concept–*Hierarchical structure*: *A tree structure can be effective in many cases where a hierarchy is an effective organization. The file tree is an example.*

CT concept–*The Internet is the computer*: *It is hard to see where the computer ends and where the Internet begins. A computer can hardly work without a network connection.*

CT concept–*Parallel processing for speed and efficiency*: *The effectiveness of parallel processing has been demonstrated by multi-CPU and multicore computers. In daily life, managing things in parallel can save time and increase productivity.*

CT concept–*Backup plan*: *If you are dependent on something, then you need a backup plan, or a plan B, if and when that thing fails. For example, if the computer and Internet stopped working how would you contact someone?*

Finally

The level of computer knowledge users should have depends on their personal needs and interests. At a minimum, basic computer literacy includes understanding how to use a computer, navigating the operating system, using common software applications, and being familiar with Internet usage and online safety. However, the more you know about computers, the better equipped you are to take advantage of the numerous opportunities and effectively navigate the digital world.

It is especially true for CTers as topics mentioned here naturally connect to quite a few CT Articles presented in this book. Because of the creative nature of the CT Article titles, this may not be immediately clear from the table of contents. But, the more progress you make in this book, the more you will realize the connections and mutual reinforcements among the materials and topics.

CT Crossword Puzzle

Computer

Across

2. A user with admin status

4. GUI 1

7. Plug-in parts of a computer

9. A display area for an app

10. Tree structure is

Down

1. GUI 3

3. Guard computer against network break-in

5. Web surfing

6. Central part of OS

8. A program under execution

7

Home Sweet Homepage :-)

A company representative might say, "Hello Mary, it is nice to meet you. Please (producing a business card) visit our homepage and find out all about me or my company." You might get an email saying, "Can you believe this? See it here." Or, a friend might invite you to dinner and say "Look at their menu, I am very much looking forward to our dinner together." These days we rely on the web every single day and it seems a computer (or smartphone) is simply a ticket to the web. Yet, what is the web? Where is it? Who owns it? Is it another name for the Internet? Why is it called the web? What makes it tick? How come it is so important? Why should I care?

We shall answer these questions and speak to ways we can make the web work for us. Of course, the information is basic to anyone in the information age, especially computational thinkers.

What Is the Web?

The World Wide Web (WWW) is just one of the services available on the Internet, along with other Internet services such as email, video chat, file transfer, SSH, Ping, DNS, remote sync, P2P, and many others.

Each computer connected to the Internet is called a *host*. **The web is part of the Internet**, even though sometimes it is hard to tell them apart. Like most Internet services, the web uses the *client and server* model to perform its duties.

Perhaps the easiest way to understand *client and server* is to look at an everyday example. We are all familiar with the retail banking service where a customer (banking client) would visit a bank office (banking host) and seek service from a teller (banking server).

The customer transacts business with the teller using a well-defined language. This customer-teller interface language (*banking protocol*) involves account number, balance, deposit, withdrawal, and so on.

The good thing about this client and server setup is that **any customer using the banking protocol can work with any teller at any bank**.

On the web, the web client is a program, known as a *web browser* (or browser for short), running on a person's computer. And the web server is another program running on a *host computer* that serves up web contents.

A person uses a browser to access the web. Well-known browsers include: Google Chrome, Microsoft Edge, Firefox, Opera, and Apple Safari. Using a browser, you can visit any website where web server programs (Figure 1) are ready and waiting to render services.

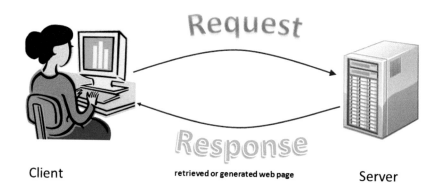

FIGURE 1: *Web Server and Client Model*

Hypertext Transfer Protocol (HTTP) is the precisely defined common language spoken between a web browser and a web server. Like our banking protocol, HTTP enables any browser to interact with any server in a standard way. HTTPS encrypts HTTP traffic for security.

Fortunately, human users don't have to speak HTTP; using a browser, all we do is point and click or use a few occasional keystrokes and the browser does the rest.

Where Is the Web?

The modern web is indeed *of the people, by the people, for the people* of the world. The web exists in the form of a wide collection of web *server hosts* located all over the world. Each server host is a computer placed on the Internet that stores contents and programming ready to handle requests from any browser (web client) that may come along. Usually, a web host can serve up many websites, each identified by a web address known as a Uniform Resource Locator (URL). Examples of URLs are

```
https://amazon.com
https://weather.com
https://my.clevelandclinic.org
https://www.kent.edu
https://chase.com
```

When entering a URL into the *Location* box of your browser, you often can skip the `http://` part. The browser is clever enough to understand. The speed of the Internet makes the actual physical location of a server host less important. However, a closer server will deliver contents to you a bit faster than one that is on the other side of the globe.

Webpages are coded in Hypertext Markup Language (HTML) that uses *markup tags* to organize page contents such as headings, sections, paragraphs, pictures, videos, tables, and *hyperlinks*. Hyperlinks use URLs to connect parts of the webpage, known as *anchors*, to other webpages, as well as other data/services, anywhere in the world. A user clicks on an anchor to follow the specified URL. The hyperlinks form an extensive web structure of interconnected webpages and hence the name World Wide Web.

Links to different contents such as pictures, audio, video, PDF and other formats allow the web to deliver any information to any visitor 24/7. What's more, URLs can also link to services such as file download, email, phone, skype, GPS coordinates, etc. for one-click/one-tap access. How wonderful is that?

It's a Brand New World!

The web brings the whole world to our fingertips and is changing our lives and the way we go about doing things in profound ways. Firing up a browser, we can immediately shop, learn, socialize, listen to music, watch video, play games, invest, and work, from anywhere at any time.

The web bridges the gap between countries and civilizations, empowers people in cities and rural areas alike, enables individual entrepreneurship, as well as encourages free sharing of information. When is the last time you drove to different stores to find products or to compare prices, visit the library, rent a movie from a store, or buy a plane ticket from a local travel agency? Where can you find yellow pages or white pages phone books?

The web is a medium for sharing. People share their pictures, funny videos, plumbing knowhow, recipes, gardening tips, DIY instructions, and so forth on the web. Others use the web to sell their crafts, artistic creations, services, used books, computers, and cellphones.

Looking for information? You can find the following on the web:

- Videos and movies to watch.

- Products and reviews from actual consumers who used them.

- Directions to any address, its GPS coordinates, and navigation to that location.

- Translations between over 100 languages and their pronunciation.

- Encyclopedic information and expert opinions/advice.

- Academic and scientific research articles/books in all fields.

Of course, you can purchase all kinds of products and services, many made available only on the web. You can attend video conferences, do banking, get health insurance, and pay taxes, too.

On a more academic side, students and teachers can access the web for online classes, lessons, teaching plans, and ready-to-use materials at K-12 and college levels. For example, you can find open technology courseware from MIT at `ocw.mit.edu`, products powering education from Google at `edu.google.com`, and technology for education at `www.iste.org` where the extensive materials also include resources aimed at "computational thinking for all".

What's more, you can even do mathematics, including algebra, trigonometry, polynomial factoring, calculus, and more on the web. For example, live demos can be found at `www.cs.kent.edu/~pwang/research/demo.html`.

Figure 2 shows an example demo of 3D plotting of a geometric surface.

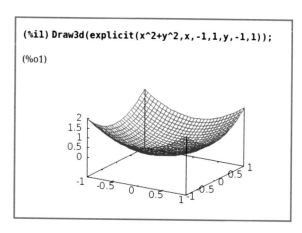

FIGURE 2: *A 3D Plot*

Indeed, it seems you can find anything and everything on the web.

The Answer Is ...

Human beings are always curious and thirsty for information. Not so long ago, people displayed the Encyclopædia Britannica in their homes as one of their most prized possessions. Today, Wikipedia, created and maintained by volunteers all over the world, is free for all on the web.

FIGURE 3: *The Answer Is on the Web*

No matter what questions you have or what information you are seeking, more than likely, the answers are on the web (Figure 3). All you have to do is look for it. Web search engines are built precisely for that purpose.

A search engine automatically and continuously visits all parts of the web and stores its findings in huge indexing databases organized for fast retrieval. Just ask the right question and a search engine can find the answers for you instantly. In this new environment, good web search skills can be very handy.

Search Engine Tips

The most popular and widely used search engine is Google. As the saying goes, "*Just Google it.*" More likely than not you'll find what you want to know.

But all web search engines are used in entirely similar ways: You enter one or more keywords for the search. The search engine looks for webpages containing the given keywords. When doing a search, it is important to provide the intended context. For example, if you enter *subway* as the keyword you may get information on the Subway restaurant instead of a transportation system. If you enter Kent you may get a city in Ohio, Pennsylvania, or even in England!

It also helps to add year, time, location, and other qualifiers to your search to make it more specific. With a precise and unambiguous search phrase, you often can get good leads immediately. If not, looking at the search results will give you ideas to refine your search. For further information, why not look up "*Google search tips*"?

While a web search engine can give you quick links to information on the web, you still need to look through the links to get the answers you want. And if you do a follow-up search, your query won't automatically be put in the context of your previous search.

FIGURE 4: *ChatGPT*

In 2023, *chatGPT* (Figure 4) became available that could answer questions in well-organized sentences and paragraphs. And it could chat with a user, back and forth, all the time within the context of the conversation. As an Artificial Intelligence (AI) research tool for the company OpenAI, it was offered for the public free of charge. You simply need to register a free account to use it.

Thus, we have the following CT rule:

> **CT concept—*Research on the web*:** *Search the web to look for any information you need, get answers to your questions, and satisfy your curiosity.*

Web Browser Tips

We all use web browsers extensively whenever we get online. There are a number of popular browsers available, Google Chrome being the most widely used. No matter which exact browser you use, it pays to know how to use it effectively. Here are some pointers that are generally applicable.

- Homepage—Every time a browser starts, it automatically loads a designated *homepage*. Why not make it the most useful site for yourself? Go to your browser *control menu* (usually three lines or three dots on the top right) and choose `preferences` to set your startup homepage.

- Sizing the browser window—Press and hold the left mouse button on the browser *title bar* (topmost bar) and drag it to reposition your browser window. Drag a window border to expand or shrink the window. Right click on the title bar to *maximize*, *unmaximize*, or *minimize* the window.

- Zoom in and out—From the *View menu*, you can zoom in/out for a better view of page contents. From the keyboard use CONTROL + (holding down the CONTROL key and press +) and CONTROL -. On a touch screen, use the pinch/unpinch gesture.

- Bookmarks bar—By placing bookmarks on the *bookmarks bar*, you make it easy to go to often-used sites. Just select the URL in the Location field and drag it to the bookmarks bar. Often the title of the bookmark is way too long. You can edit the title by right clicking the bookmark and edit the title property.

- Links—In a webpage, text and images can be links. Hovering the mouse over a link usually shows the *tooltip text* telling you more about the link before you click it. Click a link to load it into the current tab. Middle click it to open it in a new tab, and right click it to perform other operations on the link including saving the linked-to document on your computer.

- Sharing—See a webpage of interest and want to share it with someone? Simply use the *File menu* and select `email`. You can also print a hardcopy or print it into a PDF file.

- Page scrolling—The arrow keys make it simple to scroll page contents up/down and left/right. Your mouse's middle wheel button can scroll up/down, too. On a touchscreen, a finger swipe achieves scrolling. When enjoying a video in full-screen mode, you can exit fullscreen with the ESC (escape) key or tapping the touchscreen.

- Tabs—Click on a tab to switch to it. Middle click a tab to close it. Right click the tab to perform other operations.

- Browser plugins and extensions—Go to the browser control menu and select `Add-ons` or `Extensions`. Finding something you like, you can install the plugin or extension to your browser right away.

In this digital age, we all want maximum functionality for our tools and gadgets, but then many of us won't bother reading the owner's manual. So, we end up paying a lot for a very smart device and then use it as a very dumb one. So who is fooling whom? Here is a CT rule:

CT concept–*Take full advantage*: *Learn to use your device or app, configure it to your liking, explore all the features, and enjoy.*

Your Own Website

On the Internet, most popular websites include: Google, YouTube, Amazon, Wikipedia, baidu.com, yandex.ru, tiktok.com, openai.com (the chatGPT site), Netflix, Reddit, IMDb, eBay, Tripadvisor, Stack Overflow, and many others.

But the vast majority of websites are not such big ones but are the most important part of the web. Create a website for yourself, your business, hobby, family and friends, or nonprofit or charitable organization. The time and effort will be well spent, and the site will become a window to the world (Figure 5). Also, the web is a two-way street. You obtain information and services from it

FIGURE 5: *Your Own Window to the World*

and you provide information and services to it. To do the latter, many choose to set up their own website.

In planning your website, pay attention to the following:

- What are the goals and functions you want your website to achieve?

- Who are the intended audiences?

- What contents (words, pictures, videos) will the site display?

- What operations will the site perform?

- Do you have/want a logo for your site?

- What visual feel/effect do you wish the site to convey? Warm, cool, funny, serious, friendly, official, all-business, or funky?

A website can easily serve many purposes: advertising, information dissemination, selling, receiving donations, recruiting, and customer service. Website owners need to provide the site requirements and contents. But then you need help from a web developer who can do the visual design, layout, navigation scheme, and, just as importantly, the programming. Attempting to read *HTML for Dummies in 24 Hours* and do this yourself is usually a mistake.

Make sure that your site works for both regular and mobile browsers. A 2023 report[1] indicates that 92.3% of Internet users access the Internet using a mobile phone.

To place your website on the web, you first need to register a *domain name*, such as *something_nice*.com or *another_thing*.org. Go to a *domain name registrar* to find what's available and register. There is a small yearly registration fee (usually $10 to $20).

Then you need *web hosting* by a service provider such as bluehost.com, ionos.com. Faculty and students in colleges often can place their homepages up on a school web server for free.

Keep in mind that a website is the new front office for your organization or business. You need to make sure it gives a good impression and is always informative and up-to-date. Any inquiries from the site should be received and processed quickly. Any changes in business practices such as business hours, pricing, contact information, procedures, and so on should also be reflected immediately on your website. Misinformation on your site can be a disaster, and managing the website must be folded into regular routines of your business. This includes encouraging and responding to online feedback from your site.

Be Careful Online

Because the web is open and worldwide, not everything you read on it is accurate or even true.

> **CT concept—*Verify before trust***: *In getting information from the open Internet, we must be suspicious and use common sense. Check on the source, date, location, and authority of the data. Avoid hearsay and think twice before you repeat something that has not been verified, especially something dramatic from social media. Be a responsible online citizen, and don't spread rumors.*

In fact, hackers can put up a fake website with little difficulty. Therefore, you must be careful when accessing the web, entering login information, purchasing, and performing financial transactions. CT Article 5, *"Cybersecurity– How Not To Be a Fish"*, can be a good read.

Teachers should worry about students plagiarizing information in their homework or term papers. You can find free tools by searching for "best tools to check for plagiarism."

Pictures and videos can be altered digitally. News can even be based on rumors. When in doubt, do a web search and you can soon find the truth.

---

[1]Howarth, J. *Internet Traffic from Mobile Devices.* (2023, August 29). exploding-topics.com

Finally

The web is part of the Internet where web hosts store and provide information and programming. The web has these important technological ingredients:

- Web browsers—The user agents for the web functioning as a web client.

- Web servers—Programs running on web hosts that deliver web contents and services.

- HTTP and HTTPS—The hypertext transfer protocol is the language between web servers and clients.

- HTML—The hypertext markup language is used to code webpages. The latest version is HTML5.

- URL—The Uniform Resource Locator is used to link to all kinds of content and services.

- Domain names—Registered web addresses belonging to individuals and organizations.

Yet, the most important part of the web is human contributions: We all do our part to make the web useful and beneficial for everyone.

·················· CT Crossword Puzzle ············

WWW

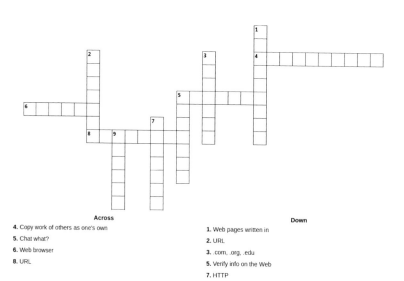

Across

4. Copy work of others as one's own
5. Chat what?
6. Web browser
8. URL

Down

1. Web pages written in
2. URL
3. .com, .org, .edu
5. Verify info on the Web
7. HTTP
9. Web contents are on

8

Cloud Computing for Everyone

In the digital age, cloud computing has been an important growth area in the computing services industry. Generally, the word "cloud" refers to computing powers on the other end of a computer network. Almost always, we are talking about well-organized hardware, software, services, and know-how across the Internet for the purpose of reducing, supplementing, or complementing local computing resources. Cloud-based resources are not pinned down at any fixed location and can be floating anywhere on the Internet. Perhaps that is why the word *cloud* is used.

How did cloud computing emerge? Who needs it? For what purposes? Advantages and disadvantages? Why should you care? We'll try to answer some of these questions here in this CT Article.

Computing Paradigms

In the early days, computers were large and expensive. They were housed and maintained by computer centers with highly trained staff. These are known as *mainframe* computers. Users accessed a mainframe by *terminals* (with CRT screen and keyboard) and shared its computing powers. Such terminals were connected to the computer center by physical cables and could display only characters, no bitmap graphics or mouse yet. Today some computer centers of large organizations still provide mainframe computing power and trained staff to their workforce with modern equipment and networks.

Miniaturization and large-scale integration of digital electronics brought rapid changes. The capacities of CPUs, memory units, and displays increased and their prices dropped at an astonishing rate. The Apple II and the IBM PC were among the first personal computers (PCs) introduced back in the early 1980s. They started to shift computing from the *mainframe paradigm* to the *PC paradigm* where users had the whole computer–hardware, software, storage, and display–all to themselves.

In the meantime, during the late 1980s, the Internet began to take shape. Based on the ARPANET (funded by the Advanced Research Projects Agency of the US Defense Department), the NSFnet, which is the US National Science Foundation's network of universities and supercomputing centers, helped create an explosive number of local and regional networks governed by the Internet Protocol (IP). Eventually, the Internet became so dominant that it virtually eliminated all historical rivals, such as BITNET and DECnet.

In late 1991, the World Wide Web (WWW), an Internet-based service, started to take root. The Internet and the web quickly grew and became ubiquitous globally, affecting almost every aspect of our daily lives.

Computing thus entered the *Internet paradigm*, combining PCs, smartphones, the Internet, and the web into a comprehensive computing environment. The new computing paradigm brought online email (Hotmail and Gmail, for example), voice and video calls (Skype and Google Hangout, for example), social networking (Instagram and TikTok, for example), audio/video sharing (Youtube and Vimeo for example), and much more. Many of these capabilities are free for individual users.

Cloud Computing

The stage was then set for the next computing paradigm, *cloud computing* (Figure 1), a confusing yet fascinating term. The *MIT Technology Review*

FIGURE 1: *Reaching for the Cloud*

article, "Who Coined 'Cloud Computing'?"[1] traces the interesting history of the term. However, in short,

> *The notion of network-based computing dates to the 1960s, but many believe the first use of "cloud computing" in its modern context occurred on August 9, 2006, when then Google CEO Eric Schmidt introduced the term to an industry conference.*

---

[1] Regalado, A. (Oct. 31, 2011). www.technologyreview.com

For a business, owning and operating all the computing hardware and software in-house can be expensive in terms of infrastructure, operation, management, maintenance, and upgrade. This is especially true for medium and small enterprises. The speed and bandwidth of the modern Internet make it possible to access and use remote (non-local) computing powers located somewhere across the Internet—that is, *in the cloud*.

This means that people in a company can access all the computing powers in the cloud with a PC or a Chromebook.

A Closer Look at the Cloud

Technology companies, such as Amazon (Amazon Web Services or AWS), Cisco, Google, IBM, Oracle, Microsoft (Azure), Apple (iCloud), CloudBees, Rackspace, SAP, Alibaba, and many others, have the economy of size to supply cost-effective cloud computing services on the Internet. Subscribers of cloud computing, organizations or individuals, simply enjoy the computing power, usually for a reasonable fee. And the rented services are available 24/7, accessible anywhere on the Internet from a desktop, laptop, Chromebook, tablet, or smartphone. Reaching the cloud is simple. Usually you will use a web browser such as Google Chrome, Firefox, Microsoft Edge, or Apple Safari and log in to your cloud account.

FIGURE 2: Cow Milking

For businesses, large and small, cloud computing can be an attractive alternative to owning, staffing, and operating their own IT equipment in house. Promoters of cloud computing ask (Figure 2), "If you need milk, would you own a cow?" Just get the milk (the computing power you need) and let someone else worry about the cow (everything related to providing the milk). Similarly, if you needed an office, would you own the whole office building?

Services on the Cloud

Cloud service providers (CSPs) offer many types of products (Figure 3) including:

- *Cloud storage*—Distributed, virtual, reliable, and fault-tolerant data storage easily accessible on the Internet/web. Well-known examples include Dropbox and Google Drive (for anyone), Microsoft OneDrive (for Windows users) and Apple iCloud (for Apple users). Often, cloud storage is also combined with file sharing, management, and/or system backup/restore functions.

- *Software as a service* (SaaS)—Software running on cloud servers accessible on-demand to subscribers, typically through a web browser. SaaS software performs office productivity (Microsoft Office 365, for example), customer relationship management, computer aided design, database management, human resource management, and many other tasks.

- *Platform as a service* (PaaS)—Virtual hardware-software servers, typically are complete with an operating system, application programming and execution environment, database, and web server. Customers can control and use the platform as well as develop custom applications on it.

- *Infrastructure as a service* (IaaS)—Virtual IT data centers complete with maintained servers, storage, and network facilities. On such infrastructure, a customer can install operating systems and develop and deploy their own applications.

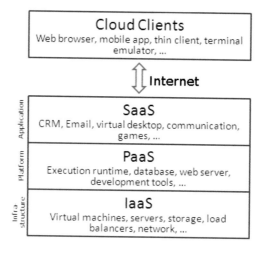

FIGURE 3: *Cloud-Based Services*

Advantages and Disadvantages

Thus, we can say the term *Cloud Computing* usually refers to leased, usage-based, computing powers accessed via the Internet that supplement or replace in-house facilities.

Cloud computing has clear advantages and disadvantages, as compared to in-house solutions.

The top advantages of cloud computing are: less up-front investment, faster to set up and start, fewer IT personnel and equipment, more reliable and physically secure, global anytime access, easy information sharing and collaboration, and simple to scale up or down. Perhaps best of all, there can be much less bother and expense for hardware/software installation, operation, update, maintenance, security, and user help.

Disadvantages of cloud computing are: relying on cloud service providers for privacy and security, less in-house control of IT services, lower, often unpredictable, network speed (compared to in-house LAN), limitations of applications running remotely rather than locally.

Cloud computing is a growing industry. It makes sense to use it for the right tasks and can be cost effective and more convenient. Individuals and IT professionals will need to weigh the pros and cons and pick the right cloud solutions. Often, a combination of in-house platforms, private cloud, and public cloud can be the best choice. Free and open cloud software, such as FOSS-Cloud (`www.foss-cloud.org`) and others, makes it much easier to create your own cloud services.

Understanding cloud computing brings more CT rules:

> **CT concept—*Internet accessibility*:** *You don't have to bring an item when traveling if you can access it from anywhere. This is especially true for digital data.*

> **CT concept—*No more physical distance*:** *Physical location and separation are no longer important; distance disappears in cyberspace. Is it still necessary to go to the office every day?*

> **CT concept—*The network is the computer*:** *A computer is almost useless without access to the Internet which brings important functions to a computer.*

Applying CT, we can rethink the modern airliners' voice and data recorders, commonly known as "black boxes." After an accident, locating or retrieving the all-important black boxes often becomes difficult or even impossible. Why not use *cloud black boxes* (Figure 4) instead? Important data can be sent securely from planes in flight to cloud storage on a continuous basis, reducing or eliminating the need to search for black boxes. With real-time data, we can better monitor airliners, control flights, and manage airspace.

FIGURE 4: *Airliner with Cloud Communication*

Cloud Services for Individuals

Perhaps the most well-known is Dropbox, a cloud storage service (Figure 5) started in 2008. According to Wikipedia[2], *"Dropbox founder Drew Houston conceived the Dropbox concept after repeatedly forgetting his USB flash drive while he was a student at MIT."*

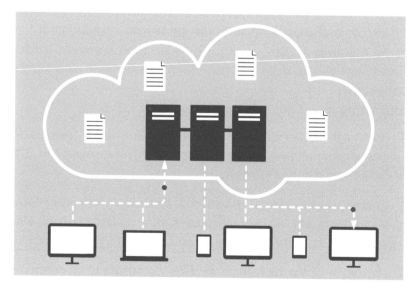

FIGURE 5: *Cloud Data Storage*

The free *Dropbox Basic* plan provides 2.5 GB of storage for an individual user. You can easily upload/download files, place files in different folders, and manage them just like you would on your own hard drive. Plus, you can share selected files publicly, with specific people, or invite others to access your Dropbox in allowable ways.

---

[2]en.wikipedia.org/wiki/Dropbox

Dropbox saves your files securely with encryption. It also helps you store and manage photos and videos. Additionally, you can automatically back up/restore your files, known as *file synching*. You can add more storage space for a fee.

Similar cloud storage and file sharing providers include Google Drive, Amazon Drive, Box, and others. Streaming services, freely available to the public to upload and share audio/video contents, include YouTube, Vimeo, Dailymotion, and more. Web-based email services and productivity suites provide individuals with email, document creation, and collaboration tools. Examples include Gmail, Outlook.com, and Google Workspace.

Cloud Applications for Companies

A *cloud application*, or cloud app, is a software program where cloud-based and local components work together. Increasingly companies are using cloud apps for business and management operations. Here is a list of cloud applications that are popular with businesses:

- **Customer relationship management (CRM)**:
  CRM systems help businesses manage their customer relationships, sales pipelines, and marketing efforts. Examples include: Salesforce, HubSpot, and Microsoft Dynamics 365.

- **Enterprise resource planning (ERP)**:
  ERP applications integrate various business functions like finance, human resources, inventory, and supply chain management. Examples include: SAP Business One, Oracle NetSuite, and Microsoft Dynamics 365 Finance and Operations.

- **Project management and collaboration**:
  These applications facilitate team collaboration, task management, and project tracking. Examples include: Asana, Trello, and Microsoft Teams.

- **File storage and sharing**:
  Cloud storage services allow businesses to store, access, and share files securely across teams and devices. Examples include: Google Drive, Dropbox, and Microsoft OneDrive.

- **Business intelligence and analytics**:
  These applications enable data analysis and visualization to gain insights into business performance. Examples include: Tableau, Microsoft Power BI, and Google Analytics.

In addition, we should mention web and mobile app hosting and system backup/recovery.

Success of Cloud Computing

The sky is the limit when it comes to the future of cloud computing.

The trend is that all kinds of computing are increasingly using the cloud or become effective and useful because of the cloud. According to a `market.us` article[3], "*The Global Cloud Computing Market size is expected to be worth around USD 2,321 Billion by 2032 from USD 546.1 Billion in 2022, growing at a CAGR of 16% during the forecast period from 2022 to 2032.*"

Here are five well-known cloud computing businesses:

- Amazon Web Services (AWS): AWS is a subsidiary of Amazon.com and has been a dominant player in the cloud computing market. It offers a wide range of services, including computing power, storage, and databases. As of 2021, AWS was the largest cloud computing provider in terms of market share.

- Microsoft Azure: Microsoft Azure is a cloud computing platform provided by Microsoft. It offers a comprehensive suite of services for building, deploying, and managing applications and services through Microsoft-managed data centers. Azure has experienced significant growth in recent years and has been competing closely with AWS for market share.

- Google Cloud: Google Cloud Platform is the cloud computing service offered by Google. It provides a suite of cloud-based services, including computing power, data storage, machine learning, and analytics. While Google Cloud Platform has been gaining market share, it generally ranks behind AWS and Azure in terms of size.

- IBM Cloud: IBM Cloud is the cloud computing platform offered by IBM. It provides a range of services, including infrastructure as a service (IaaS), platform as a service (PaaS), and software as a service (SaaS). IBM has been a longstanding player in the enterprise computing market, and its cloud services cater to businesses of various sizes.

- Alibaba Cloud: Alibaba Cloud, a subsidiary of Alibaba Group, is one of the leading cloud computing providers in China and has been expanding globally. It offers a broad range of cloud services, including data storage, database services, and artificial intelligence capabilities. Alibaba Cloud has been particularly influential in the Asian market.

---

[3] *Cloud Computing Market.* (May 2023). market.us/report/cloud-computing-market

According to a statista.com article[4], as of August 2023, the market shares of these cloud computing businesses are estimated to be: Amazon Web Services (32%), Microsoft Azure (22%), Google Cloud (11%), Alibaba Cloud (4%), and IBM Cloud (3%).

Finally

The world of computing advances with time:

$$\text{Mainframe Computing} \implies \text{PC Computing}$$
$$\implies \text{Internet/Web Computing} \implies \text{Cloud Computing}$$

Why not explore what's available for you, your business, or your company? When using the cloud, be extra careful about security and privacy of your data. Materials in CT Article 5, *"Cybersecurity–How Not To Be a Fish"* can be very helpful.

---

[4]Richter, F. *Amazon Maintains Lead in the Cloud Market.* (2023, Aug. 8). www.statista.com

CT Crossword Puzzle

On the Cloud

Across

4. IaaS

6. Where to obtain computing power for a fee

7. The opposite of on the cloud

8. Use it to access a mainframe computer

Down

1. SaaS

2. PaaS

3. A style of supplying computing power

5. Dropbox

9

A Pattern Here and a Pattern There

The word *pattern* may mean different things to different people. But here we focus on the following. According to Wikipedia:

A pattern is a regularity in the world, in human-made design, or in abstract ideas. As such, the elements of a pattern repeat in a predictable manner.

We communicate with patterns. Reading is to recognize and understand spelling or stroke patterns in a language. Speaking is to utter sound in pre-scribed patterns. To understand speech, we must first hear and detect the sound patterns, connecting them to words, filter words through grammar patterns, then interpret their meaning in the right context. We can even think of the context as the overarching pattern containing the words.

We also see the world through visual patterns—triangles and circles (ge-ometric patterns), dogs and cats, trees, cars and buses, roads, traffic signs, faces, tables and chairs, and so on. We play pattern puzzles (Figure 1). We

FIGURE 1: *Puzzle Pieces*

delight in patterns—dance to beats, sing songs, listen to music (rhythm), enjoy pictures and paintings, create sculptures, and make quilts.

Patterns are useful and practical. Just look at a barcode (linear patterns, Figure 2) and a quick response (QR) code (2D matrix patterns Figure 3); they are taken for granted these days. Patterns are everywhere. In fact, we

FIGURE 2: *ISBN Barcode for This Book*

can't live without them. Without patterns, how would we find our way home? Recognize loved ones? Tell objects apart? Diagnose health problems (symptom patterns)? Drive our cars? Or even do our jobs?

A heightened sense of patterns can be helpful, especially for computational thinkers, in almost all situations as you will see.

FIGURE 3: *QR Code for Our Companion Website*

Web Search Patterns

Humans are curious beings. One of the greatest joys of modern life is being able to find answers to questions instantly. Of course, we are talking about web searches.

Using Google or another search engine, we might enter a sequence of words, "*Old MacDonald Had a Farm*," for example, and find out all about the song. The sequence of words given is known as a *search pattern*. Knowing how to use search patterns can make a web search faster, easier, and more precise.

First, we need to realize that when given a sequence of words, Google will look for information in its database containing those words, but not necessarily in that order or even in the same sentence. The upper- or lowercase is usually ignored. Surround the words in quotation marks to insist on exact matches. For example `"white paper"` versus `"paper white"`.

Even though Google is smart, it is often useful for us to provide a specific context for our search pattern. For example, using `subway` usually gets you locations of the restaurant. `Philadelphia subway` should get you public transportation in that city. The pattern `Washington D.C. subway` gets you information on the DC Metro, in addition to restaurant locations in DC. Use `-restaurant` (the hyphen is a Google search operator) to remove that option. To indicate search within a website, use `site:computize.org recursion`, for example.

Here is an example of providing good context. The search pattern

```
site:youtube.com tennis 2023 US Open women final highlights
```

should lead directly to the exciting video to watch. Or you may first go to youtube.com and use its own search facility. To get more Google search tips, look for `Google Search Operators`.

String Search Patterns

On the computer text/document editor apps such as MS Word, Excel, Notepad++, LibreOffice (free), VI/VIM (text editor) offer many useful features including spelling help, grammar checking, text search/replace, and more.

We all know how tedious it is to look through a long document for a specific word, phrase, date, name, or some other *string of characters*. Luckily most text editors offer automatic search for any given string (of characters) within the document being processed.

Looking for a target string involves two steps: (1) You specify the string pattern to find. (2) The computer searches for *matches* to the pattern in the document.

To specify string patterns, use a notation known as *regular expression* or *regex*. This may sound complicated, but it is really simple.

1. A regex is a string consisting of **regular characters** and **metacharacters**.

2. A regular character stands for itself, indicating the character to match.

3. A metacharacter indicates your desired options for what character to match. The usual metacharacters are `{}[]()^$.|*+?` and `\` (backslash).

For example, the regex `hat` matches just that, while `h[aeiou]t` will match hat, het, hit, hot, and hut. Thus, the expression `[xyz]` matches any one of the enclosed characters, namely x, y, or z. The metacharacter `*` indicates zero or more repetitions of the previous character. For example, `Ha*` matches H, Ha, Haa, Haaa, and so on. Here is an application: `chapter[1-9]` matches chapter1, chapter2, all the way to chapter9.

The metacharacter . (period) matches any single character. Thus, `.*pdf` matches `pdf` and also any string ending in `pdf`. To match the character . we need to *escape* it (prevent its metacharacter meaning) by preceding it with \. Thus `.*\.docx` matches anything ending in `.docx`.

As you can see, regular expressions are powerful but can become complicated. For more information, search for `Wikipedia: regular expression`.

Are You a Human or a Bot?

Indeed computers are fast and efficient in matching textual patterns and are much faster than humans. But, image patterns are a whole other story. In fact, humans are so much better than computer systems in this direction. Actually, on the web, image patterns are used to test if the user is a human or a bot. Such tests are known as CAPTCHAs (Completely Automated Public Turing Test). They effectively prevent bots from registering for services, making comments, pretending to be customers, etc.

Usually, one or more images are presented for the user to detect numbers, characters, cars, boats, and animals in the images. In this example (Figure 4),

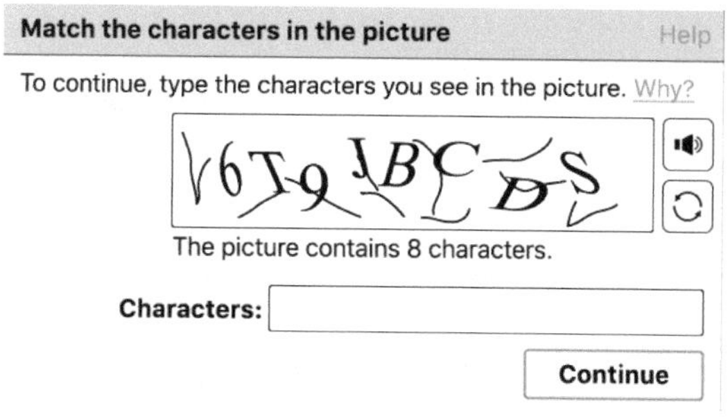

FIGURE 4: *CAPTCHA Screen*

the twisty curvy characters are easy for humans to recognize, but not for bots. The extra line segments serve to further confuse any automated character recognition attempts.

In the next example (Figure 5), a user must identify every picture, out of nine, with a bus in it. Even just having to click inside a designated area becomes an effective CAPTCHA (Figure 6). Humans and computers are built and function differently. We have full understanding of how computers work, but not the human mind. Some pattern recognition tasks are easy for humans but hard for computers, and vice versa.

FIGURE 5: *Picture CAPTCHA*

FIGURE 6: *Mouse Click CAPTCHA*

Facial Recognition

When we see a face, we easily recognize if it is a friend or stranger. However, such a simple task becomes much harder for a computer system.

Automated facial recognition systems are useful for authenticating an account holder, ticketed passenger, credit/debit card user, smartphone owner, and so on. It is also useful in video surveillance and law enforcement applications.

Basically, a facial recognition (Figure 7) system needs to isolate a face in an image (from camera or video frame), normalize the face image (to that of a passport photo, for example), extract facial features (width between eyes, length of nose, etc.), then compare the features with target images to perform recognition. Automatic facial recognition technology is relatively mature and has been applied widely. For example, faces captured from videos and pictures of the January 6 US Capitol insurrection have led law enforcement to individuals. These days, ordinary people can use websites such as PimEyes to identify others from facial images.

Beware, there are security and privacy concerns when you allow an app to collect your facial recognition information.

FIGURE 7: *Facial Recognition*

Hey, Let's Talk

In the first year at MIT graduate school, the author wrote a term paper on better computer user interface, which basically called for **talking** as the desired mode of human-computer interaction. At that time (1967), we interacted with computers via typewriter-like terminals, even at MIT.

Now we are all talking to our smartphones and computers—Alexa (Amazon Echo), Hello Google (Google app), Hey Cortana (MS Windows), Hey Siri (Apple), and so on. Even though we are limited to what can be said and understood by automatic speech recognition (ASR) systems, we feel happy and in control. ASR works by recognizing sound patterns and converting them

FIGURE 8: *Automatic Speech Recognition*

to words (text). The costly computation must be done quickly, in milliseconds, so the computer does not appear slow. In addition to overcoming background noises, ASR must also deal with male/female/child voices and accents. Finally, there are homonyms (many in English but much more in Chinese) such as 'here', 'hear'; 'two', 'too'. An ASR system must rely on context to make clever decisions. Still, today's ASR systems are far from understanding speech; they are programmed to simply respond to a fixed set of commands.

FIGURE 9: *Self-Driving Car*

Self-Driving Cars

Some say the future of transportation lies in self-driving cars (Figure 9). Such a car is certainly an advanced piece of technology integrating sensor inputs (radar, laser, infrared), geo-positioning, map data, and computer vision into one dynamic control system to drive safely from point A to point B.

Its computer vision system must identify traffic signs and signals, vehicles, pedestrians, animals, and other objects that may be on or traveling the road. That certainly is a significant task in real-time pattern recognition. The technologies are still in the developing and testing stages.

In March 2018 in Tempe Arizona, an Uber self-driving car, with test driver inside, hit and killed a woman walking at night. The woman was pushing a bicycle across the road. According to the National Traffic Safety Board[1] (NTSB), the cause was that the system lacks *"the capability to classify an object as a pedestrian unless that object was near a crosswalk"*. Putting pedestrians and other moving objects under the context of crosswalks is obviously mistaken.

In March 2019, a Tesla Model 3, with the Autopilot engaged, crashed into a truck, killing the driver, according to *Ars Technica*[2].

These tragic events tell us that automated driving has a good distance to go before becoming practical. Because of its huge potential, companies are still actively pursuing self-driving cars.

AI systems in self-driving cars are being road-tested (Figure 10) extensively to gain experience in different situations, scenes, weather conditions, and objects encountered to make improvements.

---

[1] NTSB Accident Report, NTSB/HAR-19/03 PB2019-101402

[2] Lee, T. B. *Autopilot was active when a Tesla crashed into a truck, killing driver.* (2019, May 16). arstechnica.com

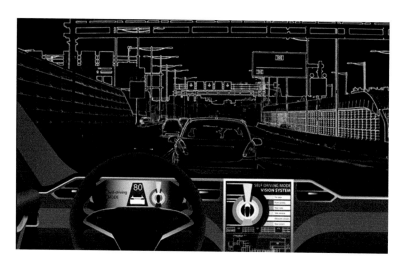

FIGURE 10: *Self-Driving Car Road Test*

Patterns in Data

Wise people learn from history and experience (known data) and find patterns for what works and what fails. These patterns can help us avoid repeating mistakes and duplicate successes.

With computing, we can collect a lot of data and find regularities (patterns) in them. Such patterns can be put to good use in specific areas. For example, data of symptoms can help disease diagnosis, data of traffic accidents can help road design and safety, data of spam can make email filters more effective, data of consumer interests can lead to more useful recommendations, and so on.

We have talked about training self-driving systems with data. Google Translate is another example. It has a huge database on existing translations among many languages and reaches into this data to do translation work. Thus, it really does not understand the material it is translating. How strangely wonderful! Google Translate also collects user feedback (more translation data) to improve its ability to translate.

A significant trend in AI is exactly in collecting and analyzing Big Data for improved business practices in client companies.

Finally–Computize

Recall that we defined *computize* as, "*To apply computational thinking. To view, consider, analyze, design, plan, work, and solve problems from a computational perspective.*"

Identifying, recognizing, matching, and using patterns are important in CT. Thus, let us apply patterns in our daily lives. For example, we can write down the pattern of a phishing email:

- The incoming email is from an unknown email address.

- The email does not address the receiver by name.

- The email promises unexpected money coming your way or talks about something urgent or important, such as your account expiring, bill overdue, resource quota exhausted.

- You are advised to follow a link or open an attachment.

Of course, you won't be fooled and will forward such email directly to: `phishing-report@us-cert.gov`.

Here is a more general situation. We all know that bad things happen when we are nervous, hurried, distracted, preoccupied, or absent-minded. Yet we also find ourselves in such moods after something bad happens. So, the pattern is *one bad thing often can lead to another*. Knowing this pattern, we all must keep calm, collected, focused, rational, and decisive to deal with a bad situation. This way we can make things better instead of worse.

How about noticing patterns when you lose your temper? forget things? become defensive/offensive? gain/lose weight? Patterns that make you productive/energetic? efficient and effective? agreeable or disagreeable? sad or happy?

These are just some examples. I am sure you can find many useful places to apply patterns to great advantages. Perhaps on Old MacDonald's farm he finds a computer—Here a pattern, there a pattern, everywhere a pattern pattern, ***ee-i-ee-i-o***!

CT Crossword Puzzle

Patterns

Across

1. Are You a Human or a Bot?

3. Dance

6. Tell objects apart with

7. Computer can identify individuals via facial ...

Down

1. Meaning of a pattern may depend on its

2. A pattern is what in data?

4. Computer can hear your

5. A string pattern language

10

AI: Aiming for Intelligence

The term *Artificial Intelligence* (AI) has seen much publicity in the media. Proponents say AI will be dominant in our digital future and companies should get on the AI bandwagon. Tractica, a market research firm, forecasted huge market growth globally for AI systems, expecting revenue to increase from about $10 billion in 2018 to $126 billion by 2025.

That is certainly significant. But what is AI? What kind of intelligence is *artificial*? In what ways will AI help? What capabilities can it bring? Could AI become smarter than humans? Or, can it potentially take over the world and replace human beings all together?

We'll try to answer such questions in ways that are simple to understand.

What Is Artificial Intelligence?

The word *intelligence* here refers to the ability to acquire and apply knowledge and skills. Intelligence is usually ascribed to human beings exclusively. But some animals are also intelligent. Dogs, for example, can learn to perform important tasks to which humans can't even come close. Basically, the goal of AI is to create man-made intelligent machines.

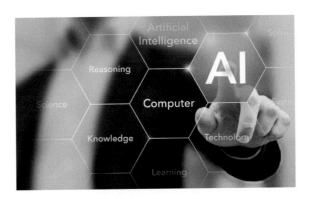

FIGURE 1: *AI Is Part of Computer Science*

AI is an area of computer science (Figure 1). As the field of AI research and development advances, the meaning of the term AI has evolved. In practice, today AI usually refers to "*a computer system's ability to exhibit some kind of smartness.*" A little history can shed more light on AI.

A Brief History of Artificial Intelligence

Of course, when we talk about intelligence we mean mental capacity and acumen, not information gathered by security agencies. As such, intelligence is not absolute but relative to some chosen baseline for comparison. Thus, natural intelligence is not easy to define and subject to different interpretations. Defining *artificial*, man-made or manufactured, intelligence then would be an even harder problem.

Alan Turing, the father of modern computer science, published a landmark paper in 1950 where he speculated about the possibility of creating machines that think. Because "thinking" is hard to define, he devised a test known as the *Turing Test*. Basically, if a machine could interact with a person via a teleprinter and the person could not tell the machine apart from a human, then it would be reasonable to say that the machine was "thinking". Turing went on to argue convincingly that a "thinking machine" was at least plausible. The *Turing Test* (Figure 2) was the first serious proposal in the philosophy of artificial intelligence. John McCarthy, one of AI's founding fathers,

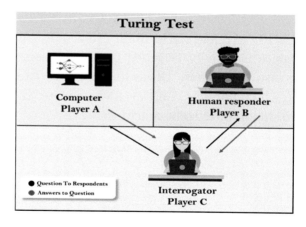

FIGURE 2: *The Turing Test*

coined the term *Artificial Intelligence* in 1955, and he organized the famous *Dartmouth Summer Research Project on Artificial Intelligence* in 1956. This meeting started AI as a field of research. McCarthy defines AI[1] as "the science and engineering of making intelligent machines, especially intelligent computer programs." And in this context, he defines ingelligence as "the computational part of the ability to achieve goals in the world."

---

[1]McCarthy, John. jmc.stanford.edu/articles/whatisai/whatisai.pdf

Henceforth, AI R&D endeavored to create systems that demonstrate their intelligence.

An early system, *ELIZA*, was created by Joseph Weizenbaum at the MIT AI Lab in 1966. ELIZA is a program that can carry on a conversation with a person by using simple rules and patterns. For example, if a user typed, "I am not feeling well." ELIZA might display, "Why are you not feeling well?" Or if the user cursed, ELIZA might respond, "Did your parents teach you such talk?" It is an attempt to pass the Turing Test without the computer really understanding what's being said. In early 2023, the impressive ChatGPT program was made available online for the public to try. Its chatting ability is far beyond that of ELIZA. Still, the question has become, "If passing (or nearly passing) the Turing Test is not enough, what does a program have to do to be considered intelligent?"

After ELIZA, programs that played games were developed. After all, if a machine can win a game with a person, then isn't the machine surely thinking or has intelligence? Such efforts include: MIT's Greenblatt Chess Program (1969), IBM's Jeopardy! (TV game show) winning system, Deep Blue Chess playing system (2011), and DeepMind Technologies' AlphaGo (2016) (Figure 3), which triumphed over the best human Go players in the world. Yet, people ascribe these impressive performances to the raw speed and data

FIGURE 3: *Google DeepMind's GO Playing AI Program*

processing powers of modern computers rather than intelligence. Take action video games for example, does anyone really believe they can win against the computer? But, that's not because it is smarter. Certainly, no one thinks a Blackjack machine is intelligent even when it can replace real dealers.

The more capable and wonderful computer systems become, the more people realize that they are still just great programs, instead of possessing intelligence.

AI Systems in Practice

Proving man-made intelligence aside, attempts and efforts to build "intelligent machines" have led to many useful programming principles, techniques, paradigms, as well as hardware devices. Their use resulted in many practical applications that enrich our lives as well as the field of AI.

FIGURE 4: *Balancing an Inverted Pendulum*

In the early days, the MIT AI Lab (now MIT CSAIL) experimented with automatically balancing an inverted pendulum to simulate a child balancing a broomstick on an open palm (Figure 4). Much later, in 2001, the Segway HT (Figure 5), a two-wheeled, self-balancing personal transporter was invented and brought to market. It was a revolutionary riding device after the bicycle. Unfortunately, for various financial and safety reasons, it was not a commercial success. Personal assistant apps, such as Google Assistant, Alexa, and Siri, use

FIGURE 5: *Segway HT Keeping Balance*

speech technologies to hear and execute user commands and to give verbal answers. They understand a given set of commands and can't really converse with the user. Pandora, Netflix, and Amazon Video can recommend songs or shows based on user experience and preference. Recommendations become better with time due to data accumulation. Google's *Nest* thermostat "learns" from your temperature preferences, activity schedule, and changes you make to the thermostat settings to adjust temperature automatically in order to save energy and keep your smart home comfortable.

Google Translate can translate words, phrases, sentences and even paragraphs from one language to another, among around 100 languages. It can even make pronunciations. You can use it from any web browser for free. Even though some translations are inaccurate, mistaken, or even ridiculous, the tool can be very useful when dealing with foreign languages or as an aid for translation-related work. It also gathers user feedback and corrections to improve its database.

These are just a few examples of many such AI programs.

Learning and Data Mining

Even though the path to AI is still long and uncertain, many useful programming techniques have been devised along the way that greatly enhance the capabilities and smartness of programs.

One such technique is *machine learning*—A program is so organized that it can receive training, automatically customize itself, or make improvements by analyzing its past successes and failures. The AI term "learning" is used even though such program behaviors are a far cry from human or even animal learning. In other words, learning in AI programs refers to "making self-improvements in performing predefined tasks through experience." It has little to do with the general ability of learning in creatures.

Another technique is *data mining*—An application will gather or be fed large amounts of data, such as "who visits what websites" or "scenes and situations encountered by an automobile driver." Statistical analyses are performed on the data to find insights or hidden correlations. Results mined from the mountains of data can often be surprising or revealing.

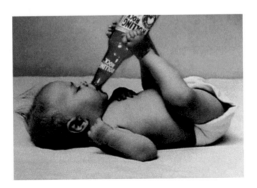

FIGURE 6: *Beer and Diaper*

An interesting story can illustrate the basic idea. In 1992, a well-known retailer had its sales data analyzed and a correlation between beer and diapers (Figure 6) was found, not by sophisticated data mining but just simple data queries. This means placing beer and diapers together on shelves can increase sales of both items.

Extracting useful information from *Big Data*, such as all phone calls intercepted in 30 days, has been a well-known technique for intelligence gathering by security agencies. Today, collecting and quickly processing large amounts of data to provide insight or gain effectiveness has become a major trend in AI.

These are just two examples of many AI programming techniques in use today. AI is being applied in all kinds of areas including marketing, manufacturing, banking/finance, agriculture, health care, image processing, security, self-driving vehicles, and many more.

Changing Context

The meaning of the term AI becomes difficult to pinpoint because it has a very complicated philosophical context that has never been generally agreed upon, and that context has been shifting with time and technology. It is almost as if when an AI program clearly succeeds in a task, such as winning the Go game, we see how it's done and say, "that's not intelligent, it is just following rules this way or that way." It is against this shifting context that we interpret the success/failure of achieving man-made intelligence.

Context is an important CT concept. In computing the ability to switch context is paramount. For example, when a computer pauses one program to resume another, the CPU undergoes a *context switch* to restore the saved state of the target process in order to resume running it. This happens all the time when we use computers, moving from editing a document to surfing the web for example.

Even within the same program, the same bit pattern is subject to different interpretations depending on its *data type*, i.e., its context.

```
'0'  00110000 (48)        '9'  00111001 (57)
'A'  01000001 (65)        'Z'  01011010 (90)
'a'  01100001 (97)        'z'  01111010 (122)
```

In the preceding table, you see that the bit pattern representing 65 as an *integer type* will represent the letter 'A' as a *character type*.

> **CT concept–*Context of symbols*:** *The meaning of any symbol depends on its context.*

We all know taking words out of their original context is a common problem. The verb *computize* means putting CT to use. For example, we should computize and prevent context-related pitfalls by avoiding words such as "last night" and "next week" in our emails.

CT concept–*Beware of context*: *Avoid context-related pitfalls in our communications.*

Applying this CT principle, we naturally realize that the meaning of the symbol AI shifts along with its context, ranging from the lofty "man-made intelligence" to the merely "added smarts in a program".

Finally

Many somewhat clever computer systems are promoted and marketed under the AI label. AI vacuum cleaners are a vivid example of such promotion or hype. The exaggeration of AI technologies has negative effects. According to a *Bloomberg Opinion* article[2], "Executives who say they've adopted the technology may be responding to hype and the fear of missing out." Politicians, funding agencies, and business managers may be similarly influenced.

Still, many AI systems do offer value, smartness, and even amazing capabilities. Those based on Big Data, such as Google Translate or face recognition systems, are in vogue. Limitations of these AI techniques include accuracy and bias in the data used, as well as insufficient background knowledge and expertise in the target areas.

Computer systems can be very impressive and powerful without relation to AI. Examples are everywhere: the Internet, the web, LibreOffice, LaTeX, MAXIMA, Skype, Zoom, turn-by-turn navigation, encryption/decryption, and so on.

The original goal of AI, that of creating man-made thinking, learning, intelligent, and even conscious machines, is still difficult to achieve. There is yet no generally agreed upon concrete criteria to replace the Turing Test for AI. More about AI can be found in CT Article 11, *"Let's Chat about AI."*

Will AI systems lead to intelligence? Who knows. Yet, who cares? If a program is sufficiently smart, useful in many applications, why not label it AI? It may be even more attractive in the marketplace. By aiming for intelligence, the industry may have hit a pot of gold; that is not such a disaster!

As to AI wiping out humans, not anytime soon.

---

[2]Bershidsky. *Business Leaders Love AI. That Doesn' t Mean They Use It.*. www.bloomberg.com

.... CT Crossword Puzzle ....

AI

Across

3. Finding patterns and relations in big data

4. Early simple chat program

7. Go winning AI program

8. Test that defines AI

Down

1. Man-made, not natural

2. Two-wheeled, self-balancing transporter

5. Beer and ...

6. Later and much better chat program

11

Let's Chat about AI

The extensive media coverage of *ChatGPT* has once again raised the profile of Artificial Intelligence (AI) and people's attention to this fast-developing technology. But what really is AI, its goals, implications, technologies, and applications? Citizens in the digital age, computational thinkers in particular, should have a basic understanding and appreciation. Furthermore, as you will see, techniques in AI can also help us acquire and improve our own computational thinking!

In CT Article 10, *"AI: Aiming for Intelligence"*, we have talked about the basic ideas of AI. Here we use ChatGPT as an opening to discuss more aspects of AI.

What Is ChatGPT?

A *chatbot* is a computer program that tries to talk with human users, usually online. ChatGPT is a new, powerful, and successful chatbot where you can ask questions, get answers, conduct a conversation as if with another person, not just anyone but a well-versed and knowledgeable person.

FIGURE 1: *ChatGPT Logo*

GPT stands for *Generative Pre-trained Transformer* (Figure 1). We asked it the question directly and here is what it said:

ChatGPT is an artificial intelligence language model developed by OpenAI that is designed to process natural language and generate human-like responses to user input. It can be used for a variety of applications, including answering questions, carrying on conversations, and providing assistance. Essentially, ChatGPT is a computer program that can 'chat' with humans in a way that mimics human conversation.

We got this definition of OpenAI from the same authoritative source:

OpenAI is a private artificial intelligence research laboratory consisting of a team of researchers and engineers working on developing advanced AI systems. The company was founded in 2015 by a group of high-profile tech industry figures, including Elon Musk, Sam Altman, (and ...). OpenAI is dedicated to creating AI technologies that are safe and beneficial for society, and their work encompasses a wide range of research areas, including natural language processing, computer vision, robotics, and more.

To have a firsthand experience chatting with ChatGPT, register an account at `chat.openai.com/auth/login` and try it for yourself. Registration is simple: your email address and a password you choose will do. No other personal information is required. Your account and usage are free. Another more advanced version, ChatGPT-4, was made available later, but requires payment.

Most find ChatGPT to be amazing and capable. It appears to have extensive knowledge and is able to answer questions and provide assistance as if it understood many things, in a wide variety of areas. For example, it can generate original music pieces in various genres/styles, write poetry, help debug code in particular programming languages, assist in problem-solving, translate whole articles to another language, and even factor simple polynomials.

ChatGPT is an example of *Generative AI*, an AI technology that generates high-quality text, images, and other content based on deep-learning models and their training data.

Impact of ChatGPT

There may be many implications of ChatGPT and its associated AI technologies. An obvious question is how ChatGPT will impact current search engines such as Google. After all, they all can answer your queries and give you useful information. However, there are major differences:

- **Forms of answers**: A search engine responds to your query with a list of webpages where you can find up-to-date information. ChatGPT formulates direct answers in well-constructed sentences. It derives the answer from its static training databases that do not contain current information such as breaking news. A search engine can display images, links, audio, and video contents, while ChatGPT is limited to sentences.

- **Ongoing Chat**: Each query to a search engine is independent of any previous queries to it. ChatGPT is different and designed to maintain an ongoing chat; that is, to converse with the user keeping the entire conversation in one coherent context.

- **Correctness of answer**: A search engine lists related webpages, and it is up to the user to obtain the correct/desired information. ChatGPT gives well-versed, fluent, and grammatically correct answers. Yet, sometimes the answer can be wrong or outdated.

Thus, ChatGPT and search engines are useful in different ways. Their advantages can merge in the future to form better/improved versions. ChatGPT does not pose an immediate threat to search engines.

Another question relates to language translation. Comparing ChatGPT with Google Translate (GTr), we can observe the following:

- GTr can translate between over 100 languages, while ChatGPT has been trained in about a dozen where English received the most attention.

- GTr uses pattern matching and has no understanding of the texts being translated. ChatGPT was designed to understand and generate human-like text in a more comprehensive and natural way than GTr.

- ChatGPT does a better job translating longer texts where context and meaning are important. GTr can be useful in single words and short phrases.

- GTr allows users to suggest alternative or better translations that can potentially improve its database. ChatGPT does not.

Of course, ChatGPT technologies can be important to improve voice user interfaces in applications such as Amazon Echo (Alexa), Hello Google, and Microsoft Windows' Cortana.

By connecting/interfacing ChatGPT or similar AI software, to different apps, smart devices, and Web/Internet, the potential is limitless. For example, in late 2023, Amazon has already combined AI and Alexa with a smart household robot (Astro). The area of AI-Generated Content (AIGC) will become more important as we move forward.

ChatGPT received much attention because it is a new breakthrough application of AI. The question is, "What is AI and how does it work?"

ChatGPT and AI

Has ChatGPT achieved Artificial Intelligence? In other words, does ChatGPT possess man-made intelligence?

In CT Article 10, *AI: Aiming for Intelligence*, we described the *Turing Test* as a way to detect intelligence in a program.

Basically, if a program can interact with a human over a communication line and make the person think another person is at the other end, then we may say that the program can think or has intelligence.

Having used ChatGPT, most people would say it passes the Turing Test with flying colors. But if you examine carefully and interact with it multiple times, you may find clues that there is no human on the other end of the line.

In 2023, we should have a new definition of AI. Here is our modern definition: *Artificial Intelligence is an area of computer science that aims to develop and provide machines with abilities that mimic, simulate, become comparable, and in many cases even surpass human beings.*

The term *artificial intelligence* is also used to describe a property of machines or programs: the smartness they demonstrate.

Let's see how AI capabilities can be built. We start with AI models.

What Is an AI Model?

Today, the most widely used method to build AI functions is to use a *model* and train it with data to make it smart. **An AI model is a set of procedures and algorithms that can be trained using data to achieve intelligent behaviors**. These include recognizing patterns, making decisions, producing predictions, and more.

The training process repeatedly alters and fine-tunes parameters in the model to get better results. Depending on the model, the number of parameters can become huge, millions even billions of parameters.

For example, ChatGPT uses a model called a *transformer network*, a type of neural network that simulates neurons and their interconnections. Using the *deep learning* technique, ChatGPT was trained with large amounts of data to learn patterns in that data.

In a chat session, ChatGPT receives a user question or comment and formulates a response, consistent with the context of the conversation. The response is generated one word at a time, using its transformer model which has been previously trained. Now the name GPT (*Generative Pre-trained Transformer*) begins to make sense!

Data Training

AI models use *machine learning* techniques to get trained. This usually involves feeding lots of data to the model in order for it to learn all the situations. The data can be prepared and labeled (supervised learning) or not (unsupervised learning).

Here is a picture of image data used in the training of self-driving cars (Figure 2). For training purposes, parts of the image can be labeled 'car',

FIGURE 2: *Self-driving Training Image*

'traffic sign', 'crosswalk', 'pedestrian', and so on. Of course, many such images are required. Yet, a self-driving system can still get confused and run over a pedestrian. Surely, the quality and quantity of data also affect the training results.

Economic Impact

AI as an industry is expected to have major impact in almost all areas of our economy, providing increased productivity, job creation and displacement, better business management, and innovation.

The economic impact of AI will be significant. According to an August 2023 report by *MarketsandMarkets*[1], the global Artificial Intelligence Market size to grow from $150.2 billion in 2023 to $1,345.2 billion by 2030, at a Compound Annual Growth Rate (CAGR) of 36.8% during the forecast period.

When AI is deployed together with other emerging technologies such as 5G/6G wireless communication, global positioning, satellite communications, Internet of Things (IoT), drones, bio and healthcare technologies,

---

[1]www.marketsandmarkets.com/Market-Reports/artificial-intelligence-market-74851580.html

agriculture/manufacturing automation, digital currencies, etc. the applications are endless.

As AI continues to evolve and become more capable, it may impact the job market in significant ways, both in creating new jobs and in eliminating and degrading existing jobs. The situation should become clearer in a few short years.

AI Models and Computational Thinking

As humans, we also learn from data and experience—the knowledge and facts we gather and happenings in our lives. Such training data, via neuroplasticity, affect our brain (neurons and connections) physically so we become better skilled and more intelligent in particular ways. Computational thinking (CT)

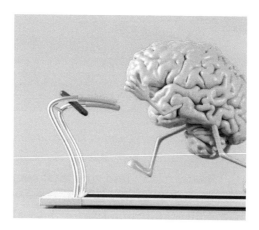

FIGURE 3: *Training a Brain*

is a mental skill. We can become better computational thinkers by doing the same; that is, by gathering more knowledge and understanding of computing and all things digital. And we can get trained by a set of CT principles and practices attached to useful labels such as '**interfaces**', '**protocols**', '**cache management**', '**iteration**', '**divide and conquer**', '**algorithm**', '**abstraction**', '**context switching**', and so on.

For example, CT Articles in this book are wonderful training data. And by getting exposed to the CT Articles, we build and reinforce our mental models to become better computational thinkers.

In the End

AI is just another technology that has many applications, and great economic impact. It has the potential of bringing many benefits to our lives and transforming the way we do things. As with any powerful tool, it can be applied to good or not so good things.

ChatGPT is an impressive breakthrough. There will be many more. Computational thinkers should keep an eye on the developments as AI, especially generative AI, becomes an increasingly important part of our digital world. Yes, ChatGPT is a loud wake-up call for us to better ourselves. We should be continuously prepared to work with new technologies and stay relevant in the job market.

The AI model methodology reinforces our belief that these CT Articles can be an effective way to train and improve our CT skills.

In terms of its ultimate goal, AI today is still far from being able to create a super being similar or superior to humans, if that is ever possible for AI.

·················· CT Crossword Puzzle ············

AI Chat

Across

4. AI systems can become better through ...

5. AI systems undergo this to improve

6. ChatGPT chats within

Down

1. ChatGPT expertise

2. AI training data can be

3. Passing the what text?

6. Conversation bot

12

A World of 1's and 0's

Digital computers use 1's and 0's, nothing else, to represent and store information. There are no exceptions—all data and all programming are coded in 1's and 0's. In other words, computers do everything using only 1's and 0's (Figure 1). Thus, inside a computer, it is a world of 1's and 0's.

How incredible! How fascinating!

FIGURE 1: *A World of 1's and 0's*

But how could this work? How can 1's and 0's play music or stream videos? understand speech? land men on the moon? operate driver-less cars?

At this point, some readers may think, "this is way over my head" and tune out. Please don't. Just continue and you'll find it very interesting and rewarding.

We use a two-step approach to describe how all this can work:

1. Simply explain why computers use only 1's and 0's.

2. In common terms, show how 1's and 0's make everything work.

Digital Hardware

Modern computers process digital signals represented by the presence or absence of an electric current or voltage. Such a signal is the smallest unit of data inside a computer and is known as a *bit* (binary digit). A bit can represent one of two opposing states: on/off, yes/no, yin/yang, up/down, left/right, true/false, and, of course, 1/0. There are many other possibilities but we conventionally refer to these two states as 1 and 0, the two binary digits. A group of 8 bits is called a *byte* and a group of bytes, usually 4 or 8 bytes depending on the computer, is called a *word*.

The Central Processing Unit (CPU) is the brain of a computer where information gets processed. A modern CPU, on a fingernail-sized silicon chip, may contain billions of transistors—fast, tiny (about 70 silicon atoms, certainly invisible to the naked eye), and cheap devices to store and process electronic signals.

Typically, the CPU (Figure 2) performs operations by retrieving and storing data in the main memory, a place to readily access information to be processed. The simplest type of main memory is DRAM (Dynamic Random

FIGURE 2: *CPU inside the Computer*

Access Memory). A DRAM bit may be formed with a single transistor and a single capacitor—using the charged and discharged status of the capacitor to represent the two states. A CPU comes with an *instruction set* for a well-designed group of built-in operations. Instructions take input and produce results in 4/8-byte words. Modern CPUs are extremely fast, executing over 100 billion instructions per second.

DRAM holds information for CPU processing, and its memory cells are *volatile*, losing their contents if power goes off. This is in contrast to hard drives, USB drives, and CD/DVD discs used for long-term data storage. It explains why every time a computer is turned on, it needs to bring the operating system back from a disk into main memory, a process known as *booting*.

In today's computers, main memories are usually 4 to 16 gigabytes ($GB=10^9$ bytes), while hard drives are much larger, approaching several terabytes ($TB=10^{12}$ bytes).

Such is the nature of digital computer hardware and it dictates that, inside the computer, information be represented and processed exclusively in the form of 1's and 0's. How interesting and challenging!

Integers

Before we immerse ourselves in a world of 1's and 0's, let's first look at our own world. In English, we represent information using words and numbers composed of a set of alphabets (upper and lower case A-Z) and digits (0-9). Other languages may use different alphabets.

Inside the computer, the alphabet has just two symbols, namely 1 and 0. In this strange world, everything must be stated in 1's and 0's. It is important to realize the 1 and 0 are just convenient symbols to indicate the two states of a bit. **Be sure to disassociate 0 and 1 as bit values from their day-to-day meaning as numbers**. Why not think of 1 as "presence" and 0 as "absence," if you wish. Now, the trick is to use bits to represent other information in systematic ways.

Let's first consider using bits to represent whole numbers 0, 1, 2, 3 and so on. Using three bits, how many numbers can we cover? Here are all 8 different patterns:

0 0 0, 0 0 1, 0 1 0, 0 1 1, 1 0 0, 1 0 1, 1 1 0, 1 1 1

These are all the different 3-letter words using the two letters 0 and 1. We can use them to represent integers 0 through 7, a total of 8 numbers.

The representation is not arbitrary. They are *base-2* or *binary* numbers. Numbers we use every day are *base-10* (decimal) where each place value is a power of 10. For example,

$$Decimal \quad 209 = 2 \times 10^2 + 0 \times 10 + 9 \times 10^0$$

Similarly for base-2 (binary) numbers, each place value is a power of 2. For example,

$$Binary \quad 101 = 1 \times 2^2 + 0 \times 2 + 1 \times 2^0$$

Increasingly larger numbers require more bits, to represent. With 32 bits we can represent 2^{32} different numbers, enough to cover integers in the range positive and negative $2^{31} - 1$. With 64 bits, we can cover far more. Arithmetic rules for binary numbers are entirely similar to decimal numbers and are easily performed in a computer.

Characters

Numbers are the most basic, but computers need to handle other types of data among which perhaps the most important is text or character data. Again, bit patterns are used to represent individual characters.

Basically, each character can be assigned a different binary number whose bit pattern represents that character. For example, the American Standard Code for Information Interchange (US-ASCII) uses 7 bits in a byte (covering 0 to 127) to represent 128 characters on a typical keyboard: 0-9, A-Z, a-z, punctuation marks, symbols, and control characters. We have, for example, these character representations:

```
'0'  00110000 (48)        '9'  00111001 (57)
'A'  01000001 (65)        'Z'  01011010 (90)
'a'  01100001 (97)        'z'  01111010 (122)
```

Note that the bit pattern for the character `'A'` can also represent the integer 65. Note also that, counterintuitively, the bit pattern for the character `'9'` is different from that for the number 9. Thus, 9 as a character is fundamentally a different symbol than it is as a number. With character encoding, a textual file simply contains a sequence of bit patterns.

The world has many languages. Unicode is an international standard for encoding text data from most of the world's writing systems. It now contains more than 110,000 characters from 100 languages/scripts. The Unicode Consortium, an international collaboration, publishes and updates the Unicode standard.

Unicode allows mixing, in a single document file, characters from practically all known languages. This is very advantageous especially in a world increasingly interconnected by the Internet and the web. Most webpages are written in HTML using UTF-8, a particularly efficient form of Unicode.

Data Context

A symbol, word, or phrase may have a very different meaning depending on the context where it is used. For example, consider the meaning of the word 'like': we like the puppy; it looks like a cat; and I was like "crazy!". Bit patterns are no exception.

You must have realized that a given bit pattern may represent a binary number or a character. For example, the bit pattern

```
01000001
```

represents 65 or the character '`A`'. The question is how to tell which one. The answer is "context." *The same bit pattern can be interpreted differently depending on the context where it is used.* We must provide a context for any given bit pattern to indicate if it is a number, character, or something else. The context can be given explicitly or deduced from where the pattern is used. For example, in evaluating the expression x + 5, we know the value of x needs to be interpreted as a number. In a computer program, the *data type* of each quantity must be declared implicitly or explicitly. The type informs a program how to interpret the data representation associated with any given quantity.

> **CT concept–*Data meaning depends on context***: *Always interpret data in their proper context and avoid separating information from its context.*

For example, we ought to avoid such terms as "today" or "next week" in emails. The awareness is an important part of computational thinking. Not doing so can have serious consequences.

In 1999, NASA's Mars Climate Orbiter burned up in the Martian atmosphere because engineers failed to convert units from British (English) to metric.

Music to My Ears

Numbers and characters are relatively easy to represent using bit patterns. But what about more complicated data such as music, picture, or video? Let's look at music first. Sound travels through air as a continuous wave. Sound pitch levels vary from low to high through an infinite number of values.

In the past, analog computers can process an electronic wave, produced by a microphone from sound, with ease. But, such analog signals are hard to store, transmit, or reproduce and have loss of fidelity problems. Digital computers can not process continuous data, such as sound, directly. Such data must first be *digitized* and become a series of numbers. It is not hard to digitize. A continuous value, that of a sound wave for example, can be digitized by taking values at a number of sampling points— the more sampling points, the more precise the representation (Figure 3). Thus, continuous data become a series of numbers that can be represented by 1's and 0's and can be stored,

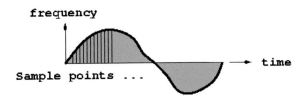

FIGURE 3: *Data Sampling*

transmitted, and received without change or loss of fidelity. The digital sound data can further be processed by clever data compression algorithms, such as mp3, to reduce data size and increase transmission speed.

A Picture Is Worth a Thousand Words

A picture is basically different colors on a surface. Thus, representing colors digitally is the first requirement. The widely used RGB (red, green, blue) color system (Figure 4) represents a color by the triple (r, g, b) where each number r, g, or b ranges from 0 to 255. For example (255,0,0) is full red, (0,255,0) full green, (0,0,255) full blue, (0,0,0) pure black, and (255, 255, 255) pure white.

Red		(255,0,0)	Cyan		(0,255,255)
Green		(0,255,0)	Yellow		(255,255,0)
Blue		(0,0,255)	Magenta		(255,0,255)

FIGURE 4: *RGB Colors*

Thus, in the RGB system, a byte is used to represent each RGB number and, in turn, a total of 256^3 different colors can be represented.

The CYMK (cyan, yellow, magenta, black) system is similarly represented. RGB is used for screen display while CYMK is used for printing.

In *raster graphics*, a picture is represented by listing the color of all its *pixels*. Each pixel (picture element) is nothing but a point in a rectangular grid over the picture. The finer the gird, the better the represented picture. In *vector graphics*, x-y coordinates, lines and other geometrical elements are used to represent a picture. Raster graphics is well suited for photographs while vector graphics is better for drawings, logos, and icons.

With digital pictures at hand, videos can then be represented by a timed sequence of pictures, together with sound data. As you can imagine, high-resolution video data can be huge, compute-intensive to render on a display. Often, added graphics hardware such as GPUs (graphics processing units) and graphics cards are used to greatly speed up display of images. Also, many highly efficient image/video data compression algorithms have been developed to reduce their size and increase transmission speed while striving to preserve picture quality.

3D Printing

Ordinary ink jet and laser printers divide a surface into a fine grid, say 300 dots per inch, and deposit precisely ink dots at specific positions on a sheet of paper. For black and white printing, we can envision a flat layer of 0's (empty spots) and 1's (ink spots) to understand the process.

Extending the idea a step further, 3D printing simply divides an object into flat horizontal layers (Figure 5). Each layer can be printed just as in 2D printing. By printing the layers one on top of another, a 3D object is formed. 3D printers use special materials instead of ink and can create intricate objects precisely. The technology is already widely used in model building, parts manufacturing, even construction. Affordable 3D printers for home use

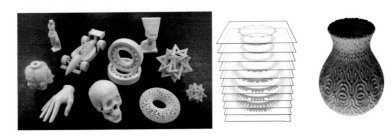

FIGURE 5: *3D Printing (image: OZEKI)*

are also available. Thus, we can envision objects as a pile of 0's and 1's. How strangely delightful!

In the End

The nature of digital hardware gives rise to a wondrous world of bits, bytes and words—a world that has only two letters in its alphabet, where any and all information consists of 1's and 0's, and where instructions are given in 1's and 0's, so are input and output, all in head-spinning speed.

Dealing exclusively with 1's and 0's may seem idiotic, yet that simplicity is the basis for reducing size, decreasing cost, and increasing speed. Do you think today's computers are powerful? Just wait, you haven't seen anything yet!

If a world with only two symbols is so nice, why not go one step further to a world of **one symbol**? Wouldn't that be even better? The answer is: *It is not possible to have only one symbol. Its presence necessarily implies its absence (another symbol). Thus, the world of 1's and 0's is it.*

CT Crossword Puzzle

1's and 0's

Across

5. Bit patterns __ information

6. 8 bits

7. Programs are also ...

8. Graphics, not raster but ...

Down

1. Represent continuous data by a series of numbers

2. ASCII code represent

3. Inside a computer numbers are

4. Bit patterns interpreted based on

5. RGB (255,0,0)

6. Zero or One

13

Secrets of the Can-Do Machine

At the center of the information revolution is the digital computer—a can-do machine like no other. At once it can be a TV, phone, thermometer, compass, music box, language interpreter, and much more. In fact, we know it can perform any task following a well-designed program—an "app" (application) as we call it these days.

It is exactly such flexibility that makes the modern computer a very different creature, namely a *general-purpose* or *universal machine*. But what features or characteristics made this possible? Are there things the modern computer can't do? What tasks are easy or hard for the computer?

We will take a closer look and try to provide some answers. By stripping away the complications, we arrive at the nature and essence of the digital computer. This way, we can reveal the reasons why it is a universal machine. We can also acquire CT principles that are useful every day.

A Universal Machine

The unique revolutionary power of the digital computer comes from its *universality*. What makes it a universal machine verses other specific-use machines is the fact that it is a *stored-program* machine. By installing and running any given program on the fly, a computer instantly becomes a different machine without rewiring or other physical modifications.

The central processing unit (CPU) is the brain of a computer where information gets processed with electronic logic circuits. A modern CPU, on a fingernail-sized silicon chip, may contain billions of transistors—fast, tiny (about 70 silicon atoms, certainly invisible to the naked eye), and cheap devices to store and process electronic signals.

The modern computer can be very complicated and hard to understand. Yet, the basics are quite simple—the CPU executes a sequence of *instructions*, one after another. The instructions and data are stored in the memory of the computer.

The instructions and data constitute a computer program. Each instruction has an *opcode*, representing the operation or action to be performed, and *operands*, values supplied for the operation. An operation may store a result in memory, perform I/O, designate which instruction to execute next, or otherwise change the *internal state* of the computer. The key is all the instructions, data, opcode, and operand values are all represented by 1's and 0's and stored in memory.

These characteristics of the digital computer are derived directly from the nature of its hardware.

The Turing Machine

Now we can go a little deeper and consider the computer's computational model, giving us a crystal-clear idea of the behavior of the computer.

Alan Turing, the undisputed father of computer science, was born on June 23, 1912, in England (Figure 1). His contributions are so important that the highest honor of computing is named the *Turing Award*. At the tender age of

FIGURE 1: *Alan Turing (1912-1954)*

24, Turing published a paper introducing a computing model, now known as the *Turing machine* (Figure 2). A Turing machine is a theoretic device that models how a computer works. A Turing machine can be described as follows:

1. The machine has a finite number of internal states. It is a *finite-state machine*.

2. Input to and output of the machine are given as symbols written on a tape that is not limited in length.

3. The collection of symbols, the machine's *alphabet*, is a finite set.

4. The symbol it is currently reading, together with its current state, determines the machine's action. An action may involve any and all of these: writing a new symbol on the tape, moving the read/write head forward or backward (or keeping it in place), entering a new state, and halting.

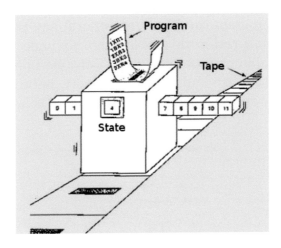

FIGURE 2: *Turing Machine*

5. The Turing machine's finite-length program specifies its different states, and exact actions for different input at each state, including state transitions.

The Turing machine pictured starts working after loading a program. It has 12 states (0 through 11) and is currently in state 4.

Modern computers are shown to be equivalent to the Turing machine. The alphabet is the set $\{0, 1\}$, data and program stored in the main memory define its states and actions, and it performs I/O. Specifically:

1. The CPU and main memory (to store programming and data constituting the internal states) are finite.

2. The tape models I/O. There is no length restriction on I/O.

3. The set of symbols $\{1,0\}$ is a finite alphabet.

4. The input (read from the tape) interpreted by the current state leads to specific actions.

5. Program actions include performing I/O (reading/writing the tape), and entering the next state (making changes to CPU and memory).

Tasks that can be performed by a Turing machine are known as *computable* or *decidable*. Those that cannot be performed by a Turing machine are *incomputable* or *undecidable*. This simply means that a task is computable if it is possible to devise an algorithm or write a computer program for it.

While undecidable problems exist, they are generally highly specialized and abstract. In most practical situations, computers can be programmed to solve a vast range of problems effectively and efficiently.

The ability to program computers to perform any task (Figure 3) comes from the fact that most real-world problems are not undecidable. They fall into the realm of decidable or computationally solvable problems. Furthermore, even for problems that are undecidable in theory, approximation algorithms and heuristics can often be used to find reasonable solutions in practice. Of

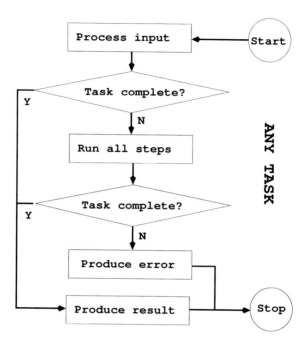

FIGURE 3: *A Computer Can Do Any Task*

course, creating effective and efficient procedures and algorithms is central to computer science. Another important topic of theoretic computer science is *computational complexity* that studies the amount of time required to solve certain classes of problems. Some computable problems can take a long time to finish, longer than the Sun's life span.

Internal State of a Computer

We mentioned the internal state of a computer before. But, the concept is so important it is worth further explanation.

The internal state of a computer refers to the current condition or situation of the computer at any given time. It includes things like what programs are running, what data is being processed, and what tasks the computer is currently performing.

To put it simply, the internal state of a computer is like the snapshot of what the computer is doing and thinking at that moment. It's like looking inside the computer's brain and seeing what it's up to.

So, when you turn on a computer, it starts with an initial internal state. As you use it, open programs, work on documents, or play games, the internal state keeps changing to reflect what the computer is doing at each moment.

In fact, if a single bit turns from 0 to 1, or vice versa, the computer has a changed state. The same goes for changes in CPU registers and counters. Hence, the number of total possible states can be huge given the size of modern computer main memory.

When an operating system performs a *context switch*, it suspends the currently running process and saves its state, then it enters a new state for running the next process. To run a previously suspended process, it first restores the saved state. Today's multi-programming operating systems perform context switches frequently, and at high speed.

Programs as Data

We know that data—text, image, audio, video, and so on—are stored in digital form in the computer. Various programs can create, utilize, and manipulate such data for many useful purposes. In CT Article 12, "*A World of 1's and 0's*" you can find how bit patterns can represent different kinds of data.

In addition, because programs themselves are also represented and stored in memory for a computer to run them, **program codes themselves can be manipulated in a computer just like data**. In fact, the key for computers being universal machines is the fact that *programs can be treated as data*.

For example, high-level programs are represented by characters. Such programs are transformed (by other computer programs known as compilers or interpreters), and translated into machine language before being executed. A machine language programs, coded in CPU instructions, can be run directly.

So, we see that computers have the ability to load, store, modify, and otherwise *manipulate programs using programs*! This means, a computer can transform and modify programs at will. A computer can even edit and alter its own programming on the fly. Therefore, it is a machine that can modify itself on the fly. In fact, this should not be surprising at all, because computers are information processing machines, and programs are just pieces of information.

Hence, we say computers are *universal machines* because they can store and run any program. When it runs a different program, the computer literally becomes a different machine, without modification or intervention at the hardware level. We take it for granted as we update, upgrade, and download apps without giving it a second thought.

Power of Abstraction

The Turing machine is a prime example of a central idea in computational thinking "abstraction."

> **CT concept–*Abstraction***: *Strip away unimportant, unrelated, or irrelevant details from concrete instances, and focus on the essential core characteristics of the subject matter.*

Through abstraction, we often can make a complicated situation much clearer by peeling away unessential aspects that often can obscure the issue. Abstraction allows us to distill the essence of an idea or concept and, therefore, gain a more profound understanding. For example, we can talk about adults, teenagers, children, liberals, conservatives, men, women, odd numbers, even numbers, and so on. But, not until we abstract to the concept of "set" and set membership, can we gain a clear concept and a language to discuss collections of objects in a general and rigorous manner.

Finally

The nature of digital hardware gives rise to a wondrous world of bits, bytes, and words—a world that has only two symbols in its alphabet. It being a stored-program machine makes it possible to download and launch apps at will.

The can-do machine can drive your car, pilot your plane, and bring space-crafts to the moon and back to Earth. Sure there are things it can't do. In practice, it can do anything provided that a program can be developed for it.

A programmer has the knowledge and skills to write programs. Therefore, in the digital age, computer programmers are the *digital smiths* who can create new tools by writing programs. Not everyone can or want to write programs. Actually, a software project often involves a small team of people, not just one person.

Humans may want to borrow the computer's can-do spirit. That way we will be more flexible in the tasks we can, or are willing to, perform. And we can try to acquire new knowledge and skills eagerly and easily! That spirit can help us become more objective, brave, and willing to try new things–breaking any self-made cage and realizing our full potential.

14

Encryption in the Digital Age

Digital information travels at the speed of light making instant communication and interactions among people, near and far, a reality. Yet, because of their open nature, data traveling on the Internet are accessible to any connected computer, making information security and privacy a real concern.

What is done to safeguard our sensitive information in the global digital village? What can individuals do to protect personal information? In CT Article 5, "*Cybersecurity–How Not To Be a Fish*," we talked about many useful cybersecurity topics. Here we will focus on *cryptography*, one of the most important techniques to secure data.

Egg Scrambling

Cryptosystems keep communication safe by encryption, a technique invented long before digital computers. The concept is simple—an original message (*plaintext*) is encrypted into *ciphertext* before communication. The ciphertext is gibberish for anyone except the intended receiver who knows how to decrypt the ciphertext back into the original plaintext.

All this sounds abstract, but it is really straightforward—you scramble a message, like scrambling an egg (Figure 1), so it becomes garbled. There is no way for anyone to find out what the original egg looks like by looking at the scrambled egg. *Hashing* is a systematic way of scrambling any message

FIGURE 1: *Egg Scrambling*

of arbitrary length into a fixed-length sequence of bits. The same original message becomes the same garbled *hash* or *message digest* after hashing. The slightest change in the original message results in a very different hash. Given a hash, there is no way to know what the original message was. There are quite a few hash algorithms. SHA-256 is currently used most often.

For example, the sentence "**This is the egg.**" has the following SHA-256 hash (a sequence of 256 bits), displayed in HEX (base 16) notation:

a6d39dfb1c20cd15b1a69506dd072354cb4c472135ccc51a0412f42d64e6e415

The hash becomes completely different if even a single character is changed in that sentence. In fact, this is exactly how your password is stored on the server where you log in. When you set your password it is first hashed and then the resulting hash stored instead. By not storing your actual password, its secrecy is preserved. When you log in, the password you enter is hashed the same way and the result is compared to the stored version. A match means your password is correct. Thus, hashing is a *one-way encryption*; there is no way to recover the original message from the hash.

But when you log in, your user ID and password are sent across the Internet. A method is needed to protect data in transit from eavesdropping, not just passwords but all data to and from you and a secure website. That leads to secure communication online.

Secure Communication

For secure communication, we need a system where the encryption can be undone or decrypted. For example, *rot13* (Figure 2) encrypts by simple letter substitution.

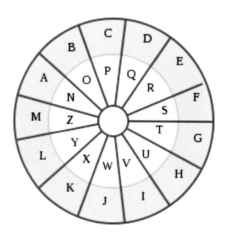

FIGURE 2: *Rot13*

Each letter in the plaintext is replaced by a letter 13 places after it, assuming there are only 26 letters and the last letter is followed by the first letter in a cycle. A rot13 ciphertext can be decrypted by applying the encryption on it again.

For example, the plaintext "Now I know my ABC" becomes the ciphertext "Abj V xabj zl NOP" using rot13. It can be entertaining to decrypt it yourself.

It is not hard to think of other more sophisticated ways. For example, senders and receivers can agree on a book to use. Ciphertext would contain a page number, line number, and word number to identify any particular word from the book. Only people who know which book and what the numbers mean can decrypt the message. Further, one of the many numbers may indicate a particular book among several possible ones to use.

These are examples of *symmetric cryptosystems* that use the same *key* to encipher and decipher messages. Communicating parties must know the key beforehand. And the key must be kept secret to others. Obviously, rot13, the book plus numbering scheme, and the WW2 German Enigma machine settings are the keys.

Symmetric Cryptosystems

Modern symmetric encryption systems (Figure 3) work on digital data. Most, if not all, of them use an encryption/decryption algorithm that is open and a key that is kept secret.

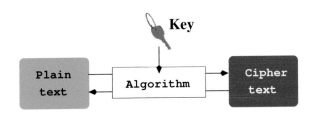

FIGURE 3: *A Symmetric Cryptosystem*

- Encryption/decryption algorithm: The algorithm performs various substitutions and permutations on chunks, typically 128- or 256-bit blocks, of the plaintext or ciphertext.

- Secret key: The plaintext (ciphertext) and the secret key are input to the encryption (decryption) algorithm. The exact transformations performed depend on the key used. The algorithm produces different output depending on the key given. Using the same key on the ciphertext, the algorithm produces the original plaintext.

A symmetric cryptosystem usually has these two characteristics:

1. Open algorithm: The encryption/decryption algorithm can be described in the open. This works because it is impractical to decode any ciphertext knowing the algorithm and not the secret key.

2. Secret key: Senders and receivers must obtain the key securely in advance, and all must keep the key secret.

The secret key is usually a bit pattern of sufficient length. The quality of the secret key is important. It should be randomly generated and be 256-bit or longer to make brute-force attacks, trying all possible keys, impractical.

When a password (or passphrase) is used as a key, it is usually put through a key derivation function, which compresses or expands it to the key length desired. Often, a randomly generated piece of data, called a *salt*, is also added to the password or passphrase before transforming it to the actual key.

The Advanced Encryption Standard (AES) is a symmetric cryptosystem for digital data established by the US National Institute of Standards and Technology (NIST) in 2001. AES has been adopted by the US government and is now used worldwide. It supersedes the Data Encryption Standard (DES), which was published in 1977. There are other symmetric ciphers, such as RC4 and Blowfish, but AES-256 seems to be the best.

Keeping Sensitive Data Safe

Let's apply computational thinking and use encryption to keep our own sensitive data and files safe. The most important is to protect *Personally Identifiable Information* (PII), which includes any data that can be used to identify an individual.

For example, bank statements, login information, business contacts, tax returns, accounting, financial, and insurance records, contracts, medical history, and so on should be kept confidential by encrypting them. Furthermore, it is advisable to keep scanned images of your important documents, such as birth certificates, passports, and driver's licenses, in files for easy usage and as backup. But, make sure these are protected, too, by encryption.

With Microsoft Word or Microsoft Office, you can save and retrieve encrypted files (Figure 4). The free Vim editor (`vim.org`) can encrypt/decrypt a file using Blowfish and a secret key. The application 'AES Crypt' (`aescrypt.com`) simply encrypts/decrypts a file with AES using a key that you choose. These tools work on multiple platforms. Similar file encryption apps are available on smartphones.

Recording all your passwords and secret keys in an encrypted *keyfile* means you can access login information and secret keys if you just remember one key,

FIGURE 4: *Opening an Encrypted Word Document*

the one for the keyfile. This can make life much easier. You may even consider encrypting your hard disks.

Symmetric cryptography is also used in HTTPS, the secure web protocol, to keep communication between a user and a website confidential. HTTPS is a must for any site requiring login. But good practice now calls for all websites to use HTTPS, instead of HTTP, in general. Every time you visit a website under HTTPS, a *session key* is agreed upon **automatically and securely** between your browser and the website first. This is the *key distribution problem* for symmetric cryptosystems. To solve this problem and for some other purposes, *public-key cryptography* was developed.

Public-key Cryptosystems

Unlike symmetric systems where the same key is used for both encryption and decryption, *public-key cryptosystems* are asymmetric and use not one but a pair of keys—one to encrypt and the other to decrypt. The decryption key is kept secret, while the encryption key can be shared publicly (Figure 5). The pair of keys are integers satisfying well-defined mathematical properties and usually produced by a key generation program. For each public key, there is only one corresponding private key, and vice versa.

The public key is made available for anyone who wishes to send an encrypted message to a recipient who uses the private key to decrypt the message. It goes without saying that the owner of the key pair will keep the private key safe and secret.

The public key usually becomes part of a *digital certificate*, which can be presented to anyone to verifiably associate the key to its owner. An owner of a key pair may also place the public key in online *key repositories* open to the public.

Thus, anyone who wishes to send a secure message to a particular receiver will use the receiver's public key for encryption. The receiver can then use the

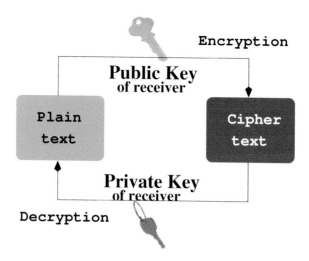

FIGURE 5: *Public-Key Encryption*

corresponding private key for decryption. Note that in this case the parties need not have communicated with each other ever before.

For example, if Eve wished to send a secure message to Adam whom she had never met before, she would first look up his public key, encrypt the message with it, then send the result to Adam.

Thinking Outside the Box

> **CT concept–*Think outside the box*:** *Break out of the mold of conventional thinking, challenge old assumptions, create, and innovate.*

Public-key cryptography is a great example. It started with the breakthrough idea, credited to Bailey W. Diffie, Martin E. Hellman, and Ralph C. Merkle, that *two parties can establish a secret symmetric key over an unprotected public communications channel.* It is infeasible for any eavesdropper of their open exchanges to deduce the key they agreed upon.

When Merkle first proposed research into the idea, it was met with skepticism and resistance from experts. But, this mid-1970 invention soon led to the even more astounding public-key cryptography, where the encryption algorithm and key can be published openly.

One critical element of public-key cryptography is the computational infeasibility to deduce the private key from the public key. Unlike symmetric encryption, public-key encryption avoids communicating secret keys. Thus, anyone and any system can send a secure message to a receiver, who has a published public key or a digital certificate, without having any prior contact with the person.

However, the speed of public cryptography is much slower than symmetric cryptography. This explains why HTTPS uses public-key encryption only in the handshake phase to establish a symmetric *session key* for the actual data transmissions.

Public-key cryptography underpins modern cryptosystems, applications, and protocols, such as digital certificates and HTTPS. It also can achieve *digital signature*.

Digital Signature

Digital signature is a way to use encryption to transform a document digitally into a signed document such that (1) the signed document cannot be altered in any way, and (2) everyone can verify it has been signed by the signer. Digital signature is different from electronic signature. The latter is simply an electronic form of a person's autograph (Figure 6). A public-key cryptosystem

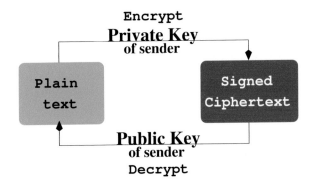

FIGURE 6: *Digital Signature*

lends itself immediately for digital signature. To sign a document, a signer simply encrypts it with the signer's own private key. The resulting document can be sent to any interested party. The signed document can be decrypted using the signer's public key. Because only the signer has knowledge and use of their private key, the document is thus verifiably signed by them. Furthermore, the integrity (unaltered property) of the original document is also maintained. Failing to protect your private key can be serious. Someone may use it to sign stuff and get you in trouble.

For example, if Eve had a key pair and wished to send a signed contract to Adam, she would use her own secret key to encrypt the contract, then send the result to Adam. The fact that Adam, or anyone else for that matter, can decrypt the result with Eve's public key to reproduce the contract proves that she indeed had signed it. It also shows the contract is unaltered because any alteration will result in decryption failure.

Normally the contract is no secret. Therefore, Eve may digitally sign an SHA-256 hash of the contract instead.

Applications

Cryptosytems can be complicated and all their details hard to understand. But they basically use clever algorithms to scramble and unscramble messages to achieve secrecy and security in many important applications. In fact, we can say that without cryptography protection of sensitive data in the digital world would be very hard indeed.

We can list some applications.

- Safe password storage and checking via hashing.

- Encryption/decryption in Microsoft Word, PDF, and other textual files.

- Direct file encryption/decryption with AES.

- Software distribution with digitally signed message digest.

- Digital certificates with owner's public key.

- Symmetric and asymmetric cryptography used in protocols and apps such as SSH (secure remote login), SFTP (secure file transfer), SSL/TLS (transfer layer security), and HTTPS (secure web protocol).

- Secure email with PGP (pretty good privacy), GPG (Gnome privacy guard), and products such as MS Office/Office365.

- Digitally signed contracts and documents, and digital certificates are widely used examples.

- Hashing and digital signature for transaction integrity in blockchains.

- Cryptography in digital currency.

Finally

The digital age brings so much power and convenience to all of us. It makes the entire world a global village. That also means all kinds of hackers and dangers lurk online. Cryptography is the weapon of choice to defend our security and privacy in the digital world. We owe it to ourselves to understand and apply it well.

Hashing, symmetric encryption/decryption, public-key cryptography, digital signatures, digital certificates, and secure protocols such as HTTPS combine to form a digital security infrastructure designed to keep our files and data safe and secure. Various apps, such as SSH or MS Office/Office365, support security features based on cryptography. As users, we can select the right applications to safeguard our private information.

.... CT Crossword Puzzle ....

Encryption

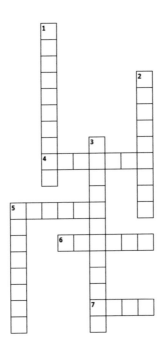

Across

4. ___ your sensitive files
5. Result of hashing is a ___
6. Digital signature can identify the ___
7. Scramble a message

Down

1. A ___ crypto system can achieve digital signature
2. A ___ crypto system uses a secret key
3. The encode/decode methods
5. Digital signature can be used to safely ___ software

15

Bitcoin Is No Coin

The digital revolution has brought many significant and wide-ranging changes to our lives—both positive and negative. Understanding the pros and cons of digital technologies and knowing how best to make use of them are part of *Computational Thinking* (CT). The widely publicized and curiously fascinating *Bitcoin*, started in January 2009, is a case in point and our focus here.

Bitcoin Is Not Money

Promoters say Bitcoin is a particular type of *cryptocurrency*—a digital currency using encryption techniques to generate currency units, verify fund transfers, and record transactions (Figure 1). Basic denominations of Bitcoin are *Bitcoin* (BTC) and *Satoshi* (1 BTC equals 100 million Satoshis). The highly advanced and convoluted nature of its technologies helps make Bitcoin fascinating and curiously inviting. However, whatever Bitcoin is, it is not money.

FIGURE 1: *An Image Representing the Bitcoin Logo*

With cash, you can purchase groceries, meals, and products. You can pay rent and mortgage, make deposits into bank accounts, and all the other things you do with the legal tender. Cash is issued by your government, which no one can refuse to accept. In contrast, bitcoin is accepted by almost no one, and there is no legal obligation for anyone to accept it as payment, and neither should you!

Bitcoin Transactions

One of the great promises of Bitcoin is anonymity because sending and receiving bitcoins do not require actual identification information. Instead *Bitcoin addresses* that belong to actual owners are used. This is similar to using screen names or pseudonyms in certain online applications. The amount of bitcoins belonging to any given address is derived from recorded incoming and outgoing transactions. This way, no self-contained tokens are used to represent bitcoins and therefore eliminating the possibility of creating a counterfeit copy.

All Bitcoin transactions are recorded publicly in online *blockchains*. A blockchain is basically a widely distributed (duplicated) database for a certain activity. A blockchain usually serves as an *immutable* (unchanging or can't be modified) ledger of transactions shared among participants. New transactions are verified, grouped into a data block, and placed at the end of a chain of such blocks, hence the name blockchain. Bitcoin and other cryptocurrencies depend on the blockchain technology. However, the blockchain technology is independent of cryptocurrencies and can be applied in many other areas and situations.

The Bitcoin blockchain lists chronologically all Bitcoin transactions ever made by all users, from the very first to the latest transaction. The Bitcoin blockchain is *transparent* (accessible to the public) and uses cryptography to safeguard its integrity. Each recorded transaction contains the amount of bitcoin to be sent to a receiving electronic Bitcoin address (usually about 30 characters in length) owned anonymously by a particular user. The user holds a corresponding secret key (often 64 characters) to access bitcoins at that address. The Bitcoin address and the secret key form a key-pair in *public-key cryptography*. Without the secret key, access is not possible.

Bitcoin Transactions Are Not Anonymous

All these elaborate arrangements provide a certain degree of protection but can not guarantee transaction anonymity. Using bitcoins involves online activities on the part of the payer and the payee. To make a transaction, payers must usually log in to a Bitcoin exchange to use a *wallet* containing their bitcoins. Users must also have interactions with shopping carts and checkout systems online. These and other required online activities provide multiple chances for tracking and can easily result in linking a bitcoin address to the identity of its real owner, and consequently to all transactions connected to that Bitcoin address via data in the blockchain—according to an article in *MIT Technology Review*[1] entitled, *"Bitcoin Transactions Aren't as Anonymous as Everyone Hoped."*

It is hard to argue that Bitcoin is more anonymous than cold cash.

Bitcoin Is Not Heaven for Criminals

In fact, Bitcoin may be the perfect trap law enforcement agencies can use to catch criminals. As the *Science* article[2] states:

> *Ross Ulbricht, the 31-year-old American who created Silk Road, a Bitcoin market facilitating the sale of $1 billion in illegal drugs, was sentenced to life in prison in February 2015. In March, the assets of 28-year-old Czech national Tomáš Jiříkovský were seized; he's suspected of laundering $40 million in stolen bitcoins. Two more fell in September 2015: 33-year-old American Trendon Shavers pleaded guilty to running a $150 million Ponzi scheme— the first Bitcoin securities fraud case—and 30-year-old Frenchman Mark Karpelès was arrested and charged with fraud and embezzlement of $390 million from the now shuttered Bitcoin currency exchange Mt. Gox.*
>
> *The majority of Bitcoin users are law-abiding people motivated by privacy concerns or just curiosity. But Bitcoin's anonymity is also a powerful tool for financing crime: The virtual money can keep shady transactions secret. The paradox of cryptocurrency is that its associated data create a forensic trail that can suddenly make your entire financial history public information.*

Bitcoin Is Not Convenient

To buy, sell, and use bitcoins online, you usually must pick a Bitcoin exchange, something better than the now defunct Mt. Gox, hopefully, and establish an account which usually also gives you an online Bitcoin wallet.

To use bitcoins you must first get some. You can purchase bitcoins which will be placed into your wallet. Payment can be with a credit card, bank transfer (ACH), or debit card (there goes your anonymity).

---

[1]Emerging Technology from the arXiv. (2017, August 23). technologyreview.com
[2]Bohannon, John. (2016, March 9). *Why criminals can't hide behind Bitcoin.* www.science.org/content/article/why-criminals-cant-hide-behind-bitcoin

You must keep your private key safe and remember it. Forget that key and you have lost all your bitcoins. They are gone forever and there is no way to get them back!

Bitcoin transactions can incur relatively high fees that are calculated according to a complicated formula making the fee amount uncertain for most users. At times, the fee can be ridiculous. "Just imagine, if you bought a $2 coffee with bitcoin, you would have had to pay $57 to make that transaction go through," said Hyun Song Shin head of research at the Bank for International Settlement[3].

Bitcoin transactions can be slow to confirm due to the possibility of *double spending* (spending already-spent bitcoins). They are also irreversible—once made, there is no cancellation of a Bitcoin transaction.

Compared to online payments by debit/credit cards, by PayPal, or by Alipay, Bitcoin is a poor and inconvenient choice at best.

Bitcoin Is Not an Investment

A bitcoin is not a coin which is made of a material that has at least some intrinsic value. Neither is bitcoin a currency backed by the full faith and credit of a government or tied to some substance such as gold or silver. It is some digital data contained in blockchains, and what value is that?

Unlike commodities or stocks, the value of bitcoins is pure speculation. There is no rational way to estimate its value at all. According to a *Financial Times* article[4]:

> *Its value peaked just before Christmas at $19,434 per virtual coin. By this week, it had plunged to more like $9,000. Down more than 50 per cent in a month and many, many billions along the way.*

The price of one bitcoin was down to around $6,200 in the third week of June 2018. At that time, US regulators opened a price manipulation probe requesting data from several cryptocurrency exchanges. CNN Money reported[5] on June 11, 2018, "The price of bitcoin slumped more than 7% after South Korea's Coinrail announced that it had been targeted by cyberthieves." Price fixing has been a reported problem and, in late May 2018, the U.S. Justice Department started a new probe into price manipulation in cryptocurrency markets.

---

[3] *Prominent Investor: Cryptocurrency Gives People an Easy Opt Out From US Dollar.* (2018) newsbtc.com

[4] Webb, M. S. *I told you investing in bitcoin was a bad idea.* (2018, January 19). www.ft.com

[5] Shane, D. *Billions in cryptocurrency wealth wiped out after hack.* (2018, June 11). money.cnn.com

Thus, investing in bitcoins is gambling at best. In fact, according to Warren Buffett[6], "bitcoin is 'rat poison'." Stay away if you know what's good for you (Figure 2).

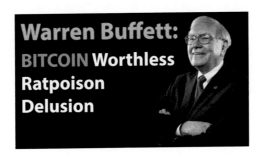

FIGURE 2: *Warren Buffett on Bitcoin*

What Is Bitcoin Mining?

Wonder how bitcoins are actually produced? New bitcoins are created through a well-defined and algorithmic process called *mining*. Anyone with the right computing hardware and software (publicly available) can participate, becoming a *miner*, from anywhere on the Internet.

The mining process involves verifying and compiling recent transactions into blocks and trying to solve a computationally difficult puzzle. Verification is straightforward—making sure the source address actually has the funds and the transaction has been signed by the address owner. The first miner who solves the puzzle is the winner and gets to place the next verified block on the block chain. The winner can also claim stipulated rewards. The rewards incentivize mining and include both the transaction fees (paid to the miner in the form of bitcoins) as well as an amount of newly issued bitcoins. The amount was 50 bitcoins in early 2009, when Bitcoin started. The winner reward amount reduces by 50% roughly every four years. The rewards are given to the winner in the form of a recorded transaction.

For each new block on the blockchain, there is only one winning miner. **All other miners are losers and can try their luck on the next block.** Globally, huge amounts of capital, equipment, and computing power are wasted in this mindless Bitcoin mining effort (Figure 3). It is estimated that Bitcoin mining accounts for about 0.60% of the world's total energy consumption. This is hugely wasteful.

---

[6]La Monica, P. R. *Warren Buffett says bitcoin is 'rat poison'.* (2018, May 8). money.cnn.com

FIGURE 3: *Array of Bitcoin Mining Processors*

A *New York Times* article[7] says:

> *Bitcoin mines cash in on electricity—by devouring it, selling it, even turning it off—and they cause immense pollution. In many cases, the public pays a price.*

It is an understatement to say that Bitcoin mining is a waste of resources and a serious act of pollution. Some countries have banned Bitcoin mining.

Furthermore, there is an upper limit for the number of bitcoins—21 million. When that number is reached, no more new bitcoins will be issued as incentive for miners. The lack of incentive for solving puzzles and adding new blocks to the blockchain can lead to a drastic reduction in the number of miners and a timebomb for the continued viable operation of Bitcoin.

Is Bitcoin Not a Scam?

Bitcoin is free-for-all to operate and deal. Some people, including former Pay-Pal CEO Bill Harris[8], say that bitcoin is a scam. Even if that is not 100% true, the entire Bitcoin enterprise is certainly continuously mired in many different kinds of frauds and scams all over the world. The situation is so serious that many Bitcoin exchanges publicize warnings about scams in an attempt to show that they themselves are somehow legit.

For example, `cointelegraph.com` has a "*Bitcoin Scams News*" page listing many instances[9]. Here are some examples:

---

[7]Dance et al. *The Real-World Costs of the Digital Race for Bitcoin.* (2023, April 11). www.nytimes.com

[8]Sharma, Rakesh. *Former Paypal CEO Calls Bitcoin A Scam.* (2019, June 25). investopedia.com

[9]cointelegraph.com/tags/bitcoin-scams

- In South Africa, a Ponzi scheme involving 28,000 investors has caused losses exceeding 1 billion rand ($80.4 million).

- Australian consumers lost approximately $2.1 million to cryptocurrency scams last year, according to the Australian Competition and Consumer Commission's annual scams report published on May 21, 2018.

- A May 18, 2018 report indicated that a Chinese government study detected 421 fake cryptocurrencies. The US Securities and Exchange Commission (SEC) created `www.investor.gov/ico-howeycoins` to demonstrate how easy it is to sell a fake cryptocurrency. Why not pay the site a visit?

  As of mid-2022, there are more than 12,000 cryptocurrencies. Due to the absolute simplicity of setting up a new cryptocurrency, the count has more than doubled from 2011 to 2012. Bitcoin remains prominent by far. Others include Doglee, Ethereum, Cronos, and Ripple.

The `bitcoin.com` site has a *"Guide to Avoiding Bitcoin Fraud"*[10] that warns against

- Fake Bitcoin exchanges and wallets

- Phishing scams, Ponzi schemes, and cloud mining scams

And these are just some of the dangers one must face and avoid, every step of the way, when dealing with a cryptocurrency such as Bitcoin.

Bitcoin Can Be Illegal

Due to lack of government supervision, regulation, or control, Bitcoin as well as other similar cryptocurrencies, can be a destabilizing factor for many economies and financial markets. The potential for tax evasion, money laundering, ransomware, illegal drug and arms trade, and even terrorism can be a serious concern.

Therefore, many countries have banned or put restrictions on cryptocurrencies such as Bitcoin. These countries include China, India, Russia, Sweden, and Thailand, among others. The list is growing.

Even people who want to use Bitcoin just for fun or privacy should be concerned. An article in the *New York Post*[11] indicated:

---

[10]support.bitcoin.com/en/articles/5997588-bitcoin-scams

[11]English, Carleton. *Blockchain for bitcoin is infected with child porn.* (2018, March 21). nypost.com

According to a bombshell report, the underlying blockchain ledger that's used to record bitcoin transactions—a massive online database that grows each time a bitcoin changes hands—contains files that are tainted with hundreds of links to child pornography sites.

The bombshell report has been published by scholars from Germany's RWTH Aachen University. Because the Bitcoin blockchain cannot be altered, the implication is serious indeed. It means those Bitcoin participants who store a copy of the blockchain can be in violation of child pornography laws. There is no telling what other illegal materials can/will be introduced into the blockchain by whoever from wherever. Remember, Bitcoin allows public access and manipulation.

All That Glitters Is Not Gold

Bitcoin, as well as cryptocurrencies like it, is a new shiny digital object. It glitters for sure, but it is not digital gold. It is hard to pin down exactly what Bitcoin is. It is not money because it is neither legal tender nor accepted in most places. It tries to provide anonymity but instead lays a perfect trap that can reveal all transactions of a user.

Bitcoin is digital and ought to be safe and convenient online, but it is not. Safety and reliability is the foremost concern for online transactions. A well-trusted payment platform that provides guarantee for goods/services delivered and payments made is essential. Banks, credit cards, PayPal, and Alipay are such platforms. Do we have similar platforms for Bitcoin?

Real estate, mutual funds, stocks, bonds, precious metals, and other well-established investments have intrinsic value and/or are well regulated to protect investors. They also provide a reasonable expectation of returns. Can a cryptocurrency which can be started by almost anyone with minimal effort be a good investment? The former US Federal Reserve Chair Janet Yellen said[12] Bitcoin was "highly speculative."

Furthermore, something is hardly harmful if it simply glitters. But Bitcoin is actually illegal in many parts of the world. The fact that criminals use Bitcoin for tax evasion, money laundering, illegal drugs, and ransom payments, among other things, should at least give us pause.

Applying CT, we should ask the following:

- "What purpose am I trying to achieve?"

---

[12]Melloy, John. *Fed chief Yellen says bitcoin is a 'highly speculative asset'.* (2017, Dec 13) cnbc.com

- "Is using Bitcoin a means to that end?"

- "Is it worth the trouble or risk?"

- "Are there other/better alternatives?"

Of course, this is generally good thinking.

Scams and Scandals

Here we list some high-profile crypto scams and scandals, along with some specific details:

- Crypto Lender Celsius (July 13, 2023): Former Celsius CEO Alex Mashinsky was arrested on federal securities fraud charges, a source told CNBC as the bankrupt crypto exchange agreed to pay a $4.7 billion settlement with government regulators. The exchange was also charged by the SEC and CFTC with scheming to defraud investors out of billions.

- FTX (2019-2022): FTX was a cryptocurrency exchange that collapsed in early November 2022 following a report by CoinDesk highlighting potential leverage and solvency concerns involving FTX-affiliated trading firm Alameda Research. Bahamian authorities arrested FTX CEO Sam Bankman-Fried who was later extradited to the US, indicted by US District Court in Manhattan, and found guilty on all seven counts of fraud, conspiracy and money laundering in early November 2023. Furthermore, in late November, the crypto exchange Binance and cofounder Mr. Zhao pleaded guilty to money laundering. Both would pay huge fines and Zhao might serve an 18-month prison sentence.

- BitConnect (2016-2018): BitConnect was a cryptocurrency lending platform that promised high returns to investors. It was a Ponzi scheme that collapsed in early 2018 after receiving cease-and-desist letters from regulators and showing a significant drop in its token value.

- Mt. Gox (2011-2014): Mt. Gox was one of the first and largest cryptocurrency exchanges. In 2014, it filed for bankruptcy after losing around 850,000 bitcoins belonging to its customers, worth approximately $450 million at the time. The loss was attributed to a combination of hacking and internal fraud.

- QuadrigaCX (2013-2019): QuadrigaCX was a Canadian cryptocurrency exchange. In 2019, the company's founder and CEO, Gerald Cotten, passed away unexpectedly. It was later revealed that he was the only one with access to the private keys necessary to access the exchange's cold wallets, which held customer funds. As a result, approximately $190 million worth of cryptocurrencies became inaccessible, leading to the company's collapse.

- PlusToken (2018-2019): PlusToken was a crypto Ponzi scheme originating in China. It promised high returns to participants and attracted millions of users. In mid-2019, the scheme collapsed, and its operators disappeared with an estimated $2 billion worth of cryptocurrencies, including Bitcoin and Ethereum.

- OneCoin (2014-2017): OneCoin was a cryptocurrency scam that claimed to have its own blockchain but had no real underlying technology. Its founder, Ruja Ignatova, promised significant returns and conducted extensive marketing campaigns. However, it was eventually revealed that OneCoin was a fraudulent scheme, and Ignatova was charged with fraud and money laundering.

- Coincheck Hack (2018): Coincheck, a major Japanese cryptocurrency exchange, suffered a security breach in January 2018. Hackers managed to steal approximately $530 million worth of NEM cryptocurrency from the exchange's hot wallet. The incident highlighted vulnerabilities in the exchange's security practices and led to increased regulatory scrutiny in Japan.

FIGURE 4: *Cryptocurrency Scam Victim*

Victims number in the millions, and the loss is estimated to be in the tens of billions, if not more (Figure 4).

Countries Banning Cryptos

In the past few years, many countries, wisely, have either completely banned all cryptocurrencies or severely restricted their access/use. Countries banning all cryptocurrency include: China, Egypt, Saudi Arabia, Qatar, Iraq, Colombia, Morocco, and others.

For example, in May 2021 China prohibited financial institutions from engaging in any cryptocurrency transactions, in June 2021 China banned all domestic cryptomining, and finally in September 2021 China outlawed cryptocurrencies outright. China is also piloting its own *Central Bank Digital Currency* (CBDC), issued by the People's Bank of China (PBoC), and officially named the digital RMB DCEP (Digital Currency Electronic Payment). CBDC is the subject of CT Article 16, "*Central Bank Digital Currency*."

In the US, the 2022 stock market downturn has brought the so-called "crypto winter" when the crypto bubble burst, losing $2 trillion in value since 2021. Some cryptocurrencies failed, others struggle. Crypto businesses such as exchanges, lending outfits, and payment and management services have closed or got in deep trouble.

The US Securities and Exchange Commission (SEC) has announced several initiatives to expand investor protections in the crypto market. Yet, the best protection against cryptocurrencies is to avoid them like "rat poison," as Warren Buffett advised.

16

Central Bank Digital Currency

Today, we take digital music and digital video for granted. As more things go digital, so do currencies. Yes, we are talking about money, the bills and coins we use in our lives. They are going digital as well.

In the not-so-distant future, sovereign countries may elect to issue their paper money also in digital form, represented by computer codes not physical objects. Such digital money is known as CBDC (Central Bank Digital Currencies). CBDCs are legal tender and backed by the full faith and credit of the issuing government, just like paper money in that country. The Bahamas has

FIGURE 1: *The Bahamian Sand Dollar*

made the first move. On October 20, 2020, the Central Bank of The Bahamas formally rolled out its CBDC, the *Bahamian Sand Dollar* (Figure 1). Other countries, in various stages of issuing their CBDC, include China (DCEP), Sweden (e-krona), EU (digital euro), Marshall Islands (SOV), and more.

The United States, on the other hand, has decided to wait for conditions to ripen as indicated by a report from the Federal Reserve System[1].

Let's take a closer look at the CBDC from a consumer's point of view.

---

[1]Lawson, Angela. *Preconditions for a general-purpose central bank digital currency.* (2021, Jan 22). minneapolisfed.org

Evolution of Money

Digital currency is the most recent step forward in a long history of transformations for money dating back to as early as 1100 B.C. when sea shells (Figure 2) and miniature bronze replicas of weapons were used in ancient China as tokens for the exchange of goods. Paper money began to appear

FIGURE 2: *Sea Shells as Currency*

around AD 700-1000 in China where paper was invented earlier (AD 105). Being much easier to carry and use than coins and precious metals (silver and gold), paper money became widely adopted as banknotes. Modern banknotes issued by central banks as legal tender are still the main form of money in all countries.

Later came electronic ways to pay and transfer money with credit/debit cards and services such as PayPal, Alipay, Apple Pay, Google Pay, etc. These are even more convenient. But such a service requires a bank account and typically involves transaction fees. They are not really forms of money but efficient ways to handle payments and transactions.

What comes next for money is digital currency. Turning bills and coins into computer codes or character strings that can be sent, received, and processed through digital communication by computing devices.

Functions of a Currency

The basic functions of any modern currency are:

- *Medium of exchange*: used in the exchange of goods or services.

- *Unit of account*: used as units to measure or express the value of goods, services, assets, debts, and contractual obligations.

- *Store of value*: used to hold wealth in a convenient and portable form over time.

- *Legal tender*: designated, in most cases, as legal tender by a government or central authority, making it a valid form of payment for settling financial obligations, taxes, and other legal requirements.

These functions collectively contribute to the stability, efficiency, and effectiveness of an economy by providing a widely accepted means of exchange and a reliable store of value.

Understanding CBDC

For a digital currency (DC) to become an alternative to cash, it ought to satisfy a set of conditions including the following:

- It must be issued by a national central bank (CB) giving it legal tender status. Also, it should be freely exchangeable with physical cash at the same value.

- It must be easily verifiable as genuine and impossible to alter, copy, or counterfeit.

- CBDCs are held in a safe and secure app known as a digital purse or wallet to run on smartphones, smart cards, and other computing devices.

- A CBDC transaction involves the transfer of DC from the payer's wallet to the payee's wallet. Ideally this can happen online or offline. Transactions happen quickly and securely; double-spending (using the same DC more than once) is impossible.

- Wallets form part of the CBDC's management and operation system which keeps track of all user accounts, balances, and transactions at all times. The system can also be used to set monetary policies and add "smarts" to wallets and transactions.

- Security aspects of a CBDC system calls for 24/7 service availability, high processing speed and capacity, data integrity, and information confidentiality.

Making It Work

Many of the preceding conditions can be met by using certain digital encryption techniques also used by cryptocurrencies such as Bitcoin or Ethereum. In CT Article 15, *"Bitcoin Is No Coin,"* you can find more information about cryptocurrencies.

A CBDC may use cryptography techniques for implementation, but it has nothing to do with the likes of Bitcoin in purpose and function. Specifically, the techniques to implement a CBDC include public-key encryption, decryption, digital signature, hashing (document digital finger printing), and fast and secure ledgers of all transactions.

To achieve the required transaction speeds, a distributed public blockchain is not advisable. A private ledger kept and shared by a few key participants, banks and authorized agents, should be used instead.

As mentioned before, multiple countries are in the process of developing CBDC using approaches suitable in their own situations. Let us look at one example.

Example–The Chinese DCEP

China is the only major economy that has already piloted its own CBDC (Figure 3) in several cities. The digital renminbi (RMB) also known as the digital Yuan, has been officially named DCEP (Digital Currency Electronic Payment). A closer look at DCEP can shed more light on many aspects of CBDC.

FIGURE 3: *Digital RMB*

(1) Brief History

In 2014 China's central bank, the People's Bank of China (PBoC), established a research group to study the feasibility of a Chinese CBDC. With progress in multiple fronts the PBoC has basically completed in 2019 the overall design, technical standards, applications development, and operations testing/debugging. Immediately, pilot testing of DCEP started in four cities (Shenzhen 深圳, Suzhou 蘇州, Xiong'an 雄安, Chengdu 成都). In 2020, seven more cities were added to expand the piloting.

The year 2021 has seen cross-border testing of DCEP with Hong Kong, and internationally with Thailand and the United Arab Emirates.

(2) Management and Operation

The primary purpose of DCEP is to serve as a preferred alternative to the physical RMB. The PBoC uses a two-tier system to issue and distribute DCEP (Figure 4). The intermediaries consist of designated banks and financial institutions. An intermediary deposits RMB with PBoC to obtain equal amounts of DCEP, which it can then distribute to end users—individuals, businesses, and merchants. In order to use DCEP, you need to register and obtain a

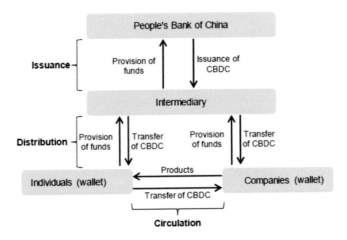

FIGURE 4: *Digital RMB Two-Tier Distribution*

DCEP wallet (Figure 5), the official secure app to receive, spend and otherwise manage your DCEP. Figure 5 shows a DCEP wallet app on a mobile

FIGURE 5: *DCEP Digital Wallet*

phone. Other forms of DCEP wallet include card with display and fingerprint sensor, keychain, smart watch, etc.

As you can see, PBoC is the control center of DCEP. For management and operation, the central bank has established two databases (DCEP banks database and DCEP issuance database) and three processing centers (DCEP authentication center, DCEP transactions recording center, and DCEP data analysis center). All these aim to achieve safe, secure, accurate, and speedy operations of DCEP.

After the pilot phases, the DCEP should be available to everyone who has a wallet and widely accepted. By law, any merchant who accepts a credit/debit card or another form of e-payment must accept DCEP in China. Because a wallet contains digital money and is not directly connected to a bank account it means DCEP functions much like cash.

(3) Degrees of Anonymity

DCEP has been designed to easily track questionable, illegal, or criminal activities such as tax evasion, bribery, and money laundering, while preserving the privacy and transaction anonymity of typical users. This is done by having four levels of wallets with different limits on the balance and per transaction amounts.

An anonymous wallet, good for common folks, can be established with one's cellphone number alone. The cellphone owner's account information is by law private and cannot be disclosed by the cell service provider to others. This means that even the PBoC cannot obtain that information without a court order. An owner needs to supply more personal information to elevate their wallet to the next level.

CBDC Advantages and Disadvantages

Having seen the basics and a concrete example of CBDC, now we can discuss its pros and cons.

Advantages of CBDC include:

1. Easier and more convenient to carry and to use

2. Say goodbye to loose change or making change

3. People without bank accounts can still use money electronically

4. No-cost fund transfer and transactions

5. Low cost to issue, track, control, and destroy

6. Safer and more secure against counterfeit, loss/theft

7. Better for fighting corruption, bribery, money laundering, and other financial crimes

8. Making cross-border transactions easier and less expensive

9. Enabling new and innovative financial products and services based on digital currency

10. Ability to better implement national monetary policies and to add features for transactions

Disadvantages of CBDC include:

1. Lacking the feeling of satisfaction from holding and counting physical money

2. Adding to the digital divide—people who do not use computing devices can find it harder to accept/use a digital currency

3. Losing your smartphone with a CBDC wallet becomes much more serious

4. Funds in a wallet don't usually earn interest

5. Central bank can potentially directly compete with commercial banks, financial institutions, and e-payment services

6. Concerns about anonymity and/or privacy for users

7. The electronic control system can become a critical point of failure or a target for hackers

8. A bug or operator error can cause serious consequences

Finally

We have briefly introduced CBDC, described its characteristics, provided some details of the Chinese DCEP as a concrete example, and listed its pros and cons. We have also largely avoided details that are too technical or complicated. A CBDC supported by a country's central bank must not be confused with cryptocurrencies regarded as "rat poison". In fact, in May 2021 Chinese regulators have barred all institutions and organizations from any cryptocurrency-related business, service, or transaction.

While some countries such as the US are taking a conservative wait-and-see approach, others are aggressively moving into the digital currency era with innovation and vision.

In the US, some states may proceed with their state-issued digital currency. For example, in May 2023, Texas Senate Bill 2334 proposed to establish a new gold- and silver-based digital currency through the office of the Texas Comptroller of Public Accounts and to back each unit of issued digital currency with a corresponding fraction of a troy ounce of gold or silver held in trust.

As many other things, currencies will also develop a digital format. And this could be the next great evolution in the history of money. Of course, an understanding of CBDC adds to our computational thinking. And hopefully, one day soon we will be lucky enough to enjoy the next form of money.

· · · · · · · · · · · · · · · · · CT Crossword Puzzle · · · · · · · · · · · ·

Digital Currency

Across

3. The Sand Dollar
6. DCEP is ___ CBDC
7. CBDC is legal ___
8. Creating new Bitcoin by ___

Down

1. A personal digital ___ stores digital money
2. Central bank digital currency
4. Some call it rat poison
5. A block chain is basically a secure public ___

17

Logic and Logical Thinking

Computers are logic machines. Digital circuits in modern computers are built with *logic gates* that perform computations on truth values. *Boolean algebra* deals with computations on truth values. Logic conditions and implications are used in software to control program execution. All these also inform us about our own logical thinking.

The ability to think and reason logically is important in general but critical for computational thinkers. Thus, also covered here is how to improve and sharpen our own ways for logical thinking.

Materials here can help you think logically and make you a better computational thinker as well.

Boolean Algebra Boolean Algebra

Logic operations are at the base of digital computers. Using a bit to represent 0 and 1 and treating 1 as *true* and 0 as *false*, all the basic logic operations AND, OR, NOT, XOR, NAND, NOR, and XNOR can be performed by logic gates. These operations form the foundation of all other computations in a computer.

The word *algebra* comes from the Arabic word *al-jebr*, meaning "reunion of broken parts." Elementary algebra, the kind we learn in middle school, deals with real numbers and symbols. The symbols stand for variables and unspecified numbers. Boolean algebra, introduced by George Boole in 1854, deals with truth values, *true* and *false* or 1 and 0, instead of numbers. Variables in Boolean algebra may take on either of the two values.

Boolean algebra has the following *basic* operations and operators:

- *Conjunction*—Denoted $A \wedge B$, A AND B, A & B, or A • B; the value of A AND B is *true* only if both A and B are *true*

- *Disjunction*—Denoted $A \vee B$, A OR B, A || B, or A + B; the value of A OR B is *true* if at least one of A and B is *true*

- *Negation*—Denoted $\neg A$, NOT A, !A, or $\overline{A}$; the value of NOT A is *true* if A is *false* and is *false* otherwise

Boolean algebra deals with expressions involving these operators, their properties, and manipulations. For example, De Morgan's laws in Boolean algebra says: $\overline{a \bullet b} = \overline{a} + \overline{b}$, $\overline{a + b} = \overline{a} \bullet \overline{b}$. There are many other such laws, making Boolean algebra very useful in the study and design of digital circuits.

Decision-Making

When drawing a flowchart or specifying an algorithm, we often need to have test conditions. Depending on the yes/no answer of a test, a procedure may take a different path through its steps (Figure 1). In logic and in programming,

FIGURE 1: *Decision Making*

a function that produces a result which is either *true* or *false* is known as a *predicate*. Programming languages usually provide *relational operators* as predefined predicates. Here is a list of typical relational operators: == (equal to), != (not equal to), < (less than), > (greater than), <= (less than or equal to), >= (greater than or equal to).

Usually, a bit pattern with all 0s is treated as *false* and any other pattern is treated as *true*. This makes sense because 0 is *false* and anything that is not 0 is *true*. An immediate result of this convention is that any function that returns a value can be treated as a predicate. Programming languages also provide *logical operators* to perform Boolean operations on truth values: && (AND), || (OR), ! (NOT).

Conditions and Implications

As you can imagine, when devising an algorithm, making the right decisions on which next step to take is critical. Typically, we use

if *predicate* then *action₁* else *action₂*

to indicate such decisions. If the *predicate* evaluates to *true action₁* is taken. Otherwise, *action₂* is taken. The else part is usually optional in the notation.

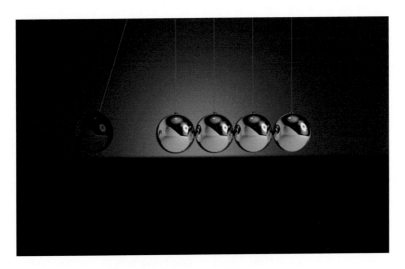

FIGURE 2: *Implication*

Correctness of an algorithm depends on using the right *implications* (Figure 2). An implication is a logical statement commonly given in these forms.

- p implies q, or $p \implies q$

- if p then q

- q if p

where p is a *premise* and q is a *conclusion*. Let's look at an algorithm that compares two input numbers x and y and returns one of the following:

1. A positive number if x is larger than y

2. A negative number if x is smaller than y

3. A zero if x is equal to y

Algorithm `numberCompare`:
Input: Number x, number y
Output: Returns 1, 0, or -1

1. If x > y, then return 1

2. If x < y, then return -1

3. Return 0

In algorithm `numberCompare`, note the implications

"control flow reaching Step 2" $\implies$ "x <= y"

"control flow reaching Step 3" $\implies$ "x == y"

Now think about why `numberCompare` can be implemented simply as "`return x - y`".

Necessary vs. Sufficient Conditions

Given the implication $p \implies q$ (p being *true* causes q to be *true*), then the following statements are true.

- p is a *sufficient condition* for q, namely p being *true* guarantees that q is *true*.

- q is a *necessary condition* for p, namely q must be *true* for p to be *true*. Also, if q is *false*, then p is *false* as well. Thus, the implication $p \implies q$ is logically the same as the implication $\overline{q} \implies \overline{p}$.

- If p is *false*, the implication says nothing about q.

- If q is *true*, the implication says nothing about p.

For example, the implication, "If x is a woman, then x is a person" certainly does not mean, "If x is a person then x is a woman." Nonetheless, if x is not a person then x cannot be a woman.

Similarly, "It is a river $\implies$ water flows in it" does not mean if water flows in it, then it is a river. In fact, it could be a water hose or a drain pipe. But, if water does not flow in it, then it is not a river.

And "If n is a multiple of 8 $\implies$ n is an even number" does not mean if n is even, then it is divisible by 8. And "If a person is over 30 years old, then the person is an adult" does not mean an adult is over 30.

Finally, "A good computer programmer thinks logically" does not mean that anyone who thinks logically is a good programmer. The person must have other training as well. Yet, it is definitely the case that without logical thinking, one cannot be a good programmer. The same can be said of good computational thinkers.

To summarize, a sufficient condition may not be necessary and a necessary condition may not be sufficient.

However, if we have both implications $p \implies q$ and $q \implies p$, then q is a *necessary and sufficient* condition for p. Likewise, p is a *necessary and sufficient* condition for q. Alternatively, we say p if and only if q or simply $p \iff q$. In such a case, p and q are both *true* or both *false*. For example, a person may vote in a United States election if and only if the person is a United States citizen, at least 18 years old, and not a convicted felon.

Don't hesitate to study the materials over again. Make logic your own natural mental tool, and it will help immensely in whatever you do. However, once logic is natural to you, don't assume others are the same. In fact, it is a good bet to assume otherwise. Because we need to work with others to achieve many tasks, guarding against falling victim to less than logical thinking on the part of others would be wise indeed.

Logical Thinking

Logical thinking is a cognitive process that involves reasoning and problem-solving in a systematic and rational manner. It is the ability to analyze and evaluate information, identify patterns, and draw logical conclusions based on evidence and facts.

But this is easier said than done. People can easily become emotional in many situations, including being optimistic, pessimistic, wishful, fearful, personal, and so forth. These feelings can negatively impact objective and evidence-based reasoning.

Logical thinking is an essential skill for decision-making, critical thinking, and problem-solving in various fields such as science, engineering, mathematics, and computer science. It is a skill computational thinkers should acquire and sharpen.

FIGURE 3: *Attention to Details*

Key points and methods of logical thinking include:

- Identifying and defining the problem or situation

- Gathering and analyzing information and data paying attention to the 5Ws and 1H (what, why, when, where, who, and how)

- Looking at the whole picture as well as paying attention to details (Figure 3)

- Anticipating potential problems and difficulties by asking "what if" questions

- Identifying patterns and relationships

- Formulating hypotheses and making predictions

- Testing and evaluating hypotheses using evidence and facts

- Drawing conclusions and making decisions based on the results

Cognitive Biases

A *cognitive bias* is a systematic error in thinking that can distort our perception, judgment, and decision-making. Such biases are mental shortcuts that our brains use to simplify complex information and make quick decisions, but they can also lead to errors in judgment or decision-making.

Cognitive biases can affect our perception, attitude, behavior, and reasoning and negatively impact logical thinking. Let's list some common cognitive biases:

- **Herd mentality bias**: Also known as the bandwagon effect, it is the tendency to follow the crowd or majority. Of course, for any proposition, getting more votes does not prove it right or wrong.

- **Confirmation bias**: The tendency to seek out information that confirms our pre-existing beliefs and to ignore information that contradicts them.

- **Availability heuristic**: The tendency to rely on easily available or memorable examples when making decisions or judgments. For example, fear of flying but not of driving.

- **Anchoring bias**: The tendency to rely too heavily on the first piece of information encountered when making decisions. For example, if you first see a bicycle that costs $1,200, then see a second one that costs $100, you're prone to see the second bicycle as cheap or not well built.

- **Hindsight bias**: The tendency to believe that an event was predictable or easily explainable after it has occurred.

- **Overconfidence bias**: The tendency to overestimate our abilities, knowledge, or accuracy of beliefs.

- **Self-serving bias**: The tendency to attribute positive outcomes to our own abilities and negative outcomes to external factors.

- **Halo bias**: The tendency to form a positive overall impression of a person or thing based on one specific trait or characteristic. For example judging a book by its cover, or a person by the car they drive.

- **Negativity bias**: The tendency to focus more on negative information than positive information.

  These are just a few examples of many cognitive biases that can influence our thinking and decision-making. It's important to be aware of these biases and to consciously work to overcome them in order to think more rationally and make better decisions.

Logical Fallacies

Logical fallacies are errors in reasoning or logical deduction that can lead to incorrect or unsupported conclusions. Logical thinking involves identifying and avoiding fallacies, which can help one arrive at more accurate and well-supported conclusions.

Here is a list of some common logical fallacies:

- **Ad hominem fallacy**: Attacking the character or motives of a person making an argument, rather than addressing the substance of the argument itself (Figure 4). This is the most commonly found logic mistake

FIGURE 4: *Ad hominem (personal attack fallacy)*

among ordinary people. Meanwhile, the reverse, "appeal to authority", discussed below, is also a common fallacy.

- **False dichotomy fallacy**: Presenting only two options as if they are the only possibilities, when in fact there are more.

- **Gambler's fallacy**: The belief that past events can influence the probability of future events, even when they are independent. For example, thinking that a coin is less likely to turn up heads after it had turned up heads 5 or 10 times in a row.

- **Slippery slope fallacy**: Suggesting that a particular action will inevitably lead to a series of negative consequences, without providing sufficient evidence to support this claim.

- **Appeal to authority fallacy**: Relying on the opinion of an authority figure as evidence for an argument, without providing sufficient evidence to support their claim.

- **Hasty generalization fallacy**: Drawing a general conclusion based on insufficient or unrepresentative evidence.

- **Post hoc fallacy**: Assuming that one event caused another event simply because it occurred before it.

- **Straw man fallacy**: Misrepresenting or exaggerating someone else's position or argument in order to make it easier to attack. The distorted position is known as a *straw man*, which is set up to be easily destroyed (Figure 5).

FIGURE 5: *Straw Man*

- **Circular reasoning fallacy**: Using the conclusion of an argument as evidence to support the premises of that same argument.

- **False cause fallacy**: Assuming that because two events occur together, one must have caused the other.

- **Appeal to emotion fallacy**: Relying on emotions or feelings to support an argument, rather than providing evidence or logical reasoning.

- **Ad ignorantiam fallacy**: Arguing that something is true simply because it has not been proven false, or vice versa.

- **False analogy fallacy**: Drawing a comparison between two things that are not truly comparable in order to make an argument.

- **Red herring fallacy**: Introducing irrelevant information or arguments into a discussion in order to distract from the main point.

Yes We Can Sharpen our Logical Thinking!

We Can Sharpen Our Logical Thinking

Computers are logic machines and they follow logic and instructions without bias. We can sharpen our logical thinking by seeing the rigorous ways computers and algorithms apply logic.

The fact is that logical thinking is a vital skill for success in many technical and non-technical areas, including and especially in our daily lives. It is critical for decision-making, problem-solving, critical thinking, effective communication, and creativity. It is a fundamental skill that can benefit everyone both personally and professionally. Of course, logical thinking is especially important for computational thinkers.

For some, acquiring logical thinking can be challenging because of overcoming cognitive biases and avoiding logic fallacies. Here are some suggestions for sharpening your logical thinking.

FIGURE 6: *The Game GO*

- **Increase experience and practice**: Seek out opportunities to engage in logical thinking, for example joining a debate team or planning an event such as a birthday party or wedding reception. Drawing flowcharts is a good activity. Also solving puzzles and playing strategy games can help (Figure 6).

- **Correct cognitive biases**: Learn to recognize your cognitive biases and consciously work to overcome them.

- **Arrest emotional reasoning**: Catch yourself when emotions interfere with rational and logical thinking. By learning to recognize when emotions are influencing one's thinking, an individual can consciously work to separate their emotions from their logical reasoning.

- **Keep an open mind**: Consider alternative perspectives and think critically. By learning from others with different backgrounds, experiences, and viewpoints, one can improve the situation.

- **Think critically**: Think clearly and pay attention to the logic in reasoning. Have a hard-to-convince mindset toward statements or arguments by others. Find logic fallacies in their reasoning so that you avoid them in yours.

With an understanding of logic, logical reasoning, potential cognitive biases, and logical fallacies, you can appreciate the importance of logical thinking. And with increasing exposure and more practice, you can become good at logical thinking which is fundamental for becoming a computational thinker.

CT Crossword Puzzle

Logical Thinking

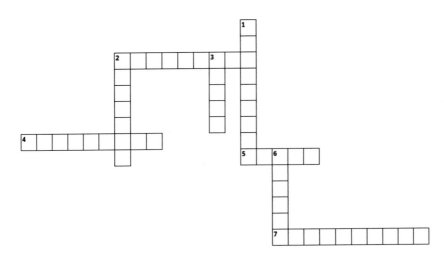

Across

2. Follow the crowd is the ___ bias

4. A must-have condition is ___

5. A truth ___ specifies the functions of a logic operator

7. A condition that guarantees a result is a ___ condition

Down

1. ___ is 20/20

2. ___ algebra provides rules on logic computations

3. Digital circuits built with logic ___

6. Logical thinkers must avoid cognitive ___

18

1 Plus 1 Equals 10

Digital data use bits to encode information. A *bit* can represent either a 0 or a 1. All data—numbers, text, images, sound, and video—must be turned into bits and stored in memory before a computer can process them. Among all data, the representation of numbers is the most fundamental.

A focus here is the representation of numbers inside computers. We'll see how a sequence of bits is used to represent numbers in what's known as the *binary notation*. And we'll see how the *place value* system works.

Concepts discussed here are critical to understanding the digital nature of modern computers, and therefore important for any computational thinker. For many, concepts explained in this CT Article can be eye-opening mental breakthroughs.

Digital Computers

Modern computers are *digital* because they store and process *discrete* rather than *continuous* information.

- Discrete data—Data are *discrete* when only certain distinct separate values are allowed. The number of chickens, age, income, are examples. Discrete values have gaps in them.

- Continuous data—Data are *continuous* when all values in a continuous range, finite or infinite, are allowed. Length, weight, volume, speed, are examples. Continuous values have no gaps separating them. Thus, even in a small range, there are an infinite number of continuous values.

In the past, analog computers processed continuous electronic waves. Such analog signals are hard to store, transmit, or reproduce precisely.

In contrast, digital computers use integers to represent information and therefore avoid these critical problems. A continuous value, that of a sound wave, for example, can be *digitized* by sampling values at a number of discrete points (Figure 1). With enough sampling points, the continuous sound wave can be recreated.

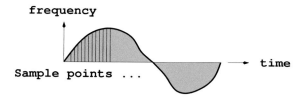

FIGURE 1: *Sampling a Continuous Wave*

Information, represented in digital form, must be stored in computer memory to be processed. The most basic memory unit is a bit, which can represent either a 1 or a 0. A *byte* is a group of 8 bits. A *word* consists of several (usually 4 or 8) bytes (Figure 2). Note that in computing, as shown in Figure 2, we count starting from 0.

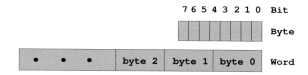

FIGURE 2: *Bit, Byte, and Word*

A computer's Central Processing Unit (CPU) performs logic operations on data. The CPU loads data from memory in order to process them, then stores the results back to memory. A *word* is normally the smallest integral data entity a CPU is designed to manipulate. The word size is measured in bits and is one of the most important hardware architecture features of a computer. For most modern computers, the word size is either 32 bits (4 bytes) or 64 bits (8 bytes). Of course the word size is determined by the size of the CPU registers. A CPU register is able to load from and store to cache/DRAM (*Dynamic Random Access Memory, a faster type of RAM*) all its bits (the whole word) as a unit at once.

For modern general purpose computers, the entire memory is an array of bytes (Figure 3), each of which can be *addressed* directly (called *byte addressing*), hence the term random access memory (RAM). A computer with word size n can address (reach directly) at most 2^n bytes in its RAM/DRAM. Often, the actual allowable size of RAM/DRAM for a computer is well below this upper bound due to other hardware limitations.

Information stored in RAM/DRAM is *volatile* and will disappear when the system is turned off. Non-volatile or *persistent* data storage is provided by one or more storage drives, including hard-disk drives (HHDs) or solid-state drives (SSDs).

In computer product specifications, memory sizes are given in byte units:

- kilobyte (KB) = 1024 bytes

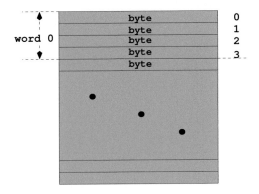

FIGURE 3: *Memory Array of Bytes*

- megabyte (MB) = 1024 KB

- gigabyte (GB) = 1024 MB

- terabyte (TB) = 1024 GB

- petabyte (PB) = 1024 TB

Typical desktop computer memory sizes range from 4 GB to 32 GB.

Ordinarily, K (kilo) is a prefix for 1000 (in the metric system), but digitally (in the binary system), K is 1024. Similarly, as far as memory or data sizes go, M (Mega) is KK, Giga is KM, Tera is KG, and Peta is KT, keeping in mind always that K is 1024[1].

Bit Patterns

The basic way to represent data in computer memory is to use *bit patterns*. A bit pattern is a particular sequence of 0's and 1's presented in a fixed number of bits. Table 18.1 shows all possible patterns made up of three bits. Each bit has two variations, 0 and 1. For each value of bit 1, there are two values for bit 0, resulting in $2 \times 2 = 2^2$ two-bit patterns. Similarly, for each value of bit 2, there are four patterns for bits 0 and 1, giving $2 \times 2^2 = 2^3$ three-bit patterns.

In general, the total number of different patterns with n bits is 2^n. Therefore, a byte can give you $2^8 = 256$ bit patterns, a 32-bit word $2^{32} = 4294967296$ bit patterns, and a 64-bit word $2^{64} = 18446744073709551616$ bit patterns.

In a digital computer, bit patterns are the only way to represent data. And, the same bit patterns can be used to represent different types of data, such as a number, character, or color. We will see how numbers are represented next.

---

[1]In actual usage, there is often confusion between the metric and binary interpretations.

TABLE 18.1: *All the Eight 3-Bit Patterns*

Bit 2	Bit 1	Bit 0
0	0	0
0	0	1
0	1	0
0	1	1
1	0	0
1	0	1
1	1	0
1	1	1

Numerals

Numerals are symbols we use to write down numbers. The numerals we use today (0, 1, 2, 3, 4, 5, 6, 7, 8, 9) are *Arabic numerals* derived from the Hindu-Arabic numeral system. Different civilizations have invented and used their own symbols for numbers. Figure 4 shows the Roman and Egyptian numerals.

FIGURE 4: *Roman and Egyptian Numerals*

Figure 5 shows ancient Chinese numerals. Simplified modern versions of these are still in use today.

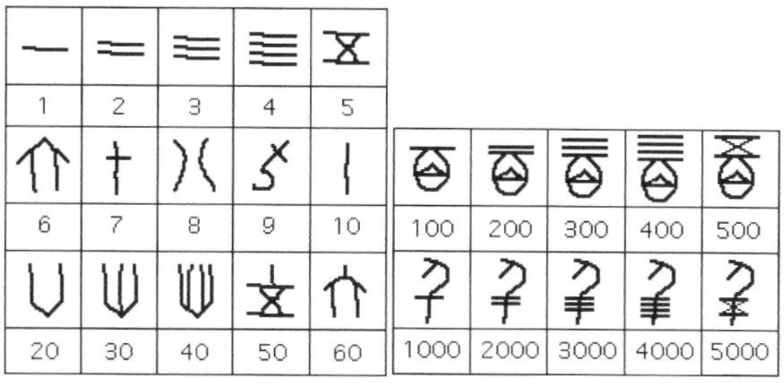

FIGURE 5: *Ancient Chinese Numerals*

Decimal Numbers

With the digits, the Arabic numerals, we can write down numbers from 0 to 9. We still need a way to represent larger numbers. We can invent new symbols, of course. But, how will we create new symbols to keep up with ever larger numbers? A systematic way must be found. An ingenious solution is the ***place value system***. For example, with three digits side-by-side, we can write down numbers up to, but not including, one thousand. Thus, the notation 379 means three hundreds, seven tens, and nine ones, or

$$379 = 3 \times 10^2 + 7 \times 10 + 9 \times 10^0$$

With the place value system, larger numbers simply require more places. Thus, we have a system for creating new symbols for numbers by combining the numerals. Such numbers, where each place represents a power of 10, are known as *base-10 numbers* or *decimal numbers*.

Binary Numbers

Binary numbers also use a place value system, just like decimal numbers, except the base is 2, not 10. We use only two numerals, 0 and 1, for binary numbers. Obviously, numbers in binary notation will be very easy to represent with bits in a computer.

Using one place, only two numbers can be represented, namely 0 and 1. To represent two in binary, we need to go to the next place. Thus, **the binary number** 10 **means two**

$$1 \times 2 + 0 \times 1$$

Thus, in binary we can say $1 + 1 = 10$.

And the binary number 11 means three

$$1 \times 2 + 1 \times 1$$

Similarly, 101 means five

$$1 \times 2^2 + 0 \times 2 + 1 \times 1$$

With four bits, we can represent numbers from 0 to 15 (Table 18.2). Keep in mind that, just as in decimal numbers, the least significant digit (bit) has the rightmost position and the most significant bit has the leftmost position. And the bit and byte positions are always counted from the right.

To get familiar with binary notation, take any binary number in Table 18.2 and add 1 to it, carrying to the next higher position as you would in doing addition, you will get the bit pattern for the next binary number. Also visit

TABLE 18.2: *Four-Bit Binary Numbers*

Dec	Binary	Dec	Binary	Dec	Binary	Dec	Binary
0	0000	1	0001	2	0010	3	0011
4	0100	5	0101	6	0110	7	0111
8	1000	9	1001	10	1010	11	1011
12	1100	13	1101	14	1110	15	1111

these interactive demos on our companion website: **Demo:** `UpCounter` and **Demo:** `DownCounter`.

It is not surprising if you find binary numbers confusing at first. After all, as far as numbers go, the decimal system is our mother tongue and is firmly ingrained in our thinking. Look at Figure 6 and see how you feel for yourself.

FIGURE 6: *Binary Cup*

Binary numbers would become easier if we memorize the powers of 2 as well as we do powers of 10. Here it goes: 2 (bit 2), 4 (bit 3), 8 (bit 4), 16 (bit 5), 32 (bit 6), 64 (bit 7), 128 (bit 8), 256 (bit 9), 512 (bit 10), 1024 (bit 11), 2048 (bit 12), and so on.

Inside a digital computer, numbers are naturally in binary, and hardware support is provided for their operations, as long as they fit in a single word. A 32- or 64-bit word can represent numbers from 0 to $2^{32} - 1$ or $2^{64} - 1$. That's a lot of numbers. Still, it is far from covering all numbers. To handle larger numbers, we can use multiple words and write software for manipulating them.

Here is a principle for computational thinkers:

> **CT concept–*Meaning of Symbols***: *Anyone can invent a symbol and assign it a meaning. The same symbol may have another meaning in a different context. Do not guess a symbol's meaning by its appearance. Always refer to its definition within the intended context.*

Numerals and numbers from different cultures, as well as the place value system, are examples of this principle.

Ancient Chinese Binary Symbols

I-Ching (易經), a Chinese text that traces back to the 3rd to the 2nd millennium BCE, introduced two symbols, yin (— —) and yang (——). Combinations of three or six yin-yang symbols form the 8 trigrams (八卦 Figure 7) or the 64 hexagrams (六十四卦).

Thus, the concept of repeating two symbols to form increasingly more symbols is an ancient one.

FIGURE 7: *I-Ching Trigrams (八卦)*

Numbers in Other Bases

While we are at it, why don't we look at numbers in other bases? Octal numbers are base 8 and use digits 0–7. Hexadecimal (hex) numbers are base 16 and use digits 0–9 followed by A (10), B (11), C (12), D (13), E (14), and F (15). The symbol 10 stands for eight in octal and sixteen in hexadecimal. The symbol 25 means

$2 \times 8 + 5$ (21 in octal)
$2 \times 16 + 5$ (37 in hex)

For interactive demos, visit our companion website (**Demo:** `OctalCounter` and **Demo:** `HexCounter`).

Three bits are needed for each octal digit and four bits for each hexadecimal digit. A byte of all 1s can represent the hex number FF (255). In general, we can use numbers in any base we desire, and we are not, limited by having two hands with 10 digits.

TABLE 18.3: *Numbers in Different Bases*

Decimal	11	17	23	29
Octal	13	21	27	35
Hex	B	11	17	1D
Binary	01011	10001	10111	11101

A principle for computational thinkers:

CT concept–*Question conventions, rules, and regulations*: *No feature in a system should be treated as rigid or sacred. Ask "what if it is changed?" and you will begin to think flexibly, acquire a deeper understanding, and, perhaps, even make a breakthrough.*

Octal and hex numbers are often used as a shorthand for the bit patterns representing them. Each octal digit specifies a 3-bit pattern, and each hex digit specifies a 4-bit pattern. Also, distinct prefixes, 0x for hex, 0o for octal, and 0b for binary are used to denote such numbers. This is especially true in programming languages. Table 18.4 shows the bits for each digit of 0o1357 or 0x2EF.

TABLE 18.4: *Octal and Hex Bit Patterns*

Octal	1			3			5			7		
Binary	0	0	1	0	1	1	1	0	1	1	1	1
Hex	2				E				F			

Mixed-Base Numbers

Decimal numbers use powers of 10 as place values; binary numbers powers of 2; octal numbers powers of 8; and hex numbers powers of 16. Talking about flexible thinking, what about asking the question why the place values must always be a power of some fixed number?

Well, there is no reason for that at all. In fact, we can use any desired value for each place. Such numbers are called *mixed-radix* or *mixed-base* numbers. For instance, how about numbers with place values 1, 60, 60, 24, 7? Would that be crazy?

Actually, we use such numbers every day, literally. We have 60 seconds in a minute, 60 minutes in an hour, 24 hours in a day, and 7 days in a week, don't we? And we have 12 inches in a foot, 3 feet in a yard, and 1760 yards in a mile. Granted, such length measurements should have long ago been replaced by the metric system.

Computational thinkers, let's apply abstraction here. The intrinsic nature of a place-value system is "assign a value for each place," and nothing more.

Meaning of Symbols

The binary number system may be eye opening for many. But what is more important is the realization of the fact that *"a symbol, any symbol, has no inherent meaning, and we can use it to stand for anything we wish."*

Thus, the symbol 10 can stand for the number ten, or the number 2, or something else, for example, "a closed eye and an open eye".

FIGURE 8: *What Is That?*

The meaning of a symbol (Figure 8) must be obtained from its definition within the context of its usage. For example, 911 can be a count, a phone number, or a disaster event. The symbol 03/04 may be March 4th or April 3rd.

Consider the statements: $1 + 1$ equals zero and $1 - 1$ equals two. Here, the symbol $+$ is used for subtraction and $-$ for addition. And why not! After all, $+$ and $-$ are not born with any meaning at all.

Human beings use symbols, in written, verbal, and other forms, to represent ideas in order to communicate with others. The process involves three steps:

1. You use a sequence of symbols to represent the idea, concept, or meaning which resides in your mind.

2. You communicate these symbols to someone else.

3. The receiver decodes the symbols back into a meaning.

Do you see where the problem lies? **There is no guarantee that the meaning received is the same as the original one.**

The situation is made worse by the fact that the same sequence of symbols may mean different things and often does. For example, the symbol O may be the number zero or an English alphabet. Similarly for the symbol l.

Consider the 4-letter word "chef." In English, it refers to a professional cook or the head cook in a restaurant. In Spanish, it is used to refer to a boss or leader. In French, it means chief or leader in a general sense, and can refer to someone in a position of authority or a person who is skilled or accomplished in a particular field.

From a computational thinking perspective, such symbol reuse is unavoidable. Because the number of symbols in use are limited, whereas ideas, concepts, and meanings are infinite. We can invent a few new symbols or sequence of symbols, but we still cannot avoid reuse.

FIGURE 9: *Texting*

Consider another 4-letter word "text." We know what it means, or do we? It means "a short message" sent or received on a cellphone! Or the act of sending such a message (Figure 9). It is a perfect example of symbols acquiring new meaning with the changing times.

Computational thinkers must keep all this in mind when initiating a communication or when receiving one, especially with texting! By being precise and careful, we can make sure that any message conveyed/received is correctly understood. Thus, we can avoid confusion, mistakes, and even save lives.

19

Cache–Efficiency Thinking

The dictionary defines the word cache as *"a store or collection of items kept in a safe place."* However, in computing, **cache** is a technical term referring to *a memory for super fast storage and retrieval of data.* In this CT Article we are going to talk about the latter.

An understanding of the cache concept can focus our attention on ready access and efficiency. Knowing how cache memory works inspires us to employ the same ideas to better manage businesses, improve our daily living, and even save lives.

Cache in the Modern CPU

A Central Processing Unit (CPU) generally repeats endlessly this cycle: (1) retrieving from main memory the next instruction then (2) executing the instruction. The problem is that a modern CPU performs step 2 much faster than step 1. In other words, main memory latency (access delay) becomes the performance bottleneck, even if it is dynamic RAM (DRAM). The solution? *CPU cache.*

CPU cache is super fast static RAM (SRAM), usually 16 MB (megabits) to 64 MB, located on the CPU chip itself, as opposed to on the motherboard. It operates between 10 to 100 times faster than DRAM, requiring only a few nanoseconds (1 ns = 10^{-9} second) to respond to a data request. The CPU cache serves as a buffer on the CPU chip for data in the main memory.

Sophisticated algorithms have been devised, implemented in the CPU *cache control unit*, to keep required data in the cache as much as possible so that the need for DRAM access is minimized. Thus, CPU cache significantly increases overall CPU speed and efficiency. This sounds complicated, but the idea is simple. For example, in our daily lives we carry a wallet (Figure 1) or purse (this is the cache). We keep often-needed items in it for instant retrieval, so much faster than looking for them in the house (the main memory). Depending on our current tasks, we can fill our wallet/purse with the right items. The tool belt for workers is another example. These daily cache devices are so efficient we don't mind managing them. In fact we won't do without them.

FIGURE 1: *Wallet Is Personal Cache*

Hit or Miss

As the CPU executes, it continuously needs to access the next instruction/data by referring to its DRAM address (**A**), usually a 32 or 64 bit quantity. If the access is for obtaining the data, it is called a *read*. Otherwise, if the access is for overwriting the data, then it is called a *write*. Given any **A**, it can be quickly determined whether it is available in the CPU cache. If it is, we have a cache *hit*, otherwise we have a cache *miss*.

Here is a simplified description of what happens when a read access to **A** takes place.

Hit: Immediately, the requested data is returned from the cache and the CPU continues execution without delay.

Miss: The requested data, together with a number of close-by items, is copied from DRAM to the cache. Space must also be found in the cache to store newly retrieved data. This usually involves the *eviction* of some well-selected in-cache data. Then the data is returned for read access. Meanwhile, CPU execution has been blocked until the data is returned.

A write access miss may cause less delay. But let's not get into details and simply say that a cache miss is expensive and can delay the CPU's progress significantly. Therefore, arrangements and algorithms are designed to maximize hits. Typical cache hit rates range from 95 to 98%.

Levels of Cache

Generally, the cache idea is using ultra-fast but expensive memory to hold select items from much slower but cheaper DRAM memory in order to achieve speed without undue increase in cost. Clever algorithms are used to maximize the hit rate so that fast memory access happens almost all the time.

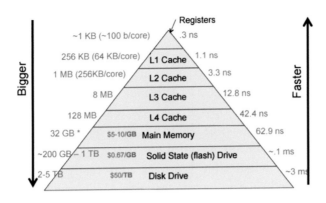

FIGURE 2: *Computer Memory Hierarchy*

Figure 2 shows the memory hierarchy of modern computers. We see from the diagram that the DRAM is about 57 times slower than L1 cache (62.9/1.1). To better illustrate the relative speeds, think about it this way. If L1 access were to take 1 second, then DRAM access would have taken nearly 1 minute. Better yet, if L1 were to take 1 day, then DRAM would have taken almost 2 months, eek!

As you can see, CPU cache has levels L1 through L3 or even L4. Each level decreases in speed and cost, but increases in size. Sophisticated logic circuits are used to manage these levels to use them in optimal ways. For a multi-core CPU, each core has its own L1 and L2, while L3 and L4 are shared among all cores (Figure 3). A cache miss happens when the needed data can't be found through all cache levels. Similar buffering happens between DRAM and

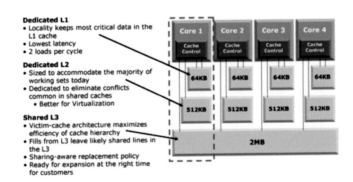

FIGURE 3: *CPU Cores and Cache Memory*

secondary memories such as flash drives and hard disks. What is the lesson here? *If an idea works why not use it everywhere it can be applied?*

For example, the web protocol HTTP has added its own way of caching to make the web faster and more efficient.

HTTP Caching

An important improvement of HTTP 1.1 over HTTP 1.0 is the introduction of caching (Figure 4). On the web, a great deal of contents are not changing often with time. These include static webpages, images, graphics, styling code, scripts, and so on. Saving a copy of such data can avoid a lot of unnecessary work of requesting and retrieving the same data over and over again from *origin servers*. Browsers (user agents) and caching proxy servers are able to serve data from their cache when they know or can verify that the data are still current and unchanged on the origin servers. A caching proxy server acceler-

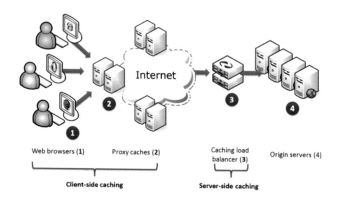

FIGURE 4: *HTTP Caching*

ates requests by providing contents from its cache. Caching proxies keep local copies of popular resources so that large organizations can greatly reduce their Internet usage and costs, while significantly enhancing performance. Most Internet Service Providers (ISPs) and large businesses employ caching proxies.

The HTTP caching scheme significantly cuts down round-trip web traffic to origin servers and reduces response time to users. This explains why it is slower the first time you visit a website, then it is lightning fast when you visit again.

Cache-Inspired CT

> **CT concept–*Cache for Speed***: *Use cache to increase efficiency and speed. In many situations, significant improvement may result from storing the right items in a cache.*

In essence, the cache idea from computing is fundamentally *prepositioning needed items in convenient locations for immediate access* to reduce delay and maximize efficiency.

Applications of this idea can be found in many situations. For driving emergencies—bringing spare tire, jump cables, flashlights, work gloves; for fire fighting—prepositioning fire stations, fire hydrants, and extinguishers; for life saving—placing police outposts, ambulance stations, emergency lighting, exit maps, first aid kits, defibrillators, and gas masks.

Let's see some more day-to-day applications. Restaurants use caching to better serve customers. Ready-to-cook ingredients for popular dishes are arranged, collected, and prepositioned near the cook station (the restaurant's CPU). This cuts down on customer's waiting time at the tables. Less popular dishes will take longer when materials must be gathered and prepared before cooking.

A busy airport has a 'taxi cache' located close to arriving passenger exits, so clever and efficient (Figure 5).

FIGURE 5: *Taxi Queue at JFK International Airport*

Cache and Obama Care

Toward the end of 2013, when a team of super coders were helping to rescue and fix the `healthcare.gov` website, one immediate technique they used was introducing a *database cache* so that frequent queries could be separated from other queries to the huge database. The database cache reduced congestion, and they were able to lower the average page access time from 8 seconds to about 2 seconds. Later, with continued improvements, the access time was reduced to below 0.35 seconds. The rescue work may well have saved the Affordable Care Act from disaster.

Don't we all wish, during the early days of the COVID-19 pandemic, that personal protective equipment (PPE) were readily available to front-line workers? That quick test kits (or any test kit) were available for immediate use? Could such preparedness have saved many lives? The question is not if pandemics will happen again but when. We need to apply the lessons learned to get ready for the next one, cache-inspired preparedness included.

Cache and Me

The cache concept is useful in a variety of situations including our own lives.

In terms of personal information processing, our brains are like the CPU. Data in the 'brain cache' are information we remember and are available immediately without going outside the brain. But our brains are unreliable and sometimes fail to recollect useful information that we need at the moment (Figure 6). The next place to keep often-used information may be our

FIGURE 6: *Trouble Remembering*

smartphones. Data kept there are also easily available, like in the DRAM of a computer, where we can go next when there is a 'brain cache miss.' Of course, there are other information sources. But they are much slower to access.

You have your home phone number and address, for example, kept in brain cache, right? But what about other important data? If you have a well-developed plan for where to keep information, could you be better off.

In our homes, we also have a hierarchy of storage spaces. Drawers, cabinets, closets, garage, and basement. Of course, we need to organize our things into these spaces to optimize ease of access. And most importantly, we need to place items back where they belong if we are going to find them easily next time. How similar is it to managing the computer's memory hierarchy?

Next, let's talk about the car. We all love our cars and we use them to go places. The car is also a place to store things. Why not treat our car like a 'cache to go', placing things we need to bring in the car way ahead of time? Such things could be items to donate, online orders to return, gifts to send, letters to mail, tools, supplies, for example. This way we won't forget to bring needed things when it comes time to drive off.

Oh yes, when driving, a good driver will always keep a bird's eye view of the car relative to other cars (Figure 7). This cached view in the driver's brain can enable evasive moves without delay. It can save lives.

FIGURE 7: *Driver's Birdseye View of Traffic*

When it comes to money management, we keep cash and credit cards in our wallet (our money cache), for larger amounts we depend on our checking accounts (our money DRAM), then there are our savings account and other even slower sources of funds. None of us will have any objection to more efficient money management.

Finally, the cache concept is about efficiency. When we are more efficient, we save time and energy, which literally can bring us more cash! Doesn't reading 'cache brings cash' out loud crash your CPU?

CT Crossword Puzzle

One Plus and Cache

Across

1. Cache highlights ___ thinking

5. Meaning of symbol is by ___

6. KB

10. CPU cache has multiple ___

Down

2. A symbol has no ___ meaning

3. Cache stores ___ used data

4. Cache access

7. In binary 10 is

8. Wallet is our quick access

9. DRAM access 57 times ___ than L1 cache

20

Time for Location, Location, Location

Brought by the digital age is the wonderful automatic navigation for driving and other modes of travel. This much appreciated capability is a result of the convergence of advanced computing, communication, and space technologies. The core technology is the Global Navigation Satellite System (GNSS) that can precisely fix positions anywhere on/near Earth. In fact, GNSS is a *global infrastructure* that enables many different location-sensitive applications, making our economies more efficient and effective.

At present, there are four GNSSs: the US GPS (*Global Positioning System*), EU *Galileo*, Russian *GLONASS*, and Chinese *BeiDou*.

A GNSS has three main components: *space* (a constellation of orbiting satellites), a *control* (ground-based devices for system monitor and control), and *user/application* (any device to receive the satellite signals for some purpose).

This CT Article focuses on a basic understanding of satellite-based positioning, how it works, and its applications and impact.

GPS for Cars

Nowadays in the US, GPS is widely used for road navigation. Using GPS you simply follow turn-by-turn directions to go to any desired destination.

FIGURE 1: *GPS Navigation for Driving*

Compared to looking for street signs, highway exits, house numbers, and following maps, GPS navigation makes life so much easier and safer, especially when traveling at night or in an unfamiliar area. Some cars come with built-in GPS navigation. Otherwise, you can use a portable device dedicated to GPS or a smartphone (with free navigation apps available). Bring your GPS device with you so you can get directions while driving, biking, and walking.

Enabling technologies for GPS navigation include the following:

- The GPS, a US owned and operated GNSS.

- A receiver (user's device) to capture and process GPS satellite signals. The received data can be used to determine the receiver's **current location**, given in latitude, longitude, and elevation, for example.

- A software application to place any given current position on a road map for directions and navigation. The map includes road/street names, traffic regulations (such as one-way streets and speed limits), addresses of houses/buildings, distances, and other data for the target travel area.

Now let's see how locations are determined based on satellite signals from GPS or any other GNSS. The principles are the same.

How Satellite Positioning Works

A GNSS consists of many, often 30 or so, individual satellites, orbiting Earth in such a pattern that, at any moment, at least four of them are in line of sight from virtually any point on the globe.

FIGURE 2: *GPS Satellite (image: Boeing)*

Think of these satellites as *lighthouses in the sky* that can help you find your own location and navigate accordingly. Surely, you need a device able to receive the satellite signals.

To make our descriptions more specific, we will use the US GPS system as an example.

GPS satellites fly in medium Earth orbit at an altitude of approximately 20,200 kilometers. Each satellite circles Earth twice a day. The satellites in the GPS constellation are arranged into six equally spaced orbital planes surrounding the Earth, so that users have direct view of at least four satellites from virtually any point on the planet.

A GPS satellite body is roughly a 2.5 cubic-meter cube (Figure 2) and weighs as much as a pick-up truck. Each GPS satellite continuously broad-

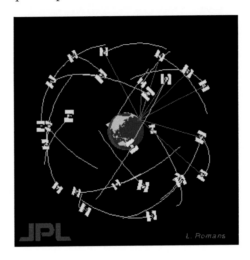

FIGURE 3: *GPS Satellite Constellation (image: NASA JPL)*

casts radio (microwave) signals that carry data indicating the satellite's clock time and precise position in space. The precise position of each satellite is determined by ground control, which tracks and maintains all the orbiting satellites. The signal data enable any receiving device (on/near Earth) to determine the receiver's range (distance) from the particular satellite. It is important that all satellites transmit their data signals in unison, at precisely synchronized times. Remember, all the satellites and, most likely, also the receiver, are moving.

Let's see how a receiver can determine its current position using **four satellites** within view at once. The geometric method is called *trilateration*. It is easier if we talk about one of these four satellites at a time.

First of all, with signal from **just one satellite**, a receiver can determine the satellite's distance from the receiver as follows.

We know light and radio signals travel at a constant speed $C = 186000$ miles per second or $C = 299792458$ meters per second. Let the signal travel

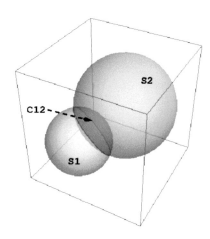

FIGURE 4: *Surface Intersection of Two Spheres*

time from the satellite to the receiver be δ seconds, where $\delta =$ (signal arriving receiver clock time)−(signal sending satellite synchronized time). With GPS, typical values for δ are about 0.06738 seconds. Then, $R = (C \times \delta)$ is the distance of the satellite to the receiver.

In other words, the receiver, on Earth or in space, is somewhere on the surface of a sphere **S1** with radius R centered at the satellite location the instant the data signal was sent.

Similarly, a second sphere **S2** centered at the second satellite used is found. Now the receiver has to be on the intersection of the surfaces of **S1** and **S2**. The intersection is a 2D circle as illustrated in Figure 4. Let's designate this circular intersection **C12**, the red line in Figure 4.

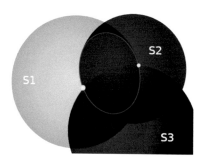

FIGURE 5: *Surface Intersection of Three Spheres*

A third satellite adds sphere **S3**. The circular intersection of **S1** and **S3** is another circle **C13** on which the receiver must be located. The circles **C12** and **C13** intersect at two points (the two yellow dots) as shown in Figure 5. You guessed it. Adding a fourth satellite narrows it down to a single point. That's the position of the receiver. The location is determined faster than a few blinks of the eye! In fact, if we assume the receiver is on the surface of Earth, we can often pick one of the two points without needing a fourth satellite. But, to get precise elevation information and other finer time/position adjustments, we want to use a fourth satellite (Figure 6).

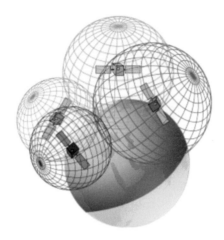

FIGURE 6: *Trilateration with Four Satellites*

Common Sense View

Perhaps mathematics or geometry is not your favorite subject, that is understandable. So let's see if we can put the GPS positioning method in layman's terms—cutting oranges.

Let's imaging a large orange as a sphere. Use a sharp flat knife and, with one straight cut, slice the orange into two pieces, a large part and a much smaller part (Figure 7). Notice the exposed cut surfaces will be flat and circular. Let's imagine a satellite at the center of this orange and the signal receiver on the skin of the cut part before you sliced it off. Similarly, imagine, at the same time, the receiver on another orange centered at another satellite. Now, Figure 4 earlier makes sense intuitively. The receiver must be on the circular curve common to these two oranges. Each orange represents a sphere centered at a GPS satellite.

If you look at Figure 5 again, you will see two intersecting flat circles meeting at two points, candidates for the receiver's position.

It is not so important that you understand all the geometry completely. In short, the distances of the receiver from four GNSS satellites are sufficient to determine the position of the receiver to a degree of precision.

FIGURE 7: *Orange Cross-Sections*

Precise Timing

An *atomic clock* can tell time to within 3 nanoseconds. A nanosecond is 10^{-9} second. Each GPS satellite uses more than one atomic clock, resulting in very precise time data in the GPS signals. Using such data, any GPS receiver can determine time to within 100 nanoseconds. Position accuracy depends on the receiver. Most receivers are correct to within 10 to 20 meters (33 to 66 feet).

Multiple receivers in close proximity can work together to increase the accuracy to within 1 centimeter.

Of course, GPS and other GNSS systems all have secret military aspects using encrypted signals and providing a degree of accuracy not available in civilian use. An example is guiding cruise missiles.

Location, Location, Location

The importance of location does not only apply to real estate. It affects many things. The ability to precisely know your location becomes important in many application areas.

And this ability has been brought to us by a convergence of modern technologies—space, atomic clocks, satellites, computers, computing, data processing, networking, and smartphones, etc.

A GNSS has these five major user application areas:

- *Location*: Determining positions on Earth or in outer space

- *Navigation*: Guiding users or objects to move from one location to another

- *Tracking*: Monitoring and managing moving objects

- *Mapping*: Helping to make various types of maps

- *Precise timing*: Keeping time using GNSS signals

According to gps.gov[1],

> *GPS boosts productivity across a wide swath of the economy, to include farming, construction, mining, surveying, package delivery, and logistical supply chain management. Major communications networks, banking systems, financial markets, and power grids depend heavily on GPS for precise time synchronization. Some wireless services cannot operate without it.*

Let's shift our attention to another GNSS, the BeiDou-3 which became operational globally in June 2020.

BeiDou Navigation Satellite System (北斗卫星导航系统)

In 2015, China began to launch satellites to build BDS-3 (third-generation BeiDou). It became the world's latest GNSS. The 35th and final satellite was launched into orbit on June 23, 2020, making BDS-3 fully operational.

BDS-3 currently offers more satellites in orbit than any other GNSS. BDS-3 provides all-weather and all-day positioning, navigation, timing, and search-and-rescue (SAR) services to its users.

The name 北斗 is Chinese for the *Big Dipper* which is easy to spot in the northern sky and can be used to locate the North Star. What an appropriate name for a modern GNSS from China!

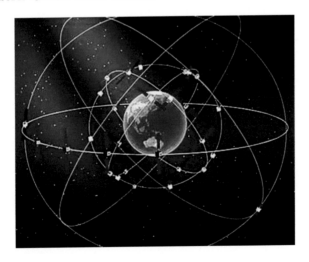

FIGURE 8: *BeiDou-3 (BDS-3) Satellite Constellation*

Here are BDS-3's main features:

- The BeiDou-3 constellation includes 35 satellites–five in geostationary orbit (GEO), three in inclined geostationary orbit (IGSO), and the remaining 27 in medium Earth orbit (MEO). The US GPS constellation however, uses six equally spaced (by 60 degrees) MEO orbits each with four satellites.

- BDS-3 satellites broadcast signals in five frequencies, namely B1I, B3I, B1C, B2a, and B2b. The B1C, B2a, and B2b are centered at 1575.420, 1176.450, and 1207.140 MHz, respectively. This helps the system to become more accurate. GPS satellite signals use only two to three frequencies. Its global services offer positioning accuracy horizontally better than 9 meters, vertically better than 10 meters and speed measuring accuracy better than 0.2 meters/sec.

- The BDS-3 is unique in supporting **two-way communication** with users, a capability not available in any other GNSS. BeiDou-compatible receiver devices can transmit data back to the satellites. This allows BDS-3 to know the current position of the user. The BDS-3 also uses inter-satellite links to help time synchronization and to enhance message communication services (MCS). BDS-3 MCS has a regional (Asia-Pacific) single message length of 14,000 bits (1,000 Chinese characters) and can transmit text, voice, and pictures. The global communication single message length is 560 bits.

Via BDS-3 we can send data and messages anytime and anywhere without depending on WiFi, cellular, or other signals. Thus, the search-and-rescue feature of BDS-3 brings the great *global 911* or *universal 120* concept a big step closer to reality.

Here is a question: How do you tell if your smartphone can use BDS-3 navigation? Of course, you can consult the specs of your phone. Or you can use a GPS testing app to see what GNSS signals you are getting. If you receive BeiDou signals, then you can navigate by installing freely available BDS-3 navigation apps. In civilian use, any positioning or navigation app you choose on your phone should automatically pick the best GNSS signals to use. Increasingly, smartphones such as the Huawei Mate 20, Google Pixel 4, Samsung S10, have dual-frequency GNSS chipsets. True multi-GNSS phones can't be too far off.

Summary

A GNSS uses *time* to determine *location*. Satellites serve as lighthouses in the sky with atomic clocks to deduce accurate locations of objects on or near

Earth. A receiver requires signals from four GNSS satellites at once to determine its own location via trilateration. Currently, there are four GNSSs: GPS, Galileo, GLONASS, and BDS-3.

A GNSS is a **global infrastructure** that is revolutionary in human history. It has many uses and makes our lives easier and work more efficient in many ways.

The ability to obtain precise time and location information at any point on or near Earth is unprecedented. It offers an automatic 3D + time coordinate system for the entire globe. Isn't that wonderful? And that should directly change the way we think about the world and how to do things in it! Thus, a computational thinker should fully appreciate GNSS and apply the unprecedented capability to better solve all kinds of problems.

Someday in the not too distant future, we may become so heavily dependent on GNSS that a blackout would be catastrophic.

CT Crossword Puzzle

Global Positioning

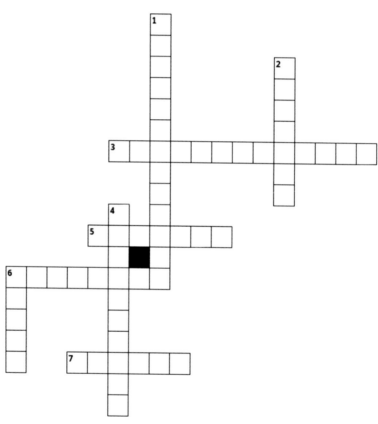

Across

3. Needs 4 satellites to perform

5. EU GNSS

6. GNSS uses time to determine

7. Chinese GNSS

Down

1. BeiDou supports user ___

2. Smartphones can receive GNSS ___

4. GPS often used for

6. Satellite positioning uses speed of

21

Face-to-Face with the Interface

Powerful digital systems have changed our lives in significant ways. We control such powerful systems through their *user interfaces* to make them work for us.

Interfaces are not limited to computers or computing. In general, the easier it is to control any given system through its interface, the better. This CT Article focuses on **the interface** from a computational thinking (CT) perspective, giving it the proper attention it deserves.

What Is an Interface

According to the *Merriam-Webster Dictionary*[1], an **interface** is *"the place at which independent and often unrelated systems meet and act on or communicate with each other"* and also *"a surface forming a common boundary of two bodies, spaces, or phases such as an oil-water interface."*

The word is a combination of "inter" and "face." Two systems face each other to interact through their respective *outer shell*. Such a shell (Figure 1)

- encases and protects the insides of a system

- provides a way to receive input from and to send output to the outside

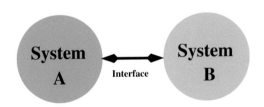

FIGURE 1: *Interface between Independent Systems*

An obvious example is the interface between a computer and its user. Computer user interfaces (UIs) have evolved quite quickly. Not so long ago, people were still using punched cards to run computer programs and getting results

---

[1]www.merriam-webster.com/dictionary/interface

from line printers. The slow turnaround time and lack of interactivity were serious obstacles. Later, the keyboard and cathode-ray tube (CRT) display combined to provide a command line interface (CLI) where a user entered commands interactivity and received results immediately on the CRT. The operating system component that provides the CLI is known as a *shell*, forms of which are still in use today. Examples are the Windows **CMD**, **Power-Shell**, and the Linux **bash**.

CLIs are fine for experts. Others had to wait until the invention of the graphical user interface (GUI). According to *WIRED*[2], "*In 1979, the Xerox Palo Alto Research Center developed the first GUI prototype.*" The Xerox Alto's GUI used a graphics display and a three-button mouse. Soon, based on this breakthrough, Apple developed Lisa, the first GUI-based computer available to the public.

Today we take the GUI for granted. What will we do with our computers or smartphones without the GUI? We need to point (mouse or touchscreen), click buttons/links, press, drag and drop, and see immediate feedback, or we will wonder if the computer is broken.

Yet, it can be even more convenient if we add voice control to the user interface. Modern speech recognition systems work rather well and allow voice input. Amazon's Echo, and Google's Hello Google are examples. However, voice is nice for short commands but tedious for lengthy input.

Nature of an Interface

An interface is where two independent systems meet and interact. For example, a simple lamp has an electric plug to insert into a socket as its interface to an electric power system (Figure 2). The plug needs to be of the right type, or

FIGURE 2: *Interfaces to Electric Power*

it's impossible to connect to the socket. The lamp also has an interface to the user, the on/off switch.

---

[2] *Web 101: A History of the GUI.* (1997, Dec. 19). www.wired.com/1997/12/web-101-a-history-of-the-gui

At an interface, one system, a user for example, is usually the *client* and the other, an application (app) for example, is the *server*. The two systems interact via the interface, which controls and regulates what interactions, in what manner and form, can take place between the two.

Using an interface, the client would communicate input such as commands and/or data to the server, and the server would return output such as results and feedback to the client in response.

The input can almost always be thought of as consisting a set of *attribute-value pairs*. For example, at a bank teller interface, the input may be

```
AccountID: 0123456
Action: deposit
Amount: 56.89
Date: June 1, 2023
Time: 14:35
Receipt: yes
```

It is up to the client (**interfacer**) to provide the correct input and for the server (**interfacee**) to check the validity of the input received. The two systems can thus interact to get the job done.

Interfaces in Computing

In addition to the UI, modern computing systems depend on various other interfaces to make their many parts work together.

At the hardware level, the motherboard of a computer provides the electrical connections by which the other parts communicate. Thus, the motherboard is a physical interface. Other standards-based electronic interfaces include USB (Universal Serial Bus), FireWire (high-speed data transfer), Ethernet (local area networking), IDE (Integrated Drive Electronics), SCSI (Small Computer System Interface) and PCI (Peripheral Component Interconnect), to name a few.

The operating system (OS) is central to a computer. It interfaces with software, hardware, and users. Each app may have its own user interface. But more importantly, an app also provides an Application Programming Interface (API) to govern how another app can control/use the particular app. In other words, two well-structured programs can interact and cooperate through prescribed APIs.

Within a software system, be it a large operating system or a particular app, you'll find *program modules* that form parts of the software system. The modules use interfaces defined by function/procedure calls to cooperate. Such an interface protects the internal working of a module from external interference, resulting in more robust program constructs known as *objects*. Today, the interface centered Object-Oriented Programming has become a well-established and widely used programming methodology.

Now we look at computer networks. At the networking level, Internet Protocol (IP) is the basic interface. On top of that there is Transmission Control Protocol (TCP) and User Datagram Protocol (UDP). And on top of these two, we have SMTP, POP, and IMAP for email; HTTP and HTTPS for the web (Figure 3); SSH and SFTP for secure login and file transfer; BitTorrent for peer-to-peer file sharing. There are many others.

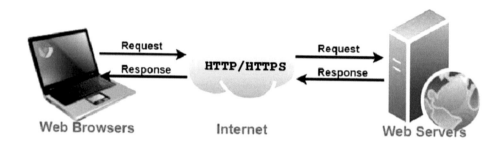

FIGURE 3: *The Web Interface*

Interfaces in Nature

Of course we understand that computers and computing depend heavily on interfaces, but so does almost everything else.

FIGURE 4: *Humming Bird and Flower Interface*

Animals use eyes, ears, nose, and skin to interface and interact with the environment. Many use gills and lungs for respiration. Mouth, teeth, and tongue form food interfaces. Flowers and nectar become specific pollination interfaces (Figure 4). Songs and calls attract mates.

Interface between Humans

Human beings are independent systems. They interface with one another easily and constantly. With speech, we easily interface verbally. Building on speech, we developed words for written communication. Additionally, we have music, dance, and poetry for other expressions.

Hence, forming an interface can be much more than where to put which color buttons on a device. It can be as complicated as developing a language, a set of symbols and their meanings, to represent concepts and operations in a sophisticated domain, such as mathematics or computer science.

Today, human interfacing has become even more instant and convenient because of phone calls, email, texting, online chat, and social media.

Abilities such as hearing, vision, voice, and physical movements come naturally. To complete our toolbox, we need skills such as speaking, handwriting, language (vocabulary, syntax, and semantics), etc. We also need to learn gestures (Figure 5) and interaction protocols such as handshake, clasped fist, bowing, elbow bump, high five, salute, hand clap, goodbye, and so on. Just

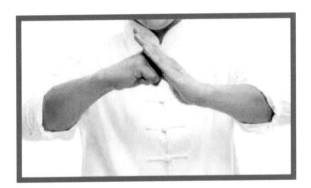

FIGURE 5: *Gesture as a Human Interface Technique*

like in the Internet, well-defined protocols specify how humans interact in formal occasions. For example, diplomatic protocols govern how government officials must behave when conducting foreign affairs.

Interface Skills Are Valuable

Becoming skillful with interfaces can be important and valuable. For example, touch typing is a good skill for almost everyone. Those who excel in it can find jobs as typists or keyboarders. Good driving skills can even land you good jobs in the shipping industry.

In the information age, the ability to efficiently and effectively use computers, apps, the web, and Internet can be lucrative. Such skills basically deal with interfaces of different kinds—text editing, word processing, spreadsheeting, tax reporting, accounting, photo/video/audio processing, and so on.

Among people, good interpersonal skills are very advantageous. They are critical for jobs in personnel relations, sales, marketing, customer service, and employee management. Lastly, but importantly, interpersonal skills are essential for career advancement.

Careful When Interfacing

Substantial tasks usually consist of parts to be completed by a number of different independent systems. They interact and collaborate to perform the entire task. Let's assume for now that each independent system is error-free and works correctly within itself. Then what can go wrong would be mistakes or errors made at some interface, because something unexpected can happen at an interface without being realized by systems on either side.

Thus, we must exercise caution when interfacing. When relating to another person, the innocent remark "see you at 7:30 tomorrow" can be a trap because there is no mention of AM, PM, or the date. It is always better to give a precise date and time to avoid potential problems. This is especially true when texting or emailing.

Be careful with numbers. A price of 15.99, for example, may be in US dollar, Canadian dollar, Euro, or RMB. A date such as 04/05/2023 could be in April or May. A temperature can be in degrees Fahrenheit or Celsius. A weight can be in pounds or kilograms. A number can even be invalid such as 560 or -7 as value for an age.

We can go on. The point is to be correct and precise when interfacing.

Here is a real incident.

After traveling nearly 10 months to Mars, the NASA Mars Climate Orbiter burned and broke into pieces in September 1999. What happened? According to CNN[3] *"because one engineering team used metric units while another used English units for a key spacecraft operation ..."* The erroneous navigation maneuver had disastrous results.

Here is another example. The *Heartbleed* security bug (disclosed in April 2014) was found in the widely used OpenSSL library (for secure online communication). It was caused by the TLS heartbeat extension failing to validate the length of input data. As a result, sufficiently long input can lead to leaking of protected and potentially sensitive data beyond the bounds of the input buffer.

---

[3]www.cnn.com/TECH/space/9909/30/mars.metric

We strive to be exact and precise when interfacing. But, we must also be aware that people can be deliberately imprecise and vague in order to misguide or even deceive. Such techniques have been developed to a fine art in elements of marketing and advertising.

Interface Design

Because of the importance of interfaces, we want to properly design them, making them easy to understand and use. To avoid mistakes, we want to make them foolproof. Take everyday appliances (Figure 6) for example, well-

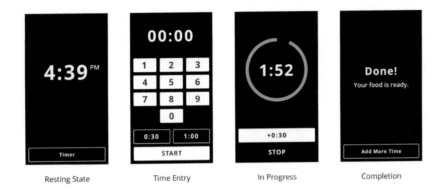

FIGURE 6: *Designing a Microwave Oven User Interface*

designed interfaces make them simple to operate and control. They not only highlight the functions of an appliance, but they also help its marketing. Actually, user interface (UI) and user experience (UX) design has become a profession. Experts help define, develop, test, and improve UI/UX as integral parts of products and software.

Here are some basic principles of interface design:

- Being logical, consistent, and easy

- Placing users in control, allowing easy editing, corrections, undo/redo operations

- Making operations easy to remember and foolproof, providing appropriate confirmation and feedback

- Supplying features for beginners and experts

- Anticipating use cases and performing thorough testing

If users feel comfortable interacting with a device (hardware or app) and regard it as user-friendly, then the UI/UX design is on the right track.

Interfaces Evolve

Some interfaces may stay constant and basically the same for a long time. But most interfaces, like other things, will change and improve with time and advancing technology.

For example, USB, one of the most successful and widely adopted computer peripheral interfaces, has evolved from USB 1.0, 2.0, ..., 3.2 to 4.0 with cable moving from type-A to type-C.

We also know that computer user interfaces moved from punched cards to GUI and even with voice input added. GUI itself has moved from desktop computers to laptops, tablets, and smartphones. Even body and eye movements are getting applications in UI.

Good old televisions have changed from CRT displays with roof-top antennae to *smart TVs* with huge high-resolution displays, Internet connections, and built-in computer chips for streaming videos from all kinds of sources apart from broadcasts. In fact, the term TV has lost its original meaning. Today there is little difference between a TV set and a computer workstation.

The modern automobile driver interfaces are a far cry from those in the Ford Model T era. Before long, there may not be a steering wheel or brake pedal (Figure 7). The cars will be driving themselves! When interfaces evolve and advance, so must systems that depend on or use them. Of course, users must also adapt and learn new skills or risk being left behind.

FIGURE 7: *Self-driving Car Interface (Image: insurancejournal.com)*

Summary

Interfaces are bridges for collaboration and interaction between independent systems.

Starting with interfaces for computers and in computing, we have expanded to all kinds of interfaces. Complicated interfaces are built upon more basic ones. It is fair to say that the interface is everywhere, and it impacts our daily lives. Have you stories of your own encounters with it?

Ignoring the interface can be costly. In the past, the American auto industry complained about cars not selling in Japan. Much to its surprise, the Japanese drive on the left side of the road, and most US cars have their steering wheels on the wrong side!

We must also be careful about potential troubles or mishaps happening at the interface. These computational thinking principles, among others, can help avoid problems at the interface:

- Communicate clearly and precisely

- Pay attention to details

- Avoid contextual problems

- Obtain confirmation and feedback

Even the best designed interface has room for improvement. And it is up to the interfacer to be aware so as to avoid problems or mistakes. It always pays for the interfacer to have enough knowledge of the interfacee side. Clearly, good mechanical knowledge of a car can make driving safer. Similarly, sufficient knowledge of potential interfacers (clients) is a must for an interface design.

We have discussed many aspects of the interface. What is the one most important takeaway? **Overlook the importance of the interface at your own peril.**

.... CT Crossword Puzzle ....

Interface

Across

5. CLI

6. Change with time

9. IP

Down

1. GUI

2. Interface source of potential ___

3. Interface living things

4. Interface skills

6. LAN

7. Interface person-to-person

8. Interface networking

22

Protocols Are Interface Rules

Generally, a *protocol* is a set of rules and conventions to follow for two parties to interface with each other to achieve some specific cooperation. These are independent parties such as individuals, organizations, clients and servers, or even countries. For example, in foreign affairs, diplomatic protocols must be strictly followed, while ordinary people must follow precise rules when writing a letter, making a phone call, or conducting business with a bank.

For example, when making a phone call we first dial a number (address of our target); when the call has been picked up, we say "Hello," and after talking we hang up the phone on both ends. These rules form the telephone protocol. Thus, protocols are everywhere, especially where there is an interface between independent systems.

But, in this article we will focus only on protocols for computer networking, in particular the Internet and the web. Improved understanding in this direction will make you a better computational thinker and can help you apply the knowledge to make interfacing with others more efficient and effective in everything you do.

What Are Networking Protocols?

For various computing devices from different vendors, under different operating systems, to communicate on a network, a detailed set of rules and conventions must be established for all parties to follow. Such rules are known as *networking protocols*.

Each separate device connected on a network is known as a *host*. Example hosts include: workstations, laptops, smartphones, smart TVs, Amazon Echo speakers, servers on the cloud, and so on. Networking makes many different services available. Each networking service follows its own specially designed protocols. Protocols govern such details as:

- Address format of hosts and processes

- Data format

- Manner of data transmission

- Sequencing and addressing of messages

- Initiating and terminating connections

- Establishing services

- Accessing services

- Integrity, privacy, and security of data transmission

Thus, for a *process* (an executing program) on one host to communicate with another process on a different host, both processes must follow the same protocol. The Open System Interconnect (OSI) Reference Model (Figure 1) provides a standard layered view of networking protocols and their interdependence. The corresponding layers on the hosts, and inside the network in-

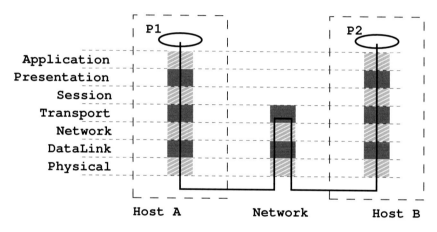

FIGURE 1: *Networking Protocol Layers (OSI Model)*

frastructure, perform complementary tasks to enable data exchange between the communicating processes (P1 and P2 in Figure 1).

Here is a brief summary of the OSI layers:

1. Physical—Provides mechanical and electrical connection specifications

2. Data Link—Organizes bits into frames

3. Network—Provides inter-network and packet movements

4. Transport—Enables data transport from source host to destination host

5. Session—Creates and ends a communication session

6. Presentation—Encodes, decodes, and translates data

7. Application—Gives network access to an end-user process

The physical, data-link, and network layers are handled by the network nodes and the transport, session, presentation, and application layers are the responsibility of the communicating hosts (Figure 2).

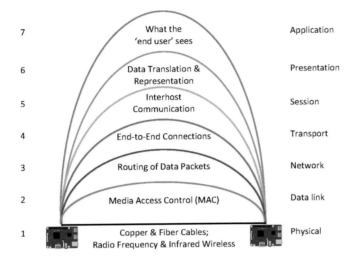

FIGURE 2: *Another View of OSI Layers*

Internet Protocols

Internet, the network that made the world a global viillage, started as a US Defense Department research project, the ARPANET.

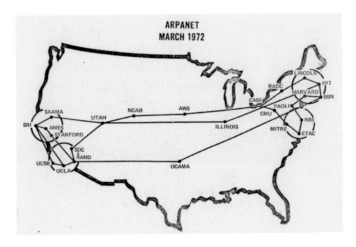

FIGURE 3: *1972 ARPANET (image: UCLA LibraryDigitalCollections)*

In 1971-72, ARPANET had 15 nodes (23 hosts) in the United States (Figure 3)—Cambridge, MA, Stanford, CA, Pittsburgh, PA, Urbana, IL,

Cleveland, OH, Los Angeles, CA, Lexington, MA, Salt Lake City, UT, Santa Barbara, CA, Mountain View, CA.

Among common networking protocols, the Internet Protocol Suite is the most widely used. The basic IP (*Internet Protocol*) is a *network layer* protocol. The TCP (*Transport Control Protocol*) and UDP (*User Datagram Protocol*) are at the *transport layer*. The HTTP (*Hypertext Transfer Protocol*) is at the *application layer* and is used for the web.

> **CT concept–*Follow protocols***: *Only by following protocols can independent parties that may have never met cooperate smoothly.*

Protocols can affect the effectiveness and speed of the entire system.

Networking protocols are no mystery. Think about the protocol for making a telephone call. You (a client process) must pick up the phone, listen for the dial tone, dial a valid telephone number, and wait for the other side (the server process) to pick up the phone. Then you must say "hello," identify yourself, and so on.

This is a protocol from which you cannot deviate if you want the call to be made successfully through the telephone network, and it is clear why such a protocol is needed. The same is true of a computer program attempting to talk to another computer program through a computer network.

The design of efficient and effective networking protocols for different network services is an important area in computer science.

IP Addresses

Just like phones on a telephone network, every host on the Internet has its own network address that identifies the host for communication purposes. The addressing technique is an important part of a network and its protocols. An Internet IPv4 address is represented by 4 bytes in a 32-bit quantity. For example, `csail`, a host at MIT, has the IP address `128.30.2.109`.

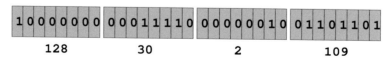

FIGURE 4: *IPv4 Address*

This *dot notation* (or *quad notation*) gives the decimal value (0 to 255) of each byte. To accommodate its explosive growth, the Internet also uses IPv6, which supports 128-bit addresses. The IP address is similar to a telephone number in another way: the leading digits are like area codes, and the trailing digits are like local numbers.

Basically, the Internet transmits information by routing *data packets* (a well-organized block of data) from a source IP address to a destination IP address.

Domain Names

Because of its numerical nature, an IP address is easy on machines but hard on users. Therefore, any host may also have a *domain name* composed of words, rather like a postal address.

With domain names, the entire Internet name space for hosts is recursively divided into disjoint domains in a tree structure (Figure 5), similar to a file tree. For example, the domain name `csail.mit.edu` identifies a host `csail`

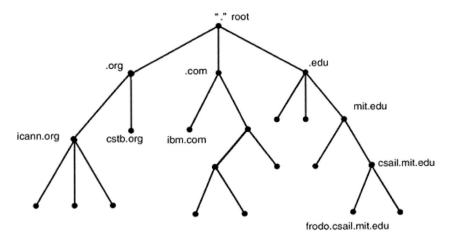

FIGURE 5: *The Domain Name Tree*

in the CSAIL Department at MIT. Domain names are for convenience. Some hosts may not need or have a domain name. The address for `frodo` puts it in the `csail` local domain, within the `mit` subdomain, which is under the `edu` top-level domain (TLD) for US educational institutions. Other TLDs include `org` (non-profit organizations), `gov` (US government offices), `mil` (US military installations), `com` (commercial outfits), `net` (network service providers), `uk` (United Kingdom), `cn` (China), and so forth. Within a local domain (for example, `csail.mit.edu`), you can refer to machines by their hostname alone (for example, `monkey`, `dragon`, `frodo`), but the full address must be used for machines outside.

All network applications accept a host address given either as a domain name or as an IP address. In fact, a domain name is first translated to a numerical IP address before being used to locate a host. The translation is done automatically via the DNS service, an Internet based domain-to-IP dynamic mapping service.

Domain names are not created equal. Some are much better than others. People pay good money for great domain names that can help their business or cause.

Domain Registration

Anyone can obtain a domain name, often for creating a website, or some other purpose. To obtain a domain name, you need the service of a *domain name registrar*. Most will be happy to register your new domain name for a very modest yearly fee. Once registered, the domain name is property that belongs to the *registrant*. No one else can register for that particular domain name as long as the current registrant keeps the registration in good order.

Internet Corporation for Assigned Names and Numbers (ICANN) accredits commercial registrars for common TLDs, including: `.com`, `.net`, `.org`, and `.info`. Additional TLDs include `.biz`, `.pro`, `.aero`, `.name`, and `.museum`. Restricted domains (for example, `.edu`, `.gov`, and `.us`) are handled by special registries such as `net.educause.edu` (for `.edu`), `nic.gov` (for `.gov`), and `nic.us` (for `.us`). Country-code TLDs are normally handled by registries in their respective countries.

Accessing Domain Registration Data

The registration record of a domain name is often publicly available. The standard Internet *Whois* service allows easy access to this information. You can do this on the web at: `www.internic.net/whois.html`, for example.

Packet Switching

Data on the Internet are sent and received in *packets*. Thus, the Internet is a packet switching network. Similar to a letter, a packet envelops a small block of data with address information so the data can be routed through intermediate nodes on the network which is shared by all connected users. The network uses routing algorithms to efficiently forward packets to their final destinations.

Because there are multiple routes from the source to the destination host, the Internet is very reliable and can operate even if parts of the network are down. Figure 6 shows the structure details of an IPv4 packet. As you can see, the packet has two parts—the packet header contains destination, source, and other meta information (functioning as an envelope), and the packet body contains the actual data to be sent through the Internet to the destination.

We now turn our attention to the most important service on the Internet— the World Wide Web (WWW) or simply the web.

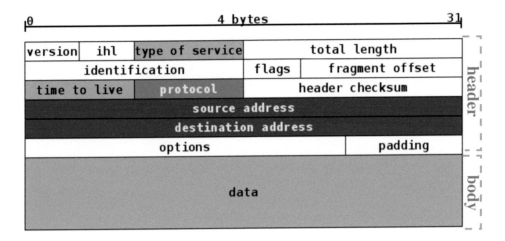

FIGURE 6: *IPv4 Packet*

Hypertext Transfer Protocol

As you may already know, web browsers and web servers communicate following the Hypertext Transfer Protocol (HTTP). It does not matter which browser is contacting what server; as long as both sides use the same protocol, everything will work.

In the early 1990s, HTTP gave the web its start. HTTP/1.0 was standardized in the first part of 1996. Important improvements and new features have been introduced in HTTP/1.1, and it is now the stable version.

HTTP is an application layer (Figure 1) protocol that sits on top of TCP/IP, which provides reliable two-way connection between the web client and web server. We don't need all the details to understand the basics of HTTP.

1. A web client, usually a browser but can be any user agent (UA), sends an HTTP *query* to a server.

2. A web server, upon receiving a query, sends back an HTTP *response*.

A query and a response form an HTTP *transaction*. Each transaction stands alone and has no protocol-provided means to be correlated with any other transaction. Figure 7 illustrates an HTTP transaction.

A simple HTTP transaction goes as follows:

1. *Connection*—A browser (client) opens a connection to a server.

2. *Query*—The client requests a resource controlled by the server.

3. *Processing*—The server receives and processes the request.

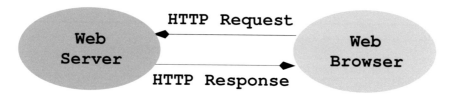

FIGURE 7: *HTTP Transaction*

4. *Response*—The server sends the requested resource, or an error, back to the client.

5. *Termination*—The transaction is finished, and the connection is closed unless it is kept open for another request immediately from the client on the other end of the connection.

HTTP governs the format of the query and response messages. Basically, each query or request consists of an *initial line*, one or more *header lines* and an optional *body*.

When using a browser to access the web, the HTTP messages between it and the web servers are kept behind the scenes. While HTTP transmits information in the open, HTTPS (HTTP Secure) is a secure protocol that simply applies HTTP over a secure transport layer protocol *Transport Layer Security* (TLS 1.2) that is derived from the earlier *Secure Sockets Layer* (SSL).

Secure Website Login

Login is also required for shopping and other business on the web. Websites often have areas and services reserved for members who are registered or have accounts with the site/organization. Each user often must log in to gain access to member-only or account-specific information or services. Access to a login page and all pages under login control normally uses HTTPS (Secure HTTP) to protect the user ID and password from eavesdropping en route in the network. For better security, it is now standard practice to require all websites, without regard to login, to use HTTPS instead of HTTP. Any webpage that uses HTTPS will display a lock symbol at the beginning of the location or address line (Figure 8). The symbol simply means HTTPS is being used for the page, and you can click on the lock symbol to check on the *digital certificate* for SSL/TSL being used. It is a good idea that you do check it. The FBI has warned the public not to be fooled by the lock symbol. It at best tells you that the HTTPS protocol is being used on that particular webpage. **A phishing website can use HTTPS as well. Yet it has been designed to steal your personal information**. HTTPS is a good thing, and all websites should use it, but we need to understand its limitations.

FIGURE 8: *HTTPS Lock Symbol*

What Is a Digital Certificate?

In secure communication, the very first concern is that the parties are actually who they say they are. A *digital certificate* is a document (computer file) signed by a certificate authority (CA) that can vouch for the identity of the certificate holder. A CA is usually a well-established third party that is in the business of verifying credentials and issuing certificates digitally signed by the CA. Certificates can be issued for different purposes and different domains: Web server, email, digital signature, payment systems, and so on. SSL/TLS certificates are widely used by web servers to enable HTTPS access. The largest CAs include Symantec[1], Comodo Group, Go Daddy, Thawte, and GlobalSign.

A CA issues a digital certificate for a customer after carefully verifying the identity and legitimacy of the person or organization (the client). Each certificate is a digital ID and contains the identity of the client, the client's public key, the expiration date of the certificate, and details of the issuing CA. A digital certificate is often issued for a certain specific purpose and is installed in applications that use it for that particular security purpose.

Figure 9 shows some details of the web server certificate used by the US Social Security Administration on its `secure.ssa.gov` site. Digital certificates follow standardized formats, for example, X509v3, and are used by security programs within applications, such as web servers, web browsers, and email clients. Servers that support HTTPS need to install valid SSL/TLS certificates. A certificate not issued by a widely recognized CA or has expired can cause a browser warning about the certificate's status, allowing the end user to accept or reject the certificate.

Certificates for CAs are issued by other CAs. A *root CA* is one that signs its own certificate.

Organizations often set up their internal certification system with a root CA controlled by their own company. This way, large companies and

---

[1]Symantec acquired VeriSign's Security Business.

This certificate has been verified for the following uses:

SSL Client Certificate
SSL Server Certificate

Issued To

Common Name (CN)	secure.ssa.gov
Organization (O)	Social Security Administration
Organizational Unit (OU)	<Not Part Of Certificate>
Serial Number	0D:91:C7:6E:43:6E:57:19:80:F7:BB:A3:98:DB:F6:E6

Issued By

Common Name (CN)	DigiCert SHA2 Extended Validation Server CA
Organization (O)	DigiCert Inc
Organizational Unit (OU)	www.digicert.com

Period of Validity

Begins On	7/14/2014
Expires On	9/30/2016

Fingerprints

SHA-256 Fingerprint	BF:98:CC:24:AF:39:0E:A0:75:24:32:1C:0D:07:AB:CE: E8:5E:34:39:87:0E:CA:5F:BD:44:94:37:4B:A7:D5:C4
SHA1 Fingerprint	13:98:7E:5C:1A:13:62:ED:7D:CD:00:DB:AC:60:06:10:96:F4:E2:95

FIGURE 9: *Sample Web Server Certificate Details*

organizations can issue digital certificates for internal use, without paying fees to commercial CAs.

HTTPS and SSL/TLS

Web servers support HTTPS for secure communication between the client and the server.

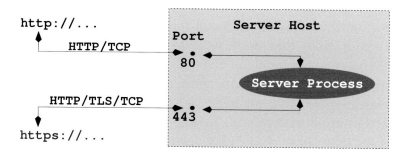

FIGURE 10: *HTTP vs. HTTPS*

HTTPS is HTTP over SSL or the newer TLS protocol (Figure 10). Note different network services use different *network ports* on servers. For example, port 80 for HTTP and port 443 for HTTPS are standard. However, non-standard ports can use protocols of their own design. SSL/TLS developed from SSL 1.0, 2.0, and 3.0 to TLS 1.0, 1.1, and 1.2. SSL/TLS provides secure communication between client and server by allowing mutual authentication, the use of digital signatures for integrity, and data encryption for confidentiality.

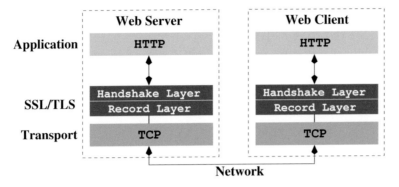

FIGURE 11: *HTTPS Protocol Layers*

To enable HTTPS, a server needs to install a valid web server certificate and enable SSL/TLS. SSL/TLS may be placed between a reliable connection-oriented transport protocol layer, such as TCP/IP, and an application protocol layer, such as HTTP (Figure 11).

Basically, TLS sets up secure communication in two steps:

1. The *handshake phase*—Mutual authentication and securely agreeing upon a randomly generated *session key* to be used in the next phase

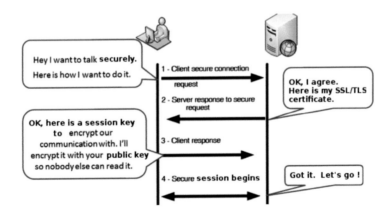

FIGURE 12: *Basic TLS Handshake*

2. The *session data phase*—Following the record layer protocol, using the session key for encryption of messages between the client and server

The handshake phase uses *public-key cryptography* for security, while the session data phase uses the more efficient symmetric encryption for speed. Each new SSL/TLS connection will establish a new session key. Figure 12 illustrates the TLS handshake process from a user viewpoint.

Finally

Hosts and processes on a network follow well-defined protocols to interface with one another. Here, we focused on the Internet protocols, IP, TCP/IP, UDP/IP, HTTP(S), SSL/TLS.

There of course are many other networking protocols including Simple Mail Transfer Protocol (SMTP) for email, FTP/SFTP for file transfer, SSH for secure shell, and DHCP for dynamic host configuration (automatically assign local IP addresses to connecting host on a LAN dynamically), and many others. A list of current Internet services, their protocols, and assigned port numbers can be found at the IANA website. Port numbers for Internet services are assigned in various ways, based on three ranges: standard system ports (0-1023), user ports (1024-49151), and the dynamic and/or private ports (49152-65535).

> **CT concept–*Protocols are interface rules***: *Only by following exact and well-defined rules can unrelated and independent entities interact successfully.*

The Internet is wonderful and used by everyone globally all the time. In fact if someone says, "the Internet is down!", then it usually means a disaster or at least a major inconvenience for all involved. The Internet as an infrastructure is like running water or electric power; you can hardly do without.

And all the various Internet services depend on protocols to work smoothly and efficiently. Computational thinkers must realize that paying attention to interfaces with machines, programs, organizations, or other people is important. And if something goes wrong at the interface, something bad can happen!

CT Crossword Puzzle

Protocol

Across

2. TCP

6. A process supplying network service

8. Multipurpose Internet Mail Extensions

Down

1. A computer connected on a network

3. Important part of network protocols

4. Open system interconnect model

5. Two parties negotiate following ___

7. A process receiving network service

23

Computer Programming by Chickens and Rabbits

The modern computer is a universal machine, because it can be programmed to do anything. Anything that is *computable*. All you need is to download and install an app, and the computer becomes a new tool instantly. No other machine is like it in that respect. Thus, its impact on the world and civilizations everywhere is much more profound than any other machine.

Therefore, a clear understanding of programming is important for computational thinkers. Here, we will give a simple explanation of programming with an easy-to-grasp example. An appreciation of program writing can show us many effective ways to solve problems that are useful in different areas, even our daily lives.

Programming Is Not Exotic

In fact, we are all familiar with programming. We follow TV programs or radio programs to enjoy our favorite shows. When we go to concerts or public meetings, we get event programs. The recipes you follow when you cook are programs. Further, you may have written (or programmed) a few recipes yourself. Yet not all recipes have the same clarity.

Some authors foresee blind spots and difficulties, making their recipes easy to follow, instead of leaving more questions than answers. The good thing is that with practice and experience everyone can write better programs.

Want to try some programming? Don't be afraid. You can do it. It is not hard. We'll show you.

Programmers Think Differently

A *programmer* is one who creates a program by writing it down as a step-by-step sequence of instructions.

A program has to be written in such a way that **anyone and everyone** can understand and follow the instructions precisely. In fact, a good program should be **foolproof**, because ultimately, a program is for an idiotic machine (the computer) to execute.

As you can see, this requires programmers to adopt a different mindset than lay persons. A programmer needs to ensure that everything is perfectly clear and that nothing is left to chance. Hence, a program is one tedious step after another. For each and every fork in the road, a plan must be laid out ahead of time for each path.

FIGURE 1: *Program Overview: Input-Processing-Output*

Definition of a Computer Program

A computer program is a step-by-step procedure that can be carried out by a computer. A program receives input, performs a sequence of steps based on the input, then produces output (Figure 1). We can specify the following criteria:

- **Finiteness**: The procedure consists of a finite number of steps and will always terminate in finite time.

- **Definiteness**: Each step is precisely, rigorously, and unambiguously specified.

- **Input**: The procedure may receive certain data from the outside as input. Allowable values for the data may vary within limitations.

- **Output**: The procedure performs specific actions and produces results as its output.

- **Effectiveness**: Each operation in the procedure is basic and clearly doable by a computer.

Program for Chicken and Rabbits

In late primary school or early middle school, an often used example of applying mathematics is the *Chicken and Rabbit Problem*: Given the total number of heads (H) and total number of legs (L), figure out how many chickens and how many rabbits are in the yard (Figure 2). For example, if there are 12

FIGURE 2: *Chicken and Rabbit Problem*

chickens and 7 rabbits, then we have 19 heads ($H = 19$). Because each chicken has 2 legs and each rabbit 4, we have $24 + 28 = 52$ legs. That is $L = 52$. Thus, if we know how many chickens and how many rabbits, we can easily calculate the total number of heads and legs.

The reverse is a bit harder. The question is, Given the total number of heads and legs as known quantities, how do we find the correct number of chickens and rabbits?

Here are some easy cases. If we know $H = 1$ and $L = 2$, then we have one chicken and no rabbit. If we know $H = 1$ and $L = 4$, then we have one rabbit and no chicken. And so on.

We'll illustrate program writing by creating a program to solve this specific problem. Let's name this program CRprog.

First, we'll look at the input and output of CRprog:

Input: The number of heads H and the number of legs L
Output: The number of chickens c and the number of rabbits r

This means the program CRprog will receive as input data H and L. Of course, these must be non-negative integers (whole numbers). Then through a sequence of steps, the program computes the correct values of c and r. Finally, it displays these values as output.

Computing c and r

Now it is time to talk about how to solve this problem. That is how to compute c (number of chickens) and r (number of rabbits) from the given input H (number of heads) and L (number of legs).

Often there is more than one way to find the answers from the input. For our problem, one way is to use brute-force by trying all possible values for r:

$$r = 0, \ r = 1, \ r = 2, \ r = 3, \ r = 4, \ ..., \ r = H$$

In other words, try "no rabbits" to "all rabbits," and we'll find the solution, sooner or later. Each trial value of r is only a **guess** that needs to be tested to see if it is right or wrong.

Brute-force search, also known as an *exhaustive search*, is a problem-solving method that systematically generates and tests each and every possible solution. Obviously, the method has many applications.

In the problem at hand, a guess r (number of rabbits) implies a corresponding guess $c = H - r$ (number of chickens), where H is the known head count.

To test the correctness of any pair r and c, we simply see if they lead to the given number of legs L. Specifically, we test if the following is true:

$$2 \times c + 4 \times r = L$$

Let's write down a flowchart for `CRprog` **brute-force** that can make the whole process more obvious.

Flowchart

In the flowchart (Figure 3) we used the *assignment symbol* `:=` which gives the computed value on the right-hand side to the variable on the left-hand side.

In the flowchart you also see an *iteration*, which is a set of steps to be executed repeatedly. In a program, an iteration is also known as a *loop*. Using iteration is what makes trying all possibilities possible and simple to specify in a program.

Specifying a Sequence of Steps

Following this brute-force strategy and with the help of the flowchart, let's write down the sequence of steps for the program. The `comment` lines are for explanations and not part of the procedure instructions.

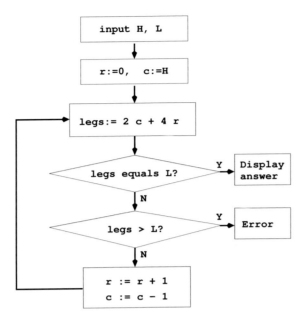

FIGURE 3: *Procedure Flowchart*

CRprog **brute-force**:

1. Receive the input values H and L
   comment: H number of heads, L number of legs

2. Let $r := 0$; let $c := H$
   comment: r initial guess for rabbits, c for chickens

3. **repeat**: Let $legs := (2 \times c + 4 \times r)$
   comment: leg count based on current r and c

4. If $legs$ equals L then goto **answer**
   comment: if $legs$ equals the given L, we found the answer

5. If $legs > L$ then goto **error**
   comment: if $legs$ is larger than L, we have a problem

6. Let $r := r + 1$; let $c := c - 1$
   comment: for our next guess, add 1 to r, subtract 1 from c

7. goto **repeat**

8. **answer**: display "c Chickens and r Rabbits"; stop

9. **error**: display "no solution found"; stop

The best way to understand a procedure is to follow the *control flow* which flows from the current position/step to the next. Follow it from the very beginning all the way to the end, and you'll get a good idea about how the procedure works.

At this time, if you are serious about learning how to program, or at least getting a good appreciation of it, you may want to try following the steps using some specific input values, such as $H = 11$ and $L = 28$. See if you get the display "8 Chickens and 3 Rabbits."

Think of it as a game. Take out a pencil and paper, and carefully follow the procedure. If this is your very first time, congratulations, because you have achieved a breakthrough not many have the chance to accomplish.

Garbage in Garbage out

It is important for a program to validate its input data at the beginning. If the input is not valid, then there is no point in going further (Figure 4).

FIGURE 4: *Garbage in Garbage out*

Try `CRprog` **brute-force** with the input $H = 0$ and $L = 0$. Does it work? This is known as an extreme case. How about $H = 9$ and $L = 15$? This input is invalid because L must be an even number. Of course, any negative or non-integral values for either H or L are invalid as well. Any L value less than $2H$ or more than $4H$ is also invalid. Can you think of other restrictions?

Please feel free to add these validity tests before step 1.

Program Efficiency

The brute-force method is not the best because it wastes computing power by trying too many guesses. Another initial guess could be r is about half of H. No matter what initial guess for r, we can compute $c = H - r$ and

$$legs = 2 \times c + 4 \times r$$

$$d = legs - L$$

If d is zero, we found the solution. If d is positive, then we have $d/2$ too many rabbits. If d is negative, we have $-d/2$ too few rabbits. In either case, $r + d/2$ is the correct number of rabbits, therefore the solution. This method takes just one guess.

But we can do even better and get the correct answer without any guessing. Using algebra on the next two equations

$$r + c = H$$
$$2 \times r + c = L/2$$

we have directly

$$r = L/2 - H$$

This means we can actually calculate the correct r and $c = H - r$ **in one step**.

Creating a Program in Stages

Given a problem to solve, we can follow a systematic approach to write a program for it as follows:

1. Think about different ways to solve the problem. Figure out an overall solution strategy.

2. Use a flowchart to design the logical structure and the flow from one step to the next.

3. Write down a procedure that checks the input, specifies and sequences the steps, and produces the answer.

4. Test run the procedure on paper with various input values, and pay attention to extreme cases.

5. Pick a computer language to code the procedure, and do actual tests by running the code.

6. Make corrections, improvements, and refinements.

Improved Version

Here are the steps of the direct computation version of the chicken and rabbit program.

`CRprog` **direct**:

1. Receive the input values for heads and legs H and L

2. Check H and L for validity; if invalid, goto **error**

3. Let $r := L/2 - H$; let $c := H - r$

4. Display "c Chickens and r Rabbits"; stop

5. **error**: display "Invalid input–no solution found"; stop

Coding

When we have the procedure figured out and precisely stated as we have demonstrated, then we are ready to put the program in a programming language of our choice.

Popular programming languages include C/C++/C#, Java, Perl, Python, JavaScript, PHP, SQL, HTML, CSS, and many more. Some of them are *general-purpose*; others are more specialized. Coding is an activity much like translation–take the step-by-step procedure given in English, or another natural language, and translate it into C++ or Python, for example.

Once in the form of computer code, a program can be run on the target computer system for testing, debugging, revision, and updating. When ready, the program can be released for general use, until the next version takes its place.

Finally a Good Start

Through the chicken and rabbit problem, we have introduced a complete example of program writing. You can see that both the brute-force version and the direct version pass the computer program criteria mentioned earlier.

The example also showed us how programming involves problem-solving strategy, planning, anticipating problems, precise steps, power of iteration, logic, and efficiency thinking.

The simple example here also demonstrated a systematic approach to programming: decide on a solution strategy, create a flowchart, list a step-by-step procedure, test, revise, and code in a programming language, finally run the code, debug, and release.

We don't want to give the wrong impression that programming is an individual effort or it is so cut-and-dry. In fact, programming is an **art** that often also takes team work. Indeed, programming is a vast and deep area of computing and computer science, including software engineering, programming languages, compilers, algorithm design and analysis, application program interface (API) design, protocols, data structures, database, and much more. Proficiency in programming is highly valuable.

One simple example cannot make anyone a programmer. But, you already had a peek into that world. Not everyone will like it. If you do, it can be a good start, or at least it can add to your computational thinking.

There is a Javascript version of this program (**Demo:** `ChicRabb`) available at our companion website that you can try interactively or download.

CT Crossword Puzzle

Programming

Across

3. Programs are also ___

4. A program achieves a certain ___

6. A program is ___ for a computer

8. A compiled program can be ___ on a computer

Down

1. ___ in ___ out

2. A program is usually written in a ___ language

5. A program receives ___

7. A program produces ___

24

Don't Stop–Do It Again!

The universe and the world around us work with rhythm and repetition. Sunrise and sunset, seasons, getting out of bed, going to work or school, coming back home, and going to bed at night. Many things repeat regularly—songs and music have reprises, visual arts and architectural designs also use repetition of patterns, animals breath in and out, and their hearts beat constantly.

All that is not surprising. But, what if I tell you that repetition is also a powerful way to solve problems? This CT Article focuses on repetition or *iteration* and formalizes it as a systematic way for problem-solving through the lens of CT. By doing this, we will gain a deeper understanding of the nature of iteration in procedures and realize that iteration can be applied to solve problems in many ways and in different areas including computing and daily living.

Simple Example

Often, we need to arrange data items in a certain order to make them easy to use. For example, words in a dictionary are in alphabetical order. Personnel records are ordered by names. Numbers are arranged in ascending or descending order, and so on. By the way, such structures in data are known as *data structures*, an important topic in computing.

To begin, let's see how iteration is applied to rearrange a list of, say, grades of eight students, into ascending order. Here is the list of grades:

$$67.5, \quad 59.5, \quad 82, \quad 93.5, \quad 77, \quad 45.5, \quad 100, \quad 76.5$$

And we want to rearrange them into

$$45.5, \quad 59.5, \quad 67.5, \quad 76.5, \quad 77, \quad 82, \quad 93.5, \quad 100$$

Here is a simple method. Find the highest grade and move it to the last position of the list. Then, repeat the operation on the rest of the list (now with one less grade) and so on, until the job is done. The list is now in ascending order. This method is actually called *bubble sort*, because in computing sorting means putting items into order.

Problem-Solving with Iteration

Iteration is a powerful tool for problem-solving. The tool can be applied if a problem, any problem, fits the following *iteration paradigm*:

1. *Do I know how to solve this problem if it is in its simplest form?*

2. *For that problem in general, do I have a way to reduce its size or complexity?*

3. *Is the reduced problem of the same exact nature?*

If the answer is yes to all three questions, you can apply iteration to solve that problem.

FIGURE 1: *Walking*

Walking to a destination (Figure 1), for example, can be solved by iteration because

1. The simplest form is when the destination is just one step away.

2. Otherwise, we can reduce the problem by one step.

3. And the reduced problem is still *walking to that destination*, the same exact nature.

Applying the Iteration Paradigm

Let's examine a couple of daily tasks that can be performed by iteration. First, the difficult task of eating a bowl of soup (Figure 2). Here the simplest or trivial case is that the bowl is already empty or almost empty. We just need to do nothing, or finish it directly and stop. However, if the bowl is full, we can

FIGURE 2: *Eating a Bowl of Soup*

take a spoonful (surprise), thus reducing the size of the task. The resulting problem is a smaller task of the same nature, that is to finish the remaining soup. Because the problem fits the paradigm, we can be sure that repeatedly taking spoonfuls will work fine.

FIGURE 3: *Delivering Newspapers*

Another example is delivering newspapers on a *paper route* (Figure 3), which is not unfamiliar to many of us. The task is to drop off today's newspaper at a list of locations in a neighborhood, usually by riding a bicycle.

Here is how that task fits the iteration paradigm. If the location list is empty or has a single entry, then we simply finish the task directly. For a long list of locations, we can reduce the list by riding to one of the locations. The list is shortened and the remaining task is still of the same exact nature. Obviously by repeatedly riding to another location, we can complete the task.

While the iteration stays the same, the order in which the locations are visited can make a difference. Ingenuity can lie in picking which location to visit next, especially when the number of locations increases and their distances vary.

Iteration Paradigm in Bubble Sort

Now let's revisit bubble sort to reveal the iteration paradigm and the repeated operations in it.

If the list to be sorted contains just one element, then we are finished by doing nothing. In general, the list will have more than one element. Then, bubble sort pushes the largest (or smallest) element to the end of the list for ascending (descending) order. The list is now reduced by one element, and the smaller problem is still a list of elements to be ordered.

The actual *pushing of the largest (smallest) element to the end of the list* is again done by iteration. The pushing task fits the iteration paradigm (you can figure this out).

The iteration repeats a number of *compare-exchange* (CE) operations. Each CE operation compares two adjacent elements of the list, and only exchanges (swaps) them when necessary so that the latter element is larger (or smaller for descending order).

Let's see how exactly it sorts a sequence of eight elements, a_0, a_2, ..., a_7 (Figure 4). Bubble sort makes multiple passes to complete its job.

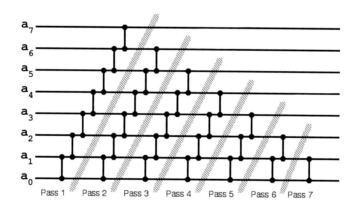

FIGURE 4: *Sorting Eight Items with Bubble Sort*

Pass 1 repeats CE operation 7 times: CE(a_0, a_1), CE(a_1, a_2), CE(a_2, a_3), CE(a_3, a_4), CE(a_4, a_5), CE(a_5, a_6), and CE(a_6, a_7), resulting in moving the largest value to a_7.

In a similar manner, pass 2 repeats CE operation 6 times and moves the largest value of a_0, a_1, ..., a_6 up into a_6; pass 3 repeats CE operation 5 times and moves the largest value of a_0, a_1, ..., a_5 up into a_5; and so on, until, finally, pass 7 repeats CE operation one last time and moves the largest value of a_0 and a_1 into a_1 to complete the sorting.

Iteration Control

To employ iteration in any application, we need to precisely control and execute all the necessary repetitions. We can look at an iteration abstractly as a construct, taking it out of the context of any particular application. We see that every iteration consists of the following elements:

- An **initialization** to set starting values in preparation for controlling and carrying out a number of repetitions of a certain operation

- An **end condition** to test if the iteration should terminate or to proceed to the next repetition

- A **body** of operations to be performed repeatedly

- An **update**, usually after completing a repetition, to set new values for controlling the next repetition

Let's put bubble sort in algorithmic form so as to clearly identify these elements. We assume the list of grades have been placed in an array of numbers a[0], ... a[n-1] and the array length is n (the total number of grades).

Recall that bubble sort repeats a number of phases, and each phase repeats a number of CE operations. Here is a flowchart illustrating the procedure for each single phase (Figure 5):

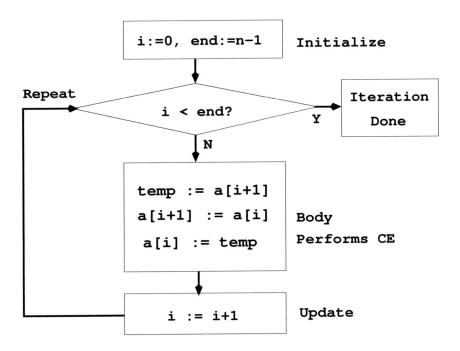

FIGURE 5: *One Single Phase of Bubble Sort*

Every iteration requires control to manage the repetitions and to start, continue, and end the repetitions correctly. Here are the essential elements of iteration control in the flowchart.

1. **Initialization**: Set the control variables `i` to zero and `end` to `n-1` once and once only in the beginning.

2. **Repetition of iteration body**: Perform the iteration body once only if `i` is less than the value of `end`.

3. **Update**: Increase the value of the control variable by one, `i=i+1`.

Following the flowchart, we see clearly one complete phase of CE operations and the largest value being pushed to the end. In the flowchart, CE uses a temporary variable `temp` to swap the values of two elements.

To complete the bubble sort, we need to perform all phases, starting with the full array of elements. By reducing the value of `end` by one, we ensure that the next phase will work on a shorter array.

Thus, **we have two iterations, one nested within the other**. The outer iteration repeats the inner iteration to execute each phase. It updates `n`, `n=n-1`, just before the next phase. And each individual phase is performed by the inner iteration which repeats CE operations.

Iterations Are Not Created Equal

Even though the speed of modern computers can help us use brute-force to iterate over large amounts of data, the efficiency of an algorithm is still very important.

Bubble sort is inefficient and seldom used in practice. This is because the number of phases grows linearly as the length of the list to be sorted grows and the list is only shortened by one element after each phase.

FIGURE 6: *Partition in Quicksort*

A much better algorithm is *quicksort* which still applies iteration but much more cleverly. With quicksort, the idea is to split the list to be sorted into two parts, smaller elements to the left and larger elements to the right. This is called the *partition* operation (Figure 6), which first picks an arbitrary element of the list as the *partition element* `pe`.

By exchanging elements, the list can be arranged so all elements to the right of pe are greater than or equal to pe. Also, all elements to the left of pe are less than or equal to pe. The location of pe is called the *partition point*.

After partitioning, we cut the list into two parts, one to the left of pe and one to the right of pe. The same partition method is now repeated on each of the two parts. When the size of a part becomes less than 2, the partition stops. When all partitions stop, the task is done. Quicksort is efficient in practice, because it often reduces the length of the list to be sorted quickly, basically cutting it in half after each partition.

Finally

We often hear the adage *"if it ain't broke, don't fix it."* Iteration certainly follows that principle by repeating what works again and again until the job is done.

Iteration has wide applications, in computing and in daily living. Any problem that fits the *iteration paradigm* is a candidate.

Each iteration involves initialization, continuation, and termination. Controlling how these are performed is important when specifying an iteration for a particular application. While an iteration is straightforward, ingenuity often lies in the way to reduce a task to small ones. In the end, iteration is not only a method to solve problems but also a new way of thinking.

When we face a new problem or task, we may have various ways to tackle it. What iteration teaches us is that we can consider vastly simplified cases to get some insight which can lead us to ways to cut the task down. As soon as we reduced the problem to one or more smaller job of the same nature, **we have the problem solved already!** Isn't that almost magical?

·············· CT Crossword Puzzle ···········

Iteration

Across

2. Iteration is a ___ for problem solving

6. ___ sort is clever and fast

7. Data are easier to use if they have ___

8. Arranging data in order

Down

1. Quicksort algorithm uses repeated ___

3. Repeating a sequence of steps

4. ___ sort is simple but slow

5. One foot in front of the other, one can go the ___

25

Internet of What? Things!

The Internet is already all encompassing. Add wireless mobile communications technologies, the Internet became accessible everywhere we go, even while jogging, driving, or taking a plane ride.

Each device connected to the Internet is called a *host*. Hosts include *clients* that access Internet-based services and *servers* that provide them. Communications over the Internet follow the Internet Protocol (IP). For example, desktops, laptops, and smartphones are clients. They are used to access and interact with servers that provide various services including the web, audio/video streaming, banking, e-commerce, and so on.

That is the traditional view of the Internet. The power and usefulness of the Internet can be greatly extended with **Internet of Things** (IoT) where we also connect devices called *things*.

Here we discuss IoT, its purposes, applications, impact, and potential. A good grasp of IoT as a technology will make you a better computational thinker.

In the Beginning

The phrase *Internet of things* was coined by Kevin Ashton in 1999, when the Internet was still in its infancy. The initial idea was to connect everyday devices and objects to the Internet, enabling them to interface with one another and be controlled by users via the Internet.

FIGURE 1: *Bread Toaster*

The very first IoT device was a toaster (Figure 1) built and demonstrated by John Romkey and Simon Hackett in 1989. The toaster was connected to a network via TCP/IP (an Internet protocol) and had **one** control to turn the toaster on/off. Toast darkness was determined by controlling how long the power was kept on. Even though this toaster had little practical value by itself, it really was *the toaster that changed the world*!

The concept of IoT began to take shape in the early 2000s, as technology advanced and more devices became capable of connecting to the Internet. At this stage, the focus was primarily on connecting devices such as smartphones, laptops, and computers to the Internet.

As the technology evolved, the scope of IoT expanded to include other devices such as sensors, cameras, and other smart devices. These devices could be used to gather data and provide insights into various aspects of our lives, such as home security, energy consumption, air quality, and even personal health.

With the advent of machine learning and artificial intelligence (AI), IoT devices became smarter and more capable of processing data in real-time. This led to the development of advanced applications—such as smart homes, voice-controlled assistants, smart cities, connected vehicles, fully automated ports—that can revolutionize the way we live, work, and interact with the world around us.

Today, new IoT technologies and applications emerge all the time. As more **things** (devices and objects) become connected to the Internet, the potential for IoT to transform our lives in countless ways continues to grow.

IoT Devices

So, what things or devices are ready to become part of an IoT network? Basically, an IoT-ready device has these main characteristics:

- **Connectivity**: The device is able to connect to the Internet or a network using a wireless or wired connection. It should support standard network protocols such as WiFi, Ethernet, Bluetooth, Zigbee, or cellular.

- **Sensors**: The device has one or more sensors that can measure and collect data. Such a sensor may detect temperature, humidity, light, motion, and so on.

- **Processing Abilities**: The device possesses sufficient processing ability to perform its intended functions, such as collecting, sending, receiving, and processing data, running machine-learning algorithms, or responding to user input/commands.

- **Efficient Power Usage**: An IoT device is usually small and runs on batteries. It should be designed to conserve power and maximize battery life. This is particularly important for devices that are intended to operate in remote or hard-to-reach places/locations, where frequent battery charging or replacement may be difficult or even impossible.

- **Security**: The device often has built-in security features to protect against unauthorized access, data breaches, and cyberattacks. This could include encryption, authentication, access control, and secure communication protocols.

- **Compatibility**: The device is compatible with standard IoT platforms and protocols, allowing it to be easily integrated into an IoT network.

Overall, an IoT-ready device should meet specific needs and be compatible with standard IoT protocols and platforms.

Household IoT

The most popular IoT consumer devices (Figure 2) include smartphones, smart TVs, smart printers/copiers, smart speakers, connected thermostats, home security systems, domestic robots, smart bulbs, energy monitors, connected appliances, smart door locks, and connected car devices. For example,

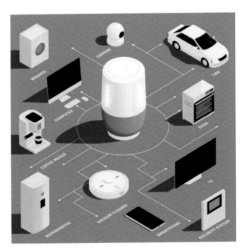

FIGURE 2: *Smart Consumer Items*

Amazon Echo is an IoT smart speaker backed by an Internet-connected voice assistant. It understands voice commands in major languages including English, German, Spanish, Italian, and Chinese. The device can help set alarms, manage your purchases, provide weather and news information, play music, and make calls via your enabled cellphone.

Here are some more examples: Google Home, smart thermostats like Nest and Ecobee, smart home security systems like Ring and SimpliSafe, smart lighting systems like Philips Hue and LIFX, and smart locks like August and Yale.

Remote Monitoring Systems

An important IoT application is in remote monitoring systems with cameras that allow users to check on their elderly or disabled parents from their own homes. These types of devices are becoming increasingly popular as people seek ways to monitor and care for their aging loved ones from a distance.

Such a remote monitoring system typically consists of video cameras, microphones, or other sensors placed in the elderly person's home, which can be accessed remotely by family members using a smartphone app or web portal. Some systems also include features such as two-way audio communication, motion detection, and alerts that notify family members of any unusual activity or changes in the elderly person's behavior or condition. Wearable devices for remote vital signs monitoring can help greatly in such cases.

In addition to providing peace of mind for family members, these types of systems can also help elderly individuals remain independent and stay in their own homes for longer. They can also provide valuable insights into the elderly person's daily routines and habits, which can be used to identify potential health or safety issues early on.

Smart Cities

Moving out of households, IoT can be deployed city-wide (Figure 3).

FIGURE 3: *Smart City*

Let's first look at control and management of city traffic. Smart traffic lights and signs are great examples of IoT applications that are designed to improve traffic flow and reduce congestion in urban areas. These devices use sensors, cameras, and other technologies to collect and analyze real-time traffic data, which is then used to adjust traffic signal timing and provide drivers with up-to-date information on traffic conditions.

Several cities around the world have implemented smart traffic lights and signs . Examples include Singapore, Barcelona, and Los Angeles.

Additional smart city IoT applications include:

- **Smart waste management**: IoT sensors are used to monitor waste bins to optimize garbage collection routes.

- **Smart energy management**: IoT devices are used to optimize energy use in buildings, streetlights, and other city infrastructure.

- **Smart parking**: IoT sensors monitor available parking spots, enabling the system to guide drivers to the nearest space available or to indicate estimated wait time for a free spot.

- **Smart water management**: IoT sensors can monitor water usage, detect leaks, and optimize water distribution, improving efficiency and reducing waste.

- **Public safety**: IoT devices such as cameras and sensors can help monitor public spaces and detect potential safety threats, improving public safety and emergency response.

- **Air quality monitoring**: IoT sensors are placed at well-selected locations to monitor air quality in real-time, detecting pollutants and providing data to help city officials make decisions about pollution control measures.

Also IoT has many applications in transportation, including air traffic control, sea port control, trucking, and package delivery.

People-less Ports

Yangshan Deep Water Port in Shanghai (上海洋山深水港 China, Figure 4) is a fully automated sea port that uses IoT technologies to speed up and optimize port operations while improving efficiency, safety, and security. In particular, the port uses a variety of sensors and IoT devices to collect real-time data on various aspects of port operations, such as container location, traffic flow, and equipment performance. This data is then analyzed by the port's centralized control center, which uses artificial intelligence and machine learning algorithms to optimize port operations.

FIGURE 4: *Yangshan Deep Water Port, China (image: VGC 2023)*

For example, sensors placed on container cranes can monitor the movement of containers and track their location. This information can be used to optimize the positioning of the cranes and to reduce wait times for ships. Similarly, sensors placed on unmanned guided vehicles (UGVs) can monitor their location and performance, allowing the control center to optimize their routing and improve efficiency.

In addition to optimizing port operations, IoT technologies can also improve safety and security in the port. For example, sensors can be used to detect potential hazards, such as overheating equipment or leaking containers, and to alert port authorities in real-time. This can help to prevent accidents and reduce the risk of damage to cargo or equipment.

The largely unmanned fully automated container ports in China use a combination of advanced IoT, Beidou (北斗) satellite navigation, 5G (mobile), AI, and driverless vehicle technologies. As of April 2023, in addition to Yangshan, China has two other such ports: Qingdao (青岛) Port and Tianjin (天津) Port and is completing a fourth.

IoT Network Protocols and Topology

Having seen various applications, it is now time for us to take a closer look at the IoT technology itself, namely its protocols and network configurations. Of course Internet Protocol (IP) is the most basic for communication over the Internet. In addition an IoT network (Figure 5) and the connected IoT-ready devices may use one or more of the following IoT protocols:

- **Zigbee**: Zigbee is a wireless protocol that is commonly used in home automation and industrial control applications. It supports mesh networking, low-power consumption, and a range of data rates.

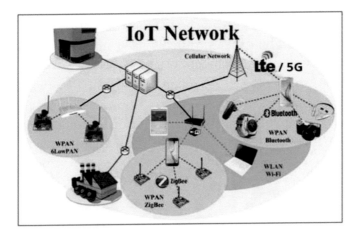

FIGURE 5: *An IoT Network*

- **CoAP (Constrained Application Protocol)**: CoAP is a simple protocol that is designed for use in constrained networks, such as those found in IoT devices. It is used for data transfer between devices and servers, and supports resource discovery and management.

- **Bluetooth**: Bluetooth is a wireless protocol that is widely used in consumer electronics for short-range communication. It is often used in IoT devices for communication between smartphones and other devices.

- **MQTT (Message Queuing Telemetry Transport)**: MQTT is a simple messaging protocol that is commonly used in IoT networks for its low bandwidth and power requirements. It is used to send messages between devices and servers, and it supports a publish/subscribe model for data communication.

- **LoRaWAN (Long Range Wide Area Network)**: LoRaWAN is a wireless protocol that is designed for long-range communication in low-power devices. It is often used in IoT applications for remote monitoring and control.

- **HTTP (Hypertext Transfer Protocol)**: HTTP is a standard protocol used for web-based communication, and it is often used in IoT networks for communication between devices and servers. It is commonly used for data transfer and control of IoT devices.

- **4G LTE and 5G (mobile network)**: These are used for IoT applications involving mobile devices usually over a wide area.

These are just a few examples of the IoT protocols that an IoT-ready device may need to support. The exact protocols used in a network will depend on the specific use case and requirements of the network.

These various protocols are useful in forming IoT networks for different purposes. Different applications also require appropriate IoT network configurations (called *network topology*) to better perform intended tasks (Figure 6). In small-scale IoT networks, the most common topology is a star topology,

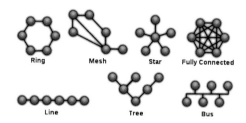

FIGURE 6: *Various Network Topology*

where all leaf-node devices are connected to a central hub or gateway, such as a WiFi router, smartphone, or cable modem. This hub or gateway acts as a mediator between the devices and the Internet, and it allows for easy management and control of the network. Another common topology for small-scale IoT networks is a mesh topology, where devices communicate with each other directly, creating a self-organizing network that can handle failures and ensure reliable communication.

In large-scale IoT networks, the topology becomes more complex and may include a combination of various topologies. For example, a hierarchical topology may be used, where smaller sub-networks are connected to larger networks through gateways or routers. This can help manage the flow of data and ensure that the network is efficient and reliable. Another common topology for large-scale IoT networks is a tree topology, where devices are connected in a hierarchical structure with a single root node at the top.

In general, the topology of an IoT network depends on the specific use case, the number of devices, the geographical distribution of the devices, and the requirements for reliability, security, and scalability.

IoT Takes Flight

Recent years have seen the rapid development of drones that are relatively light weight and inexpensive. Drones can become IoT devices because they can be equipped with cameras, microphones, satellite positioning, and other types of sensors. And they can be connected to IoT networks via wireless mobile links. Thus, drones can collect all kinds of data and transmit them in real-time.

Drones can provide valuable insights into areas that are difficult to access, such as remote or dangerous locations, and can be used for a variety of purposes, such as surveillance, inspection, mapping, and delivery of items.

Advances in mobile networking, especially 5G technologies, are crucial in enabling using drones as IoT devices. With high-speed connectivity and low latency, 5G networks can support the real-time data transfer necessary for drone operations, allowing for more precise control and safer flights. 5G also enables the use of high-resolution cameras and other sensors that produce large amounts of data, which can be processed quickly and efficiently.

FIGURE 7: *Smart Agriculture (image: digi.com)*

The integration of smart drones as IoT devices, powered by 5G mobile network technologies, opens up a new dimension of possibilities for various industries, enabling them to gather critical data and insights that were previously inaccessible. Here are some real-world examples:

- **Agriculture**: Drones with multispectral cameras and other sensors are used to monitor crops, detect crop diseases, and assess soil moisture levels (Figure 7). This information can be used to optimize crop yields, reduce the use of fertilizers and pesticides, and improve overall farm management. For example, the American Farm Bureau Federation used drones to survey crop damage caused by Hurricane Florence in 2018. The drones can also efficiently and quickly spray fertilizers or pesticides on crops.

- **Clean Energy**: Drones can help inspect and maintain power lines, wind turbines, and other energy infrastructure. Using drones with thermal cameras, companies can detect problems such as hotspots, which can be indicative of potential failures. In 2018, Southern Company used drones to inspect a 50-mile stretch of transmission lines in Alabama.

- **Construction and mining**: Drones are used to monitor construction sites, conduct surveys, and inspect buildings. Using drones with Lidar sensors, construction companies can create highly detailed 3D models of sites, which can be used for planning and design purposes. Skycatch, a company specializing in drone surveying, has worked with construction companies such as Bechtel and Mortenson to survey construction sites. Drones and other IoT devices, often in combination with AI, help improve health, security, efficiency, and control in the mining industry.

- **Emergency response**: Drones can be used to provide situational awareness and support during emergencies. For example, drones equipped with thermal cameras can help locate missing persons in search and rescue missions. Drones serving as emergency mobile transmission towers can quickly restore mobile communication to a remote disaster area. In 2019, DJI, a leading drone manufacturer, partnered with the European Emergency Number Association to develop guidelines for the use of drones in emergencies.

- **Retail**: Drones can be used to deliver packages and products to customers. In 2016, Amazon began testing its Prime Air delivery service, which uses drones to deliver packages to customers within 30 minutes of ordering. Other companies, such as UPS and DHL, are also testing drone delivery services.

- **Entertainment**: Synchronized drone shows can be a big draw for important festivals and other public events, especially at night. Such a spectacular and crowd-pleasing show also presents a unique venue for advertising and public announcements. It also demonstrates the power and potential of combining IoT, 5G, drones, and real-time control of a large number of unmanned flying objects (Figure 8).

These are just a few examples of how drones are being used as IoT devices. Weather balloons also become flying IoT devices that use LoRaWAN gateways, for example, for weather monitoring and forecasting purposes. There are also IoT enabled/enabling blimps. As the technology continues to develop and become more widespread, we can expect to see even more innovative use cases emerge.

IoT Market

The stakeholders in the IoT marketplace are diverse and include hardware manufacturers, software developers, cloud service providers, telecommunications companies, system integrators, and end-users.

FIGURE 8: *A 500-Drone Light Show (image: CGTN)*

The size of the IoT market is difficult to estimate precisely, as it includes a wide range of products and services across multiple industries.

However, according to a report by *Fortune Business Insights*[1], "*The global Internet of Things (IoT) market size was valued at USD 544.38 billion in 2022 and is projected to grow from USD 662.21 billion in 2023 to USD 3,352.97 billion by 2030, exhibiting a CAGR of 26.1% during the forecast period.*"

In the End

Starting from a simple and silly idea of connecting a household toaster to the Internet, IoT has grown, expanded, and evolved into something significant. In fact, IoT has opened up a new dimension of the Internet.

With the convergence of new devices, sensors, protocols, networking techniques, drones, and 5G mobile networks, IoT has transformed, in may respects, the way we live, work, conduct business, play, and much more. The IoT market size is significant and will grow rapidly going forward.

Embedding sensors, processing and networking power in physical objects, and connecting them to the Internet is a small step indeed. But gather enough small steps, you get a brand new situation. Electronic circuit integration and chip technology development are also examples obvious to computational thinkers.

That is the "quantity to quality" law of transformation, a consistent law as civilizations evolve and advance. The idea of sharpening a stone to make a simple tool has led to much bigger things indeed. Computational thinkers understand this well and are ready to take any new idea and maximize its impact.

---

[1]fortunebusinessinsights.com/industry-reports/internet-of-things-iot-market-100307

.... CT Crossword Puzzle ....

IoT

Across

4. IoT lets you ___ remotely

5. IoT make cities ___

7. The I in IoT

8. IoT market is ___

Down

1. IoT makes smart flying ___

2. IoT enables fully ___ sea ports

3. IoT started with a household ___

6. The T in IoT

26

Chips Are Everywhere!

In late 2022, the Biden administration announced new restrictions on American companies. Under that restriction, chip manufacturers that take US funding cannot make new, high-tech investments in China or other "countries of concern" for at least a decade. The US also moved to enlist help from allies. Thus begins the so-called *chip war*. Global politics and struggles among great powers are not our subject here. We will talk about what chips are, their usefulness in our daily lives, how they are designed, manufactured, and distributed, as well as their economic importance, and future directions. Of course, such an understanding is important in the digital age, especially for computational thinkers.

What Is a Chip?

Obviously, we are not talking about potato or corn chips. A *computer chip*, or chip for short, is also known as a microchip, an integrated circuit or IC. It is a collection of electronic circuits built on a small piece of special material such as silicon. These chips are critical for modern computing, as they can be designed to do different jobs such as logic processing (CPU), data storage, or some other application. On the chip, *transistors* act as miniature switches that can turn an electric current on or off. Furthermore, the on/off state of a transistor is also controlled electronically making it the perfect device for building electronic circuits. A chip usually contains many complicated electronic circuits which are constructed by creating many transistors made of silicon in an interconnected pattern as designed. Chips are usually the size of a fingernail or smaller (Figure 1). In early January 2023, Intel announced its i9 CPU chip containing 2.95 billion transistors.

Brief History

Chip making dates back to the mid-20th century, when the first electronic computers were being developed. The first computers were built using vacuum tubes, which were bulky, expensive, slow, and generated a lot of heat.

FIGURE 1: *Some Packaged Chips*

In the late 1940s and early 1950s, researchers began experimenting with using transistors as an alternative to vacuum tubes. Transistors were smaller, more reliable, and used less power than vacuum tubes, which made them ideal for use in electronic devices.

The invention of the integrated circuit in 1958 by Jack Kilby of Texas Instruments and Robert Noyce of Fairchild Semiconductor marked a major milestone in chip research and development. Integrated circuits allowed multiple transistors to be fabricated on a single piece of semiconductor material, making it possible to build smaller and more complex electronic devices.

In the 1960s, the development of large-scale integration (LSI) and very large-scale integration (VLSI) made it possible to fabricate even more transistors on a single chip. This paved the way for the development of microprocessors, which are the Central Processing Units (CPUs) of modern computers.

Throughout the 1970s and 1980s, chip development focused on increasing the speed and performance of microprocessors, as well as reducing their size and power consumption. This led to the development of new materials, such as silicon dioxide, and new manufacturing processes, such as photolithography, that allowed for even more transistors to be packed onto a single chip.

In the 1990s and 2000s, chip research and development continued to focus on increasing performance and reducing power consumption, as well as developing new types of processors, such as graphics processing units (GPUs) and application-specific integrated circuits (ASICs).

Chips Are Everywhere

Nowadays, most devices use chips: computers, cellphones, GPS navigators, smart appliances and objects, light bulbs, watches, cars, airplanes, and networks.

FIGURE 2: *Many Objects with Chips*

Here are some day-to-day objects that often contain chips to make them smart or work better (Figure 2):

- **Smartphones**: Smartphones contain a wide range of chips, including microprocessors, memory chips, and wireless communication chips, which allow them to perform a variety of tasks, such as accessing the Internet, running apps, and taking photos. Also, most have receiver chips to process satellite signals from GPS, Beidou, and other Global Navigation Satellite Systems (GNSSs).

- **Laptops**: Laptops also contain a variety of chips, including microprocessors, GPUs, and memory chips, which allow them to run complex software and perform tasks such as video editing and gaming.

- **Smart home devices**: Smart home devices such as smart thermostats, security cameras, and smart speakers often contain chips that allow them to communicate with other devices and perform tasks such as monitoring temperature, detecting motion, and playing music.

- **Automobiles**: Automobiles contain a wide range of chips (Figure 3), including microprocessors and sensors, which are used to control various systems such as the engine, transmission, and brakes.

- **Fitness trackers**: Fitness trackers contain chips that allow them to track and monitor physical activity, as well as measure heart rate and other biometric data.

FIGURE 3: *Inside of a Smart Car*

- **Gaming consoles**: Gaming consoles such as the Xbox and PlayStation contain powerful microprocessors and GPUs that allow them to run complex video games.

- **Smartwatches**: Smartwatches contain chips that allow them to perform various tasks, such as displaying notifications, tracking fitness, and making phone calls.

- **Smart TVs**: Smart TVs contain chips that allow them to connect to the Internet, run apps, and stream video content.

- **Digital cameras**: Digital cameras contain chips that allow them to capture and process images, as well as store them on memory cards.

- **ATMs**: ATMs contain chips that allow them to connect to banking networks and perform transactions, as well as provide security features such as encryption and authentication.

- **Wearable medical devices**: Wearable medical devices such as pacemakers (Figure 4) and glucose monitors often contain chips that allow them to measure and transmit data about the patient's health to healthcare professionals.

- **Smart lighting systems**: Smart lighting systems contain chips that allow them to be controlled remotely via smartphone apps or voice assistants, as well as to adjust brightness and color temperature.

No matter which way you turn, you are likely to find chips embedded in something around you. If there were no chips, there would not be the digital age. And that is not an exaggeration.

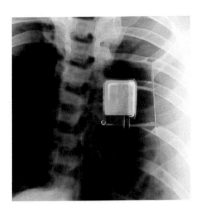

FIGURE 4: *Pacemaker Implant*

Types of Chip

Chips can be designed and built for various purposes. The following are some common types of chips for information processing:

- *CPU (Central Processing Unit) Chip*: It executes instructions and performs calculations required to run software and applications. A CPU chip typically consists of multiple processing cores that can handle tasks concurrently.

- *GPU (Graphics Processing Unit) Chip*: GPUs are specialized chips designed to handle graphics-related computations, such as rendering images, videos, and animations. They excel at parallel processing, making them useful for tasks like gaming, video editing, and machine learning algorithms that involve complex mathematical calculations.

- *AI (Artificial Intelligence) Chip*: AI chips are specifically designed to accelerate artificial intelligence tasks. They are optimized for processing large amounts of data and performing high-speed calculations required for machine learning and deep learning algorithms. AI chips often incorporate specialized architectures like neural networks or tensor processing units (TPUs) to enhance AI performance.

- *FPGA (Field-Programmable Gate Array) Chip*: Unlike traditional chips, FPGAs can be programmed and reprogrammed to perform specific tasks or functions. They are highly versatile and customizable, making them suitable for a wide range of applications, including telecommunications, industrial automation, and cryptography.

- *ASIC (Application-Specific Integrated Circuit) Chip*: ASICs are custom-designed chips built for a specific application or task. Unlike FPGAs, ASICs cannot be reprogrammed, but they offer superior performance and power efficiency for the intended purpose. ASICs are commonly used in specialized devices like cryptocurrency mining rigs and networking equipment.

- *SoC (System-on-a-Chip)*: SoC refers to a chip that integrates multiple components of a computer system onto a single chip. It typically includes a CPU, GPU, memory, and other system components. SoCs are commonly found in smartphones, tablets, and other embedded systems.

Of course, there are also chips for various types of computer memories.

How Are Chips Made?

From idea to product, the process of developing a microchip involves several major steps, including design, verification, fabrication, testing, and packaging:

- **Conceptualization and Design**: The first step in developing a new chip is to conceptualize the idea and create a design. This involves defining the specifications of the chip, selecting the appropriate materials and manufacturing processes, and designing the layout of the chip. The time and cost for this step can vary widely depending on the complexity of the chip and the resources available to the design team.

- **Verification**: Once the design is complete, it needs to be verified to ensure that it meets the required specifications. This involves simulating the behavior of the chip using specialized software tools and identifying any errors or design flaws. The time and cost for this step can also vary widely, depending on the complexity of the chip and the tools available.

- **Fabrication**: After the design has been verified, the chip can be fabricated. This involves using specialized manufacturing processes to etch the design onto a piece of semiconductor material, such as silicon. The time and cost for this step can also vary widely, depending on the complexity of the design and the fabrication processes used.

- **Testing**: Once the chip has been fabricated, it needs to be tested to ensure that it meets the required specifications. This involves using specialized equipment to measure the performance and functionality of the chip. The time and cost for this step can also vary widely, depending on the complexity of the chip and the testing equipment used.

- **Packaging**: After the chip has been tested, it needs to be packaged into a form that can be used in electronic devices. This involves encapsulating the chip in a protective material and connecting it to pins or leads that allow it to be connected to a circuit board. The time and cost for this step can also vary widely, depending on the complexity of the packaging process and the resources available.

Each of these step can take weeks or months. Overall, the process of developing a computing chip from idea to product can take anywhere from months to years.

Chip Manufacture Costs

The mass production of chips is capital-intensive. The investments in the construction of fabrication and testing facilities can be especially substantial.

A fabrication facility, also known as a fabrication plant (Figure 5) or "a fab," can cost billions of dollars. A fab—which includes 1,200 multimillion-dollar tools and 1,500 pieces of utility equipment—takes about 3 years, $10 billion, and 6,000 construction workers to complete.

FIGURE 5: *Chip Fabrication Plant or FAB*

Similarly, the cost of building a testing facility can be significant, depending on the complexity of the testing equipment required. For example, a testing facility for advanced microprocessors may require specialized equipment such as electron microscopes, X-ray diffraction machines, and other high-tech tools that can cost millions of dollars each.

Therefore, the cost and time required for the entire chip development process, from concept to mass production, can vary greatly depending on the scale of the operation and the complexity of the chip. For smaller operations or less complex chips, the costs and timelines may be more manageable. However, for larger operations or more complex chips, the costs and timelines can be significant and require substantial investment over an extended period of time.

Here are some of the necessary software, hardware, and manufacturing equipment needed in each step of the chip development process:

1. *Conceptualization and Design*

   - **Electronic design automation (EDA) software**: This is used to create the design of the chip.

   - **Computer-aided design (CAD) software**: This is used to create 3D models of the chip design.

   - **Workstations and high-performance computing (HPC) clusters**: These are used to run simulations of the chip design to test for functionality and performance.

2. *Verification*

   - **EDA software for verification**: This is used to verify the functionality and performance of the chip design.

   - **Formal verification software**: This is used to verify that the chip design meets the required specifications.

   - **HPC clusters**: These are used to run simulations for verification.

3. *Fabrication*

   - **Photolithography equipment**: This equipment is key to chip-making. It uses light to transfer (print or etch) the circuit patterns for the chip design onto the semiconductor material (Figure 6). ASML, a global industry leader based in the Netherlands, offers one of the best photolithography equipment for chip making that uses Extreme UltraViolet (EUV), an incredibly short wavelength of light to print small, complex designs on microchips.

   - **Chemical vapor deposition (CVD) equipment**: This is used to deposit layers of materials onto the semiconductor material.

   - **Etching equipment**: This is used to remove unwanted material from the semiconductor material.

   - **Ion implantation equipment**: This is used to implant impurities into the semiconductor material to create the necessary electrical properties.

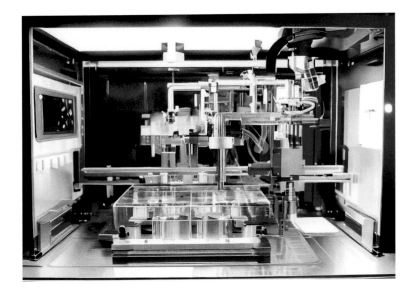

FIGURE 6: *Photolithography Equipment for Chip-making*

- **Metrology equipment**: This is used to measure the dimensions and properties of the chip features to ensure they meet the required specifications.

4. *Testing*

- **Test equipment**: This includes various types of testing equipment, such as oscilloscopes, logic analyzers, and power supplies, which are used to test the functionality and performance of the chip.
- **Probe cards**: These are used to make electrical connections between the chip and the testing equipment.

5. *Packaging*

- **Wire bonding equipment**: This is used to make connections between the chip and the leads or pins of the package.
- **Molding equipment**: This is used to encapsulate the chip in a protective material, such as plastic.
- **Automated test equipment (ATE)**: This is used to test the packaged chip to ensure it meets the required specifications.

As you can see, the equipment and software required for each step of the chip development process can be quite specialized and expensive. Many of these tools and technologies require specialized knowledge and training to use effectively, which is why chip development often requires a team of experts with diverse skill sets.

Currently, the major directions for chip research and development are in further miniaturization, increasing power efficiency, and special-purpose applications. We can be sure that the future of chips remains bright and exciting.

Chip-Inspired Computational Thinking

Looking at the chip technologies we can find several inspirations for computational thinkers:

- *Divide and conquer*—Chip design and manufacturing is a very large and complicated undertaking, even though the resulting chip is tiny. The entire task is broken down into smaller ones and distinct steps to be handled individually.

- *Step-wise refinement*—New generations of chips are created by making improvements and incremental advances to the previous generation of chips. For example, circuit integration have gone through "small-scale integration" (SSI), "medium-scale integration" (MSI), "very-large-scale integration" (VLSI), and "ultra-large-scale integration" (ULSI).

- *Bottom-up problem-solving*—Using silicon transistors as basic building blocks, forming logic gates, then up to simple circuits, then eventually to a complete chip.

- *Iteration of a virtuous cycle*—Better chips result in more powerful computers which are used in the design, manufacturing, and testing of new chips. The cycle goes on.

Listed here are just some ideas. Computational thinkers are sure to learn other lessons from the varied aspects of chip-making and apply them in different places.

Careers in the Chip Industry

Many different educational paths can lead to careers in the chip industry. Examples of majors and studies that can be helpful for those looking to enter the field include: electrical engineering, computer science, materials science, physics, and mathematics.

It's important to note that the chip industry is highly technical and specialized, and many roles require advanced degrees or specialized training. Therefore, in addition to choosing an appropriate major or study, individuals interested in pursuing a career in the computing chip industry may also need to seek out internships, certifications, and other opportunities to gain practical experience and skills.

Finally

A chip is tiny, complex, and powerful. With the naked eye, we can hardly see it. Yet, a microchip is one of the most wonderful artifacts we have ever made.

Chips are everywhere and affect almost all aspects of our lives. A good understanding of chips is important in the digital age, especially for computational thinkers.

Some may take chips for granted or do not fully appreciate the tremendous creativity, difficulty, effort, time, infrastructure, funding, and rapid evolution required in their design and manufacturing. These are certainly significant challenges.

The matter is further complicated by international factors such as intellectual property rights, manufacturing expertise, technical standards, and trade policies, which affect the development and use of chip technologies. In addition, the chip industry is an important part of the global economy. All these are reasons why international division of labor in the form of supply chains has been essential in chip R&D and manufacturing.

The micro chip is at the center of the digital revolution and we can look forward to more advances, breakthroughs, applications, and wonderful improvements in our lives brought about by the small but powerful chips.

27

Problem-Solving: Algorithmic and Recursive

To become a computational thinker, we need just two things: (1) To have a good understanding of computing and digital technologies and (2) to be inspired and apply that knowledge to solve problems and improve the way we do things in all areas and in our daily lives. As we stated in the introduction of this book, CTers problemize, and that is exactly the kind of problem-solving we are discussing here. At the center of computing is the idea of automation. Computers are universal machines that can be programmed to perform almost any task. They allow us to automate solutions to problems. Such solutions can be performed by computers repeatedly, reliably, precisely, and with great speed. Not all problems lend themselves to automated solutions, but computational thinkers prefer solutions that can be automated.

The stages of computer automation are *conceptualization, algorithm design, program design*, and *program implementation*. Specifying and implementing solution algorithms requires precise and watertight thinking. Also required is anticipation of possible input as well as execution scenarios. Few are born with such talents. But, we all can become better problem-solvers by studying cases, experimentation, and building our solution repertoire. Often, there are multiple algorithms to solve a particular problem or to achieve a given task. Some may be faster than others. Some may use less resources. Others may be easier to program or less prone to mistakes. Analyzing and comparing different solution approaches is also an important part of problem-solving.

Solving Puzzles

A good way to begin thinking about problem-solving is perhaps by looking at a few puzzles.

Egg-Frying

The Problem: A pan can fry up to two eggs at a time (Figure 1). We need to fry three eggs. Each egg must be fried for 1 minute on each side. Design an algorithm to fry the three eggs in as little time as you can manage.

FIGURE 1: *Egg Frying*

The slowest method would fry one egg at a time, cooking each side for 1 minute. It would take a total of 6 minutes.

A better method would fry two eggs, turning them over after 1 minute, and cooking them for another minute. After that, fry the third egg. This method takes a total of 4 minutes.

Is this the best we can do? Well, no. We can do better.

1. Start with frying two eggs for 1 minute.

2. Take one of the half-done eggs out of the pan, turn the other egg over, and add the third egg in the pan, fry for 1 minute.

3. Take out the egg that is done, flip the other egg over, and add back the half-done egg, fry for 1 minute.

4. Take both eggs out and terminate.

Each step takes 1 minute. The whole procedure takes 3 minutes to get the job done.

Again, is this the best we can do? Well, yes. How do we know? Can we prove that no method can be faster?

Here is a proof. The three eggs require 6 egg-side-minutes of frying. The pan can supply a maximum of 2 egg-side-minutes per minute. Thus, at least 3 minutes are needed to produce 6 egg-side-minutes, no matter how the frying is done.

Liquid Measuring

The Problem: We have a 7-oz (ounce) cup and a 3-oz cup (Figure 2). Unfortunately, neither has any volume markings on it. We have a water faucet but no other containers. Find a way to measure exactly 2 oz of water.

FIGURE 2: *Two Cups*

We see the allowable operations are filling water from the faucet, pouring water from one cup to the other, and emptying the cups. Here is how we can proceed.

1. Fill the 3-oz cup completely.

2. Empty the 3-oz cup into the 7-oz one.

3. Repeat steps 1 and 2 one more time.

4. Fill the 3-oz cup again completely.

5. Pour water from the 3-oz cup into the 7-oz cup until it is full.

6. Two ounces of water now remain in the 3-oz cup.

Let's now switch the 7-oz cup to an 8-oz cup. Can you solve the same problem? What if we switch it to a 6-oz cup?

Connecting Nine Dots

The problem: The more-or-less well-known *nine dot puzzle* challenges us to connect a grid of nine dots (Figure 3) with four or fewer straight lines without lifting the pencil or retracing any line.

FIGURE 3: *Nine Dot Puzzle*

The solution has been widely used as an example of *thinking outside the box*. Obviously, the box in this example is outlined by the nine dots. The *sofpower.com* logo (Figure 4) shows one solution with four lines.

FIGURE 4: *Sofpower.com Logo*

Magic Tray

The Problem: A magic tray is a perfect square and has four corner pockets (Figure 5) whose openings look exactly the same. Inside each pocket is a cup hidden from view. The tray also has a green light at the center.

Cups inside the pockets can be either up (1) or down (0). The light will turn red automatically if all four cups are in the same orientation.

Your job is to turn the light red by performing a number of steps. Each step consists of reaching into one or two pockets to examine and optionally re-orient the cups. No other operations are allowed. Remember, you can't see the cups. Figure 5 shows one possible configuration to give you an idea.

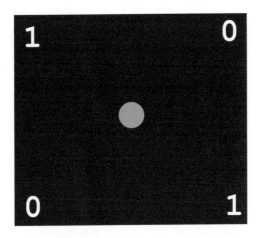

FIGURE 5: *Magic Tray Puzzle*

To complicate things, the tray immediately spins wildly after each step. When it stops spinning, there is no way to tell which pockets you had examined in the last step.

Your job is to create an algorithm to turn the light red, no matter what the initial orientations of the cups are. Remember, an algorithm must specify exactly what to do at each step and guarantee termination after a finite number of steps. Therefore, to keep reaching into pockets and turning cups up (or down) is not a solution, because you may be extremely unlucky and reach into the same pockets every time.

One observation we can make is that we may choose to reach into pockets along a side or on a diagonal. But there is a chance, however small, that we may reach into the same side/diagonal all the time. Our algorithm must work even if it never examines all four pockets. This puzzle is fun and hits home the algorithm ideas perfectly. We will leave the reader to work out this algorithm. It should take no more than seven steps. A solution can be found at our companion website (**Demo: MagicTray**).

Let's move on from puzzles for now.

Recursion

A circular definition is usually not good and to be avoided, because it uses the terms being defined in the definition, directly or indirectly. For example, *Bright: looks bright when viewed*; *adult: person not a child* and *child: person not an adult.* A circular definition is like a dog chasing its tail. It goes on and on to no end. Figure 6 shows two mirrors reflecting infinitely into each other to illustrate the recursion concept visually.

However, a term or concept can be defined *recursively* when the definition contains the same term or concept without becoming circular. A *recursive*

FIGURE 6: *Infinity Mirror*

definition has *base cases* that stop the circling at the end. For people first exposed to recursion, the concept can be confusing. But, it is simple once you understand it. Please read on.

In mathematics, a *recursive function* is a function whose expression involves the same function. For example, the factorial function

$$n! = n \times (n-1) \times (n-2) \times ... \times 1, \text{ integer } n > 0$$

can be recursively defined as

For $n = 1$, $1! = 1$ (base case)
For $n > 1$, $n! = n \times (n-1)!$ (recursive definition)

In computing, a recursive function or algorithm calls (invokes) itself either directly or indirectly. Here is the pseudo-code for a recursive `factorial` function.

Algorithm `factorial(n)`:
Input: Positive integer `n`
Output: Returns `n`!

1. If `n` is `1`, then return 1

2. Return `n` × `factorial(n-1)`

The "return" operation terminates a function and may also produce a value. Step 2 returns the value `n` times the value of `factorial(n-1)`, which is a call to the same function itself (Figure 7).

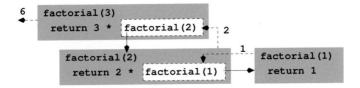

FIGURE 7: *Recursive Calls and Returns*

To solve a problem recursively, we reduce it to one or more smaller problems of the same nature. The smaller cases can then be solved by applying the same algorithm *recursively* until they become simple enough to solve directly.

CT concept–*Remember Recursion*: *Think of recursion when solving problems. It can be a powerful tool.*

To appreciate the power of recursion and to see how it is applied to solve non-trivial problems, we will study several examples.

Greatest Common Divisor

Consider computing the greatest common divisor (GCD) of two non-negative integers a and b, not both zero. Recall that $gcd(a, b)$ is the largest integer that evenly divides both a and b. Mathematics gives $gcd(a, b)$ the recursion

1. If b is 0, then the answer is a

2. Otherwise, the answer is $gcd(b, \ a \ mod \ b)$

Recall that $a \ mod \ b$ is the remainder of a divided by b. Thus, a recursive algorithm for $gcd(a, b)$ can be written directly:

Algorithm gcd(a,b):
Input: Non-negative integers a and b, not both zero
Output: The GCD of a and b

1. If b is zero, return a

2. Return gcd(b, a mod b)

Note, the algorithm gcd calls itself, and the value for b gets smaller for each successive call to gcd (Table 27.1). Eventually, the argument b becomes zero and the recursion unwinds: The deepest recursive call returns, then the next level call returns, and so on until the first call to gcd returns.

An interactive gcd (**Demo: InteractiveGCD**) can be found at our companion website.

TABLE 27.1: *Recursion of* gcd(1265,440) = 55

Call Level	a	b
1	1265	440
2	440	385
3	385	55
4	55	0

Recursive Solution Formula

The Recursion Magic: *Answer two simple questions and you may have magically solved a complicated problem.*

For many, recursion is a new way of thinking and brings a powerful tool for problem-solving. To see if a recursive solution might be applicable to a given problem, you need to answer two questions:

- Do I know a way to solve the problem in case the problem is small and trivial?

- If the problem is not small or trivial, can it be broken down into smaller problems of the same nature whose solutions combine into the solution of the original problem?

If the answer is yes to both questions, then you already have a recursive solution!

A recursive algorithm is usually specified as a function that calls itself directly or indirectly. Recursive functions are concise and easy to write once you recognize their basic structure. All recursive solutions use the following sequence of steps:

(i) Termination conditions: Always begin a recursive function with tests to catch the simple or trivial cases (base cases) at the end of the recursion. A base case (remainder zero for **gcd**) is treated directly and the function returns.

(ii) Sub-problems: Break the given problem into smaller problems of the same kind. Each is solved by a recursive call to the function itself passing arguments of reduced size or complexity.

(iii) Recombination of answers (optional): Finally, take the answers from the sub-problems and combine them into the solution of the original bigger problem. The function call now returns. The combination may involve adding, multiplying, or other operations on the results from the recursive calls.

For problems, like the GCD, where no recombination is necessary, this step becomes a trivial return statement. However, in the factorial solution, we need to multiply by n the result of the recursive call $factorial(n-1)$.

The *recursion engine* described here is deceptively simple. The algorithms look small and quite innocent, but the logic can be mind-boggling. To illustrate its power, we will consider the *Tower of Hanoi* puzzle.

Tower of Hanoi

Legend has it that monks in Hanoi spend their free time moving heavy gold disks to and from three poles made of black wood.

FIGURE 8: *Tower of Hanoi Puzzle*

The disks are all different in size and are numbered from 1 to n according to their sizes. Each disk has a hole at the center to fit the poles. In the beginning, all n disks are stacked on one pole in sequence, with disk 1, the smallest, on top, and disk n, the biggest, at the bottom (Figure 8). The task at hand is to move the disks one-by-one from the first pole to the third pole, using the middle pole as a resting place, if necessary. There are only three rules to follow:

1. A disk cannot be moved unless it is the top disk on a pole. Only one disk can be moved at a time.

2. A disk must be moved from one pole to another pole directly. It cannot be set down some place else.

3. At any time, a bigger disk cannot be placed on top of a smaller disk.

To simplify our discussion, let us label the first pole A (source pole), the second pole B (parking pole), and the third pole C (the target pole). If you have not seen the solution before, you might like to try a small example first, say, $n = 3$. It does not take long to figure out the following sequence.

move disk 1 from A to C
move disk 2 from A to B

move disk 1 from C to B
move disk 3 from A to C
move disk 1 from B to A
move disk 2 from B to C
move disk 1 from A to C

So, it turns out that you need seven moves for the case $n = 3$. As you get a feel of how to do three disks, you are tempted to do four disks, and so on. But you will soon find that there seems to be no rule to follow, and the problem becomes much harder with each additional disk. Fortunately, the puzzle becomes very easy if you think about it recursively.

Let us apply our recursion engine to this puzzle in order to generate a sequence of correct moves for the problem: *Move n disks from pole A to C through B.*

(i) Termination condition: If $n = 1$, then move disk 1 from A to C and return.

(ii) Subproblems: For $n > 1$, we shall do three smaller problems:

 1. Move $n - 1$ disks from A to B through C

 2. Move disk n from A to C

 3. Move $n - 1$ disks from B to C through A

 There are two smaller sub-problems of the same kind, plus a trivial step.

(iii) Recombination of answers: This problem is solved after the sub-problems are solved. No recombination is necessary.

 Let's write down the recursive function for the solution. Two recursive calls and a move of disk n is all that it takes.

Algorithm `hanoi(n, a, b, c)`:
Input: Integer n (number of disks), a (name of source pole),
   b (name of parking pole), c (name of target pole)
Output: Displays a sequence of moves

 1. If $n = 1$, display "Move disk 1 from a to c" and return.

 2. `hanoi(n-1, a, c, b)`

 3. Display "Move disk n from a to c"

 4. `hanoi(n-1, b, a, c)`

Each of steps 2 and 4 makes a recursive call. This looks almost too simple, doesn't it? But it works. To obtain a solution for seven disks, say, we make the call

```
hanoi(7, 'A', 'B', 'C')
```

During the course of the solution, different poles are used as the source, middle and target poles. This is the reason why the `hanoi` function has the `a, b, c` parameters in addition to `n`, the number of disks to be moved at any stage. Figure 9 shows the three-step recursive solution for `n = 5`:

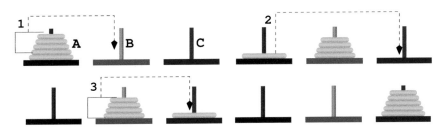

FIGURE 9: *Tower of Hanoi (Five Disks)*

1. Move four disks from pole A to pole B (`hanoi(4, 'A', 'C', 'B')`)

2. Move disk 5 from pole A to pole C

3. Move four disks from pole B to pole C (`hanoi(4, 'B', 'A', 'C')`)

Now, what is the number of moves needed for the `hanoi` algorithm for n disks? Let the move count be $mc(n)$. Then we have:

- If $n = 1$, then $mc(n) = 1$.

- If $n > 1$, then $mc(n) = 2 \times mc(n - 1) + 1$.

The above definition for $mc(n)$ is in the form of a *recurrence relation*, and it allows us to compute $mc(n)$ for any given n.

But, we can also seek a close-form formula for $mc(n)$.

$n = 1 \quad mc(1) = 1$
$n = 2 \quad mc(2) = 2 + 1$
$n = 3 \quad mc(3) = 2^2 + 2 + 1$
$n = 4 \quad mc(4) = 2^3 + 2^2 + 2 + 1$
...

Generally:

$$mc(n) = 2^{n-1} + 2^{n-2} + ... + 2 + 1 = 2^n - 1$$

An interactive Tower of Hanoi game (**Demo:** `TowerOfHanoi`) can be found at our companion website. Because $2^n - 1$ moves will be needed for n disks, you should test the program only with small values of n. But the monks in Hanoi are not so fortunate, they have 200 heavy gold disks to move, and the sun may burn out before they are finished!

But the logic behind the *recursion engine* provides a problem-solving strategy unparalleled by other methods. Many seemingly complicated problems can be solved easily with recursive thinking.

More to Come

Here, we have seen several important examples of problem-solving using algorithmic thinking. The recursion paradigm is especially amazing and wonderful.

Continued discussion of problem-solving can be found in CT Article 28, "*Problem-Solving: Backtracking and Heuristics*".

28

Problem-Solving: Backtracking and Heuristics

In this CT Article we continue to discuss computational thinking for problem-solving. First, let's look at the *backtracking paradigm*; that is, proceeding with building a solution until running into a dead-end, then retreating to try another possibility. Do this repeatedly until a solution is found or all possibilities have been exhausted.

Next, we'll look at *heuristics*, a different way to solve problems that are hard to handle with algorithms.

Eight Queens

The Bavarian chess player Max Bezzel formulated the Eight Queens problem in 1848. The task is to place eight queens on a chess board so that no queen can attack another on the board.

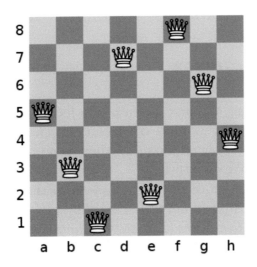

FIGURE 1: *Eight Queens*

As you may know, a queen can attack another piece on the same row, column, or diagonal. And the question is how many solutions there are. It turns out that there are 12 basic solutions (Figure 1 shows one). Other solutions can be derived from these by board rotations or mirror reflections for a total of 92 distinct solutions.

We know a necessary condition for a solution is that each column and each row must contain one and only one queen. To satisfy this necessary condition, there are eight possible column positions for row 1, 7 for row 2, and so on, for a total of 8! = 40320 queen placements. A brute-force way to find solutions is to check all 8! cases for diagonal attacks.

But we can do better than that by using a solution technique called *backtracking*. The idea is to place the queens, one at a time in successive columns (or rows), making sure the next queen is placed in a non-attacking position in relation to previously placed queens.

If the procedure finished placing all eight queens, we have a solution. If it got stuck (no queen for the next column) along the way, we backtrack to the previous queen and move it to its next possible position.

If it has no next position, then we backtrack further. Compared to the brute-force method, backtracking examines far fewer cases.

To illustrate backtracking, let's look at a Four Queens problem.

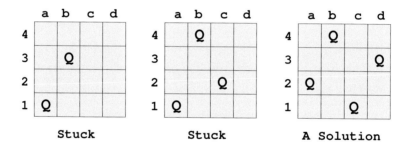

FIGURE 2: *Four Queens Backtracking*

We begin by placing the first queen in the first column at board position (1,a) (Figure 2, left). Next we place our second queen in the second column at board position (3,b). We then found that there is no place for the third queen in the third column. We are stuck.

So, we go back and move the second queen to the next possible position in the column at board position (4,b). This allows us to place the third queen in the third column at position (2,c), only to find there is no position for the fourth queen (Figure 2, middle).

Again, we need to go back and change the position of a previous queen. It turns out that we have no next positions for the third or second queen. We are forced to move the first queen to its next possible position (2,a).

From this position, proceeding in the same manner as before, we finally arrive at a solution (Figure 2, right). This is clearly faster than the brute-force approach.

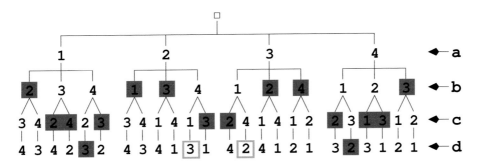

FIGURE 3: *Solution Tree*

The efficiency of backtracking comes from abandoning further queen placements after getting stuck. To illustrate the savings, let's look at the solution tree for the Four Queens problem (Figure 3), where the first level nodes give the row positions for the first queen (in column **a** on the board), the second level positions for the second queen (column **b**), and so on.

The solid shaded nodes are dead-ends. The paths leading to the two boxed nodes represent the only two solutions. You can see in Figure 3 how many tree branches are pruned by backtracking, resulting in significant computational savings.

General Backtracking

We used the Eight Queens problem to introduce the backtracking technique, which is generally applicable to solve problems by building a solution one element at a time. For a queens problem, we can place one queen at a time until all queens are placed. Other such problems include maze escaping (Figure 4), crossword, and Sudoku puzzles.

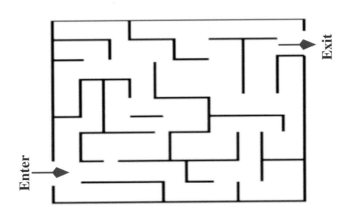

FIGURE 4: *A Maze Puzzle*

But backtracking is not just for games. It has wide applicability in solving practical problems, such as the *knapsack problem*, packing items of different weight or size into a container. The goal is to maximize the total dollar value, for example, of the packed items.

Similar to the queens problem, the knapsack problem is a type of *combinatorial optimization* problem where different combinations of items, satisfying given conditions known as *constraints*, are examined to optimize certain desired values.

For the queens problem, we have the non-attacking constraint, and we want to find different ways to place the maximum number of queens on the board. For the knapsack problem, we want to find different ways to pack the given items in order to maximize the value of the packed items under certain measures.

Tree Traversals

Perhaps you already know that files in a computer are organized in a tree structure Figure 5.

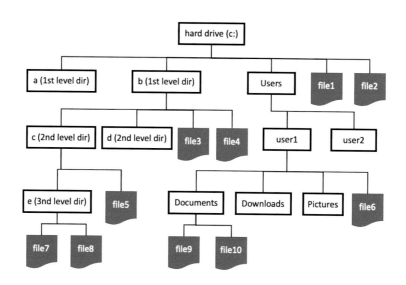

FIGURE 5: *Windows File Tree*

In general, a tree structure is a very useful way to organize hierarchical data. Family trees are well known. Internet domain names are also organized into a tree structure. On a computer, sometimes we need to search for a file because we have forgotten its folder location, or we are not sure of the file's precise name. Or, we want to find all files whose name contains a certain character string. Most operating systems provide a way for users to do such searches. It can be as easy as typing in a sub-string of the file name and a computer program will look for files with matching names in the entire file tree. This is very convenient, indeed. In fact, you can also find files containing certain words. That can come in handy when you remember parts of the file contents but not the file name.

But, how can such search operations be performed? Well, we need a systematic way to visit each node on the file tree, known as a *tree traversal*. A file tree traversal enables a program to visit all files, following folders and sub-folders, and to match file names or contents with user input.

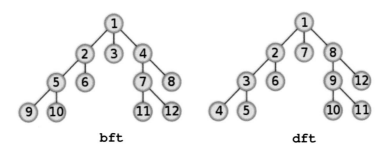

FIGURE 6: *Tree Traversals*

The two most common tree traversal algorithms are *depth-first traversal* (dft) and *breadth-first traversal* (bft). With bft, we visit the root, then its child nodes, then grandchild nodes, and so on. With dft, we visit the root, then we **dft** the first child branch, **dft** the second child branch, and so on. Figure 6 shows the node-visit order for a tree using bft and dft.

Implementation of the bft is straightforward. Because dft is defined recursively, we can use a recursive algorithm to implement it.

Algorithm `dft(nd)`:
Input: `nd` the starting node for dft traversal
Effect: visiting every node in the tree rooted at `nd` in dft order

1. Visit `nd`

2. If `nd` is a leaf node (no children), then return

3. Otherwise, for each child node `c` of `nd`, from first child to last child, call `dft(c)`

Trace this algorithm when the input node (`nd`) is the root of the tree in Figure 6 and verify the dft order given in the figure.

CT concept—*Make use of tree structures*: *Keep the tree structure in mind when you problemize. It can be found everywhere and* *can be used effectively in many situations, especially when hierarchies are involved.*

Let's take a fresh look at the solution tree (Figure 3) for the Four Queens problem we have seen. Now, we see that the backtracking algorithm employed there is simply a dft of the solution tree while applying the non-attacking condition at each node. A solution is found whenever a valid last level leaf is reached.

Complexity

The speed of modern computers adds a new dimension to problem-solving, namely by brute-force. We are no longer limited by our own speed or processing capabilities. Instead, we can ask the computer to examine all cases, or explore all possibilities, even when their numbers become quite large.

For example, we can solve the Eight Queens problem by checking each of 8! ways of placing the queens. The backtracking algorithm is a faster way to explore all of the solution tree, which has 8! branches. However, if the number of queens, n, increases much beyond 8, then the brute-force method, even with backtracking, will soon prove to be too slow. This is because the number of possible solutions $n!$ grows big very quickly as n increases.

> **CT concept–*Weigh speed vs. complexity*:** *Fast computers enable solutions by brute-force. But, they are no match for rapidly growing problem complexities.*

To get a feel of how fast $n!$ grows as n increases, let's consider a task of simply running a loop that does nothing for 20! (20 factorial) iterations. Assuming a fast computer with a CPU clock rate of 10 GHz (10^{10} Hz), and each iteration takes just 1 clock cycle, we can compute how long the task will take:

$$20! = 2432902008176640000$$

$$\frac{20!}{10^{10}} = 243290200.817664 \text{ seconds}$$

$$\frac{243290200.817664}{24 \times 60 \times 60} = 2815.85880576 \text{ days}$$

That is more than 7.5 years! It will take much, much longer if each loop iteration actually does something.

The term *complexity* is used in computer science in two ways: (i) the inherent difficulty of computational problems, and (ii) the growth of time/space required by an algorithm as its input problem size increases.

Indeed, not all problems or algorithms are created equal. For example, binary search grows proportional to $log_2(n)$ in complexity, where n is the length of the sorted list. Finding the maximum/minimum value in an arbitrary list grows linearly with the list size. The bubble sort algorithm has complexity n^2, while the quicksort algorithm has an average complexity of $n \times log_2(n)$.

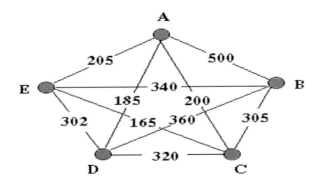

FIGURE 7: *Traveling Salesman Problem*

Traveling Salesman Problem

The well-known *traveling salesman problem* (TSP) asks this simple question: Given a set of cities and the distances between each pair of cities, what is the shortest route to visit each city and return to the starting city? Figure 7 shows an instance of this problem involving five cities. Such a problem has proven to be difficult when the number of cities grows. For n cities, there are $(n-1)!$ possible routes to check. This *combinatorial growth* is also seen in the queens problem.

Heuristics

When faced with a high-complexity problem that quickly outstrips the computational powers of computers, what is a problem-solver to do? Well, giving up is the last option. We must be resourceful and try our best to come up with something: a shortcut, approximation, oversimplification, or experience-based rule of thumb. In other words, we will try *heuristics*.

In computing, a *heuristic* is a technique to solve a problem more quickly or efficiently when brute-force or rigorous algorithmic methods are too expensive (practically impossible), or to get some solution instead of insisting on an exact or optimal one. This is often achieved by trading accuracy, precision, optimality, or completeness for computational feasibility.

In daily life, well-known examples of heuristics include stereotyping and profiling. Let's look at some examples in computing. We already know that the Eight Queens puzzle becomes too big for a slightly larger number of queens. But, we can apply the following heuristic to at least get a solution.

> **CT concept–*Remember heuristics***: *Apply heuristics when problem complexity outstrips computational power.*

Here is a *queens heuristic*, where we form a list, *positions*, of row positions for queen placement based on the number of queens:

1. Let $N \geq 4$ be the number of queens. Let *even* $= (2, 4, 6, ...)$ be the list of even numbers, and *odd* $= (1, 3, 5, ...)$ be the list of odd numbers, less than or equal to N.

2. If N *mod* $6 = 2$, then swap 1 and 3 in *odd* and move 5 to the end

3. If N *mod* $6 = 3$, then move 2 to the end of *even*, and move 1 and 3 to the end of *odd*

4. *positions* = *even* followed by *odd*

Applying this heuristic to $N = 7$, we get *positions* $= (2, 4, 6, 1, 3, 5, 7)$. For $N = 8$, we get *positions* $= (2, 4, 6, 8, 3, 1, 7, 5)$. For $N = 20$, we get

$$positions = (2, 4, 6, 8, 10, 12, 14, 16, 18, 20, 3, 1, 7, 9, 11, 13, 15, 17, 19, 5),$$

and we did not wait for years!

For the TSP, there are quite a few heuristics. A TSP *tour* is a round trip visiting each city once and returning to the origin city. The simplest and most intuitive is the *nearest city* heuristic, which calls for always traveling to the nearest new city from the current city. To find the nearest city at every step, we need to perform a total of

$$(n - 1) + (n - 2) + ... + 2$$

comparisons. The number is proportional to n^2.

The *greedy heuristic* sorts all, at most $\frac{n(n-1)}{2}$, segments between city pairs, and forms a sorted list, L. It then constructs a tour, usually shorter than the nearest city heuristic, by adding segments, one at a time, to the tour and removing them from L:

1. Add the shortest segment from L to the tour and remove it from L.

2. From L, add the shortest **valid** segment to the tour. A segment is invalid if it causes a city to be visited twice unless it's the nth segment.

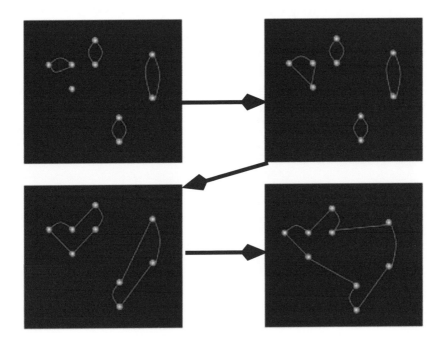

FIGURE 8: *Neighborhood Tour Heuristic*

3. Repeat step 2 until the tour is complete.

Note that segments of the tour may not be connected until construction is complete. Another TSP heuristic constructs a complete tour by forming disjoint neighborhood sub-tours and merging them together. Figure 8 illustrates the neighborhood tour heuristic for TSP.

A sub-tour is a tour involving a subset of the cities. The heuristic starts with n sub-tours, each consisting of an individual city.

Then it merges sub-tours following these rules:

- From all current sub-tours, pick the two closest sub-tours and merge them into a larger sub-tour.

- When merging two sub-tours, find the best way that minimizes the merged sub-tour.

Finding good algorithms to automate problem solution is at the center of modern computing. There are many good techniques including, brute-force iteration, chipping away, recursion, top-down divide and conquer, bottom-up building blocks, tree traversal, backtracking, and others.

For problems that are too complex, the challenge is to come up with clever heuristics to at least get some results.

Next: Problem-Solving Paradigms

In this CT Article we have seen more applications of computational thinking in interesting specific cases. All these details bring us to the question, "What are the general principles of computational thinking for effective problem-solving that have wider applicability and usefulness?"

That is exactly the topic of CT Article 29, "*Problem-Solving: Paradigms and Applications.*"

29

Problem-Solving: Paradigms and Applications

One of the main purposes of computational thinking (CT) is to better solve problems. Some would even say CT is basically a problem-solving methodology. Therefore, a computational thinker should have good problem-solving abilities and an attitude or mental orientation for problemizing.

After discussions in the previous two CT Articles (27 and 28), we are now ready to look at *problem-solving* itself in general (Figure 1).

FIGURE 1: *Thinking about Problem-Solving*

Problem-Solving Paradigms

We shall briefly explain some important general problem-solving paradigms, methods, and approaches and give examples.

- **Research Online**: Take advantage of the Internet, the web, social media, search engines, Wikipedia, YouTube, and AI systems such as Chat-GPT to find information and answers relating to a problem. For many problems, this should be your go-to approach initially. Don't forget to consult experts or professionals when needed.

  For example, my refrigerator or AC is not cooling or my plant has a disease. Indeed almost any other problem you encounter.

- **Decomposition** or **Divide and Conquer**: This involves breaking down a large or complex problem into smaller, more manageable parts or sub-problems. This approach allows you to focus on one part of the problem at a time and solve it before moving on to the next.

  For example, to plan a birthday party, you can have an invitation list, venue, food/drinks, and entertainment as sub-problems.

- **Abstraction**: This involves identifying the essential features of a problem and ignoring the irrelevant details (Figure 2). Abstraction allows you to simplify a problem and focus on its core components.

FIGURE 2: *Abstract Heart Gesture*

For example, to create a backyard garden, you may want to first focus on the overall visual effects before getting into the types of plants, flowers, and building materials.

- **Algorithmic Thinking**: This involves developing step-by-step procedures or algorithms for solving problems. Algorithms provide a clear and unambiguous set of instructions that can be followed to solve a problem.

For example, to plan a vacation abroad, you may create a flowchart based on a countdown to the planned departure time. Sequence the steps depending on which to do first and which next.

- **Pattern Recognition**: This involves identifying patterns (Figure 3) or trends in data that can be used to make predictions or solve problems. Pattern recognition allows you to identify similarities and differences between different data sets.

FIGURE 3: *Big Dipper in the Night Sky*

For example, to identify a phishing email, you can spot the unfamiliar sender id, irregular reply address, vague subject line, strange tone of the message, and push for you to open an attachment, visit a website, or click a link. The give away is the asking for your sensitive information.

- **Logical Reasoning**: This involves using deductive reasoning to analyze and solve problems. Logical reasoning involves identifying the premises of an argument and drawing conclusions based on those premises.

For example, to solve a Sudoku puzzle, you can use logical reasoning to eliminate numbers from each cell based on the numbers already present in the same row, column, and 3×3 box. Or, to catch scammers, you may want to follow the money trail.

- **Top-Down Method**: This approach involves starting with a broad view of a problem and then breaking it down into smaller, more specific sub-problems. It allows you to focus on the high-level structure of a problem before diving into the details.

For example, to plan a dinner party, you might start with the objective/goal of the party, venue, budget, list of guests, food (dishes and drinks), any dietary considerations of individual guests, and the order of presentation of the courses, and so on.

- **Bottom-Up Method**: This approach involves starting with specific details and building them up into a larger goal. It is useful when dealing with problems where the details are well-defined but the overall structure is flexible. By combining a set of standard components, we can build a variety of end products (Figure 4).

FIGURE 4: *The Lego Approach*

For example, consider building a prefabricated house. You use standard components to create modules, put them together to form sections, and combine sections to make a house. Even skyscrapers are built from the ground up one floor on top of another.

- **Recursion**: This involves first solving the most trivial case of a problem, then a way to reduce the size of more complicated cases resulting in one or more smaller ones of the same nature that can be solved using the same method. We have talked about recursion in CT Article 27.

  For example, to calculate the factorial of a number N, namely $N!$, you can use a recursive function that multiplies $(N-1)!$ by N.

- **Iteration**: This involves repeating a set of steps or a process multiple times until a desired outcome is achieved. It is useful for refining solutions and improving their quality.

  For example, for a cross-country car trip, we can go from city to city or stop to stop, repeatedly.

- **Heuristics**: This involves using rules of thumb or educated guesses to solve a problem when an optimal, systematic, or algorithmic solution is too slow, too hard, or not feasible. It is useful when dealing with complex problems where finding an optimal solution is computationally infeasible.

For example, consider security checking at crowded public places such as train stations or airports. *Profiling*, or looking for suspicious actions or behaviors in the crowd, is often effective. Other heuristics include common sense, stereotyping, educated guess, and even intuition.

- **Backtracking**: This involves systematically exploring all possible solutions to a problem by trying one option after another and backtracking when a dead-end is reached. It is useful for solving problems with a large search space.

For example, for maze (Figure 5) escaping, you can use backtracking to explore all possible paths until the correct path is found.

FIGURE 5: *A Garden Maze*

- **Trial and Error**: This involves trying out different solutions until a desired outcome is achieved. It is useful when dealing with problems where the solution is not immediately clear.

For example, to solve a crossword puzzle, you can use trial and error to try out different word combinations until the correct solution is found.

- **Incremental Improvements**: Also known as *step-wise refinement*, this involves first building a solution quickly overlooking many distracting details. Then, make small changes to the solution to improve its performance or quality. It is useful to get something working first then use it to find the improvements and refinements.

For example, to create a software program, you can build an initial version 1.0. Then use it to get experience, user feedback, and so on, then make incremental improvements to add new features, fix bugs, and optimize its performance over time, resulting in version 2.0.

- **Parallelization**: This involves breaking a problem down into smaller sub-problems that can be tackled independently and concurrently. This allows solving the sub-problems simultaneously on multiple processors (Figure 6) or cores. It is useful for solving problems that are computationally intensive and can be broken down into smaller, independent tasks.

FIGURE 6: *Working in Sync*

For example, to look for someone or something in an area, we can divide the area into a grid and employ multiple searchers simultaneously, each responsible for a sub-area.

- **Optimization**: This involves finding better or even the best possible solution to a problem within a given set of constraints. It is useful for solving problems where there are many possible solutions, but only a few of them are optimal.

  For example, to optimize the production schedule for a factory, you can use mathematical optimization techniques such as linear programming to find the schedule that maximizes production while satisfying constraints such as labor availability and machine capacity.

- **Modularity**: This involves breaking a system down into smaller, independent modules or components that can be developed and tested separately. It is useful for solving problems that are too large or complex to be solved as a whole.

  For example, to run a restaurant, you can divide up the operations into reservations, hosting, table service, kitchen, bar service, and so on.

- **Structuring Data**: Solution methods can become easier, faster, and more efficient if the data involved in the problem or solution process are organized to have certain structures that the solution method can utilize to advantage.

  For example, a dictionary of words is an obvious example. Records kept by time and date, airline flights by departure and destination cities, addresses by city, state, and zipcode, files and folders stored in a hierarchical (tree) structure, customers waiting in a queue, are additional examples.

Of course, there are many other CT paradigms, methods, and approaches used in problem-solving. By using a combination of these techniques, you can solve complex problems in a structured and effective manner.

In fact, the more familiar you are with computational and digital technologies, the better you can solve all kinds of problems.

Applications in Daily Living

Let's see how useful the CT problem-solving paradigms are in our daily lives.

FIGURE 7: *Trip Planning*

- **Planning a trip**: When planning a trip (Figure 7), you can use decomposition to break down the trip into smaller tasks such as booking flights, reserving accommodations, and planning activities. You can also use heuristics to find the best time to book flights and accommodations based on historical pricing data, and trial and error to find the best deals. Additionally, you can use optimization to find the best itinerary that maximizes your time and minimizes your expenses.

- **Solving household problems**: When facing household problems, such as a leaky faucet or a malfunctioning appliance, you can use decomposition to break down the problem into smaller components and identify the root cause. You can also use trial and error to try out different solutions until you find one that works, and incremental improvements to optimize the solution over time.

- **Managing personal finances**: When managing your personal finances, you can use data abstraction to simplify your budget and identify areas where you can cut expenses. You can also use optimization to find the best investment strategies that maximize your returns while minimizing your risks.

- **Choosing a career**: When choosing a career, you can use top-down design to identify your career goals and then break them down into smaller steps such as researching job opportunities and acquiring relevant skills. You can also use data abstraction to simplify the job market and identify the most promising career paths, and heuristics to identify industries and job roles that match your interests and skills.

- **Learning a new skill**: When learning a new skill, you can use bottom-up design to start with the basics and gradually build up your knowledge and expertise. You can also use iteration to practice your skills and refine your technique over time, and feedback loops to identify areas where you need to improve.

- **Making decisions**: When making decisions, you can use logical reasoning to analyze the pros and cons of different options, and heuristics to identify biases and errors in your decision-making process. You can also use backtracking to explore different options and find the best solution, and trial and error to test different strategies until you find the one that works best for you.

Handling Crises

It is true that no one can be lucky all the time. When something bad happens, such as a loved one had an accident or your kitchen caught on fire, how do you avoid panic so you don't get into more trouble yourself. There is a reason why people say, "misfortunes never come singly." This is indeed a problem worth solving ahead of time.

Here are some tips for dealing with emergencies:

1. **Stay calm**: In an emergency situation, it's natural to feel panicked or overwhelmed. However, it's important to try to stay calm and focused in order to make effective decisions and take correct actions (Figure 8).

2. **Be very careful**: It is natural to be in a hurry when dealing with a crisis. But that is exactly the time to be extra careful. It wouldn't help at all if you get hurt yourself or worse.

3. **Call for help**: If the situation requires immediate medical attention, call emergency services or seek help from a nearby hospital or clinic. If the situation involves a safety threat, call the police or other appropriate authorities.

FIGURE 8: *Staying Calm Can Save Lives*

4. **Take immediate action**: If there is a specific action that you can take to address the situation, take it as soon as possible. For example, if someone is choking, perform the Heimlich maneuver immediately.

5. **Follow emergency protocols**: If you are in a workplace or public setting, follow the emergency protocols that are in place. These protocols may include evacuation procedures, emergency contacts, and other important information.

6. **Communicate with others**: If there are others involved in the situation, communicate with them clearly and calmly. Try to provide reassurance and guidance as needed.

7. **Seek support**: After the immediate crisis has passed, seek support from friends, family members, or professionals if needed. It's important to take care of yourself and seek help if you are struggling with the emotional impact of the situation.

Normally, it's important to be prepared and take a structured approach to problem-solving. But, the priority in an emergency is to take immediate action to deal with the urgent present problems. By staying calm, taking action, and seeking help as needed, you can help to minimize the impact of the emergency and protect yourself and others.

In the End

In our three CT Articles on problem-solving (27-29), we have discussed many topics and hopefully gained a much better understanding and became better at solving problems of many kinds. In fact, we have demonstrated how CTers would *problemize* all the time, everywhere.

However, in addition to the paradigms, methods, and approaches discussed earlier, here are a few more important aspects of computational thinking for problem-solving—creativity, collaboration, continuous improvement adapting to change, and ethical considerations.

Computational thinkers, by incorporating these aspects into your problem-solving approach, you can develop more effective solutions and make a positive impact on the world around you.

. . . . CT Crossword Puzzle . . . .

Problem Solving

Across

3. A procedure invoking itself is ___

5. a ___ b is remainder of a divided by b

7. A recursion needs to ___ at the end

9. Combinatorial ___ increases very rapidly

Down

1. Tower of ___ puzzle illustrates recursion well

2. Problem-solving skills can be applied ___

4. The traveling ___ problem has combinatorial growth

6. Hitting a dead-end, go back to find another way

7. Depth-first tree ___

8. When an algorithmic approach is too slow/hard, we can try ___

30

Parallel Computing: Ways To Cooperate

The history of modern computing is a story of the pursuit of speed. And indeed the increase in processing speeds has been remarkable.

On July 16, 1969, the US launched Apollo 11 that carried astronauts Neil Armstrong, Buzz Aldrin, and Michael Collins to the moon. Armstrong and Aldrin became the first humans to set foot on the lunar surface on July 20, 1969. The onboard Apollo Guidance Computer (AGC) was a compact digital computer responsible for providing guidance, navigation, and control for the spacecraft during various mission phases, including the critical lunar descent and ascent. The AGC had a clock speed of 1.024 MHz (megahertz), which means it executed approximately 1 million instructions per second.

Fast-forward to mid-2023, modern personal computers, laptops, and smartphones typically have processors with clock speeds measured in gigahertz (GHz), which are thousands of times faster than the AGC. Contemporary CPUs can execute billions of instructions per second (GIPS). What a difference.

As you may have guessed, to keep making a single CPU smaller and faster can't work forever. And you are right. We have basically reached the limit of single CPU speeds.

So what to do to get the computer to be even faster? The idea is actually commonsense, "use more CPUs." It is like if a job is too much for one person, divide up the job and get more people to help.

In a computer, more people means more independent processing elements (PEs) in the computer hardware. A PE can be a CPU or a *core*. Dividing up the job means designing our programs (apps) to have tasks to assign to the available PEs. The approach is known as **parallel computing**.

The idea is simple to understand, but the devil has always been in the details. Making multiples of anything work together is not easy. Making hardware and software to support parallel computing can be tricky indeed.

This CT Article will explain how that is done, including the methods, challenges, and solutions. Such knowledge about parallel computing is directly applicable to managing multiple concurrent tasks, or teams of people who cooperate and work together in parallel.

Sequential Processing

FIGURE 1: *Pie Baking*

The ordinary view of a program is this:

1. The program starts to run.

2. It executes a sequence of instructions one-by-one in the given order.

3. The program stops and finishes.

Indeed, we have the same view for procedures, algorithms, and flow charts. Figure 1 shows the sequential process of pie baking.

Thus, sequential program execution means one program runs from start to finish, then another program runs. It is a simple and straightforward approach. However, strict sequential processing is seldom used in practice.

Even a PC with just one CPU can appear to do things in parallel by a technique known as *time slicing*—switching the CPU rapidly among processes (running apps) giving each process a slice of CPU time so they all appear to make progress and be responsive to user input. The operating system does a *context switch*, saving the current process state and replacing it with the state of the next one, to run the next process.

FIGURE 2: *Traffic Cop in Rome*

Parallel Processing

A CPU in today's PCs usually has multiple *cores*. High-end PCs may actually offer multiple CPUs each with multiple cores. Thus, they offer multiple PEs to run different tasks at the same time, or in parallel. Figure 2 shows parallel activities in real life.

A core is part of the CPU and offers independent execution capabilities to the CPU. Each core can run any *thread* belonging to any process. This means application programs can be written with multiple threads to take advantage of the available PEs. Figure 3 shows a quad-core CPU where the cores are organized into two pairs sharing levels of cache memory.

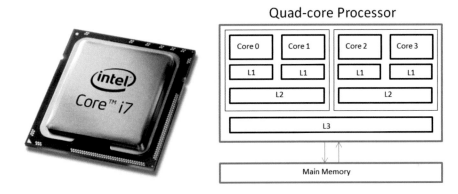

FIGURE 3: *Quad-core CPU*

Of course, an operating system needs to implement controls for parallelism. In short, parallel software is also important to achieve parallel computing. A parallel program breaks up tasks into parts to be run by the available PEs. A CPU can run any entire process while a core can run any thread (an independent part of a process).

The arrangement is like managing a busy restaurant—equip it with several kitchens (CPUs and cores) so that a number of chefs, cooks, and assistants (various independent tasks) can work simultaneously to get the job done.

> **CT concept–*Parallel programming is advantageous*:** *Multiple threads can make programs not only easier to write, but also run faster and more responsively.*

Challenges for Parallel Programs

To support parallel processing, the hardware, operating system, and software programs (apps) all need to do their part. We'll now see how apps can utilize parallelism via *threads* and the challenges thereof. We can think of each thread as a worker in the kitchen.

What Is a Thread?

A program under execution is called a *process*. A process consists of routines, data, stack, and operating system code and structures.

Within a process, control usually follows a single *execution thread*, starting with the first step, through a sequence of steps, and ending with the last step. This is the *single thread* programming model.

To perform tasks in parallel, multiple concurrent *threads of execution* (*multithreading*) can be used. As an independently running entity, a thread is much easier to create than a new process. Hence, a thread is sometimes known as a *lightweight process*.

Advantages of Multithreading

Single-threaded programs are good for simple calculations. Dynamic, interactive, or *event-driven* programs usually consist of multiple active parts that naturally perform independently and interact or cooperate in some way to achieve the intended goals. An event-driven program basically performs tasks in reaction to external events such as user input or signals from other processes or threads. For example, consider satellite based navigation systems (Figure 4).

FIGURE 4: *Satellite Navigation in Car*

Separate threads can take care of user control, map rendering/update, satellite signal tracking and location determination, and so on.

As another example, a video game program has independent parts for user controls, graphical rendering, motion generation, score keeping, etc. A single-threaded video game would be enormously complicated, if not impossible. A multithreaded program can model each of these parts with a different thread. Also, a web browser is a natural candidate for multithreading. Figure 5 shows parallel processing in a chocolate assembly line.

FIGURE 5: *A Chocolate Assembly Line*

Furthermore, graphical rendering and user control processing take place simultaneously. Responsive handling of such concurrency is difficult in a single-threaded program.

Challenges of Multithreading

Basically, a multithreaded program has to coordinate several independent activities and avoid the possibility of them *tripping over one another*. Multithreaded programs involve four important new aspects not present in ordinary single-threaded programs: *mutual exclusion, synchronization, scheduling*, and *deadlock*. A good understanding of these concepts will help you better handle real-world activities and better manage cooperation with others.

Mutual Exclusion

Threads running in parallel usually need to cooperate to achieve intended tasks. Cooperation typically involves different threads accessing the same program constructs. When multiple threads share a common resource, a piece of data or a file, for example, simultaneous access by more than one thread can take place. Such simultaneous access is called a *race condition*, and there is no telling which thread may win the race and the outcome of the entire program can be unpredictable or erroneous. For example, if two threads increase the same variable `counter` by one at the same time, the resulting count can be wrong. To avoid simultaneous access, it is necessary to arrange *mutually exclusive access* to shared quantities. When programmed correctly, only one

FIGURE 6: *Mutex*

thread at a time can access the same quantity protected by *mutual exclusion* (mutex).

Consider writers cooperating on a magazine article. If two writers work on the same article from different workstations concurrently, disaster strikes. Mutual exclusion in this case can be arranged by insisting that every writer *lock* the article before working on it. No one else can obtain access to the article until it is *unlocked*.

Mutual exclusion is actually commonplace. Think about passengers on an airliner. Every passenger must lock the restroom door after entering it and unlock it to exit. Other passengers must wait until the door is unlocked before entering. That is simply politeness. In parallel computing, we call it *mutual exclusion* (Figure 6).

Synchronization

Mutual exclusion avoids threads tripping over one another. But you still need a way for threads to communicate and coordinate their actions in order to co-operate. Threads make progress at independent and unpredictable rates. Thus, it is necessary to coordinate the order in which some tasks are performed.

If a task **must not be started** before some other tasks are finished, it is important to make sure that is the case. For example, imagine each thread is a worker in an assembly line. Then a thread must wait until another thread has finished a part it needs. Such time-related coordination of concurrent activities is called *synchronization*. For example, we all obviously know that synchronization is critical for symphony orchestras (Figure 7).

Consider workers in a kitchen making bread. One is working on preparing the dough; another will take the dough that is ready to start baking it. The baking worker must wait until the dough is ready.

FIGURE 7: *Synchronization*

Thread synchronization usually involves delaying a thread until certain conditions are met or certain computations by other threads are done.

A thread is said to be *blocked* if its continued execution is delayed until a later time.

Thread Scheduling

When a process involves multiple threads, the available CPU and/or cores execute all threads in rapid succession. Exactly which currently executing thread is stopped and which waiting thread is run next (Figure 8) depend on the *scheduling policy* of the thread system and the priority settings of the threads involved.

FIGURE 8: *Ready and Waiting*

Deadlock

In a situation where multiple threads are interdependent in many ways, with resources shared under mutual exclusion and sub-tasks under synchronization, there is the possibility of *deadlock*. Figure 9 shows a traffic deadlock situation. Deadlock happens when threads are waiting for events that will never happen.

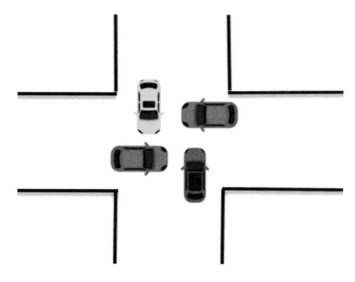

FIGURE 9: *Deadlock*

For example, thread A is waiting for data from thread B before producing output for B. B is waiting to receive some output from A before it can produce data for A. In real life, two friends wishing to talk but neither is willing to call first; is an example of deadlock. Of course, in parallel computing as well as in real life, we must avoid such problems.

> **CT concept–*Cooperating parallel programs need coordination***: *Otherwise, they can run into problems and won't work well or at all.*

Finally

In parallel processing, we make use of multiple CPUs/cores and write multi-threading programs for operating systems as well as important apps such as web browsers. This way we can increase execution speed and perform tasks more quickly and effectively. In fact, having multiple simultaneous activities is natural in real life as well as in computing. Computational thinkers should break out of the box of single-threaded thinking. That is a thinking dictated by sequential procedures, algorithms, or single-PE computers. Instead we should all embrace parallelism in computing as well as in real life where things happen in parallel naturally.

Parallel computing is an important area and we have only scratched the surface of that topic. Even then, we can see the links between parallel processing and everyday activities and understand that making independent agents cooperate is often the right choice. We also realize that many tasks or activities are inherently concurrent. We simply need to face the associated challenges such as mutual exclusion, synchronization, scheduling, and deadlock.

·················· CT Crossword Puzzle ·············

Parallel Computing

Across

4. An independent running activity within a process

5. A program in execution

7. A thread is a ___ process

8. Processes avoiding resource conflicts

10. CPU rapidly switching giving each process a ___ of time

Down

1. Coordinating the time sequence of events

2. Multi-thread programs are ___ and responsive

3. A CPU may have multiple ___ for parallelism

6. User interface programs are driven by ___

9. Processes blocking each other from making progress

Becoming a Computational Thinker: A Summary

Congratulations on reaching the end of the book. It may have taken some time, but you have completed the task and accomplished a lot for sure. Some CT Articles may be more interesting than others and some even worthwhile revisiting. Hopefully, you are finding applications of CT everyday and everywhere.

With ever increasing pace, our world is becoming digital and more interconnected. In this new world, CT can make us not only more successful but also feel in control. Such feeling comes from a deeper understanding of our digital environment and how it works. Dare we say that computational thinkers live more at ease because they fit in better?

To wind up, we'll summarize the dos and don'ts of a computational thinker.

Computational Thinker Dos:

- Thinks logically and analytically

- Takes a systematic and methodical approach

- Pays attention to details and ask "what if" questions

- Thinks outside of the box, innovates, and creates

- Keeps an open mind and considers all possibilities

- Pays attention to collaboration and communication

- Learns and improves, works toward "version 2.0"

Computational Thinker Don'ts:

- **Overconfidence**: Overconfidence can lead to complacency and can cause you to overlook important details or fail to consider alternative solutions. It's important to maintain a healthy level of skepticism and be willing to challenge your own assumptions.

- **Confirmation bias**: Confirmation bias occurs when we only seek out information that confirms our existing beliefs or assumptions, and ignore information that contradicts them. This can lead to inaccurate conclusions and prevent us from considering alternative solutions.

- **Tunnel vision**: Tunnel vision occurs when we become too focused on one particular aspect of a problem and fail to consider the broader context. This can lead to oversimplification and prevent us from identifying more complex or nuanced solutions.

- **Lack of creativity**: While logical reasoning and analytical thinking are important, it's also important to be creative and open-minded when approaching complex problems. Failing to think creatively can limit your ability to come up with innovative solutions.

- **Neglecting ethical considerations**: As a computational thinker, it's important to consider the ethical implications of your work and ensure that your solutions are socially responsible. Neglecting ethical considerations can lead to unintended consequences and undermine the positive impact of your work.

A computational thinker can always become a better computational thinker. Here are a few things one should be careful about when analyzing a situation or making a decision:

- Becoming emotional

- Being optimistic or pessimistic

- Jumping to conclusions

- Assuming a context without checking

- Over-reliance on authority

- Trusting words over deeds

CT for Health and Happiness

Providing problem-solving skills and approaches, CT can indeed contribute to improving people's health and overall well-being. CT can impact positively both the physical and psychological aspects.

First, the following are the physical aspects:

- *Monitoring and tracking*: CT can be applied to physical health by utilizing various technologies and tools for monitoring and tracking vital signs, physical activity, sleep patterns, and nutrition. This data-driven approach allows individuals to gain insights into their physical well-being, identify patterns or issues, and make data-informed decisions to improve their overall health.

- *Personalized health management*: By applying CT, individuals can develop personalized algorithms and routines for physical health management. This can include creating exercise plans tailored to their fitness level and goals, optimizing nutrition based on specific dietary needs, and establishing sleep patterns that promote optimal rest and recovery.

- *Preventive care*: CT encourages a proactive approach to health. By analyzing health data and patterns, individuals can identify potential risks and take preventive measures to maintain good health. This can involve regular screenings, vaccinations, and lifestyle modifications to reduce the chances of developing certain health conditions.

Now, below are the psychological aspects:

- *Cognitive flexibility*: CT emphasizes adaptable thinking and problem-solving. This mindset can help individuals develop cognitive flexibility, enabling them to approach challenging situations and emotions with resilience. It encourages individuals to consider multiple perspectives and explore alternative solutions to psychological issues, fostering mental well-being.

- *Emotional regulation*: CT involves breaking down problems into manageable parts and analyzing them logically. These skills can be applied to emotional regulation by helping individuals identify and understand their emotions, break them down into smaller components, and develop strategies to address them effectively. This can involve techniques such as mindfulness, meditation, or seeking professional help when needed.

- *Self-reflection and self-awareness*: CT encourages iterative problem-solving and continuous learning. Applying these concepts to psychological well-being can involve self-reflection and self-awareness exercises. By analyzing one's thoughts, behaviors, and emotions, individuals can gain insights into their mental state, identify patterns or triggers, and make conscious choices to improve their overall psychological health.

Of course, computational thinkers know that CT is not a substitute for professional medical or psychological care.

Finally: Happiness

Let's say a few words about **happiness**. In CT the *context switch* concept is highly relatable to the idea that *happiness is a mindset*. Context switching refers to the process of saving the **current state** of a running task, such as a program or a thread, and restoring the state of a different task to allow it to run. This switch enables the computer to efficiently manage and allocate its resources among multiple tasks.

What is a mindset? It is a state of mind. And what is a mental context switch? It is a change of the state of one's mind, leaving one state of mind and entering another.

Happiness is not solely dependent on external circumstances but is influenced, in fact determined, by how we perceive and interpret the world around us. For example, our interpretation of a traffic jam depends on our eagerness to get somewhere in a hurry. So, if we manage to modify our interpretation and deliberately adopt a positive or sunny one, then we will feel much better. Therefore, if we consciously shift our mental and emotional state, a context switch, we feel happy. Thus, we say indeed, "*happiness is a state of mind.*"

Wishing you health, happiness, and every success in the digital age. And thank you for being a reader. Your feedback is most welcome.

To Your Happiness and Success

Index